The PLO under ʿArafat: Between Gun and Olive Branch

SHAUL MISHAL

The PLO under 'Arafat
Between Gun and Olive Branch

YALE UNIVERSITY PRESS
New Haven and London

Designed by Nancy Ovedovitz and set in Times Roman type by
Rainsford Type. Printed in the United States of America by
Alpine Press, Stoughton, Mass.

Library of Congress Cataloging-in-Publication Data

Mishal, Shaul, 1945–
    The PLO under 'Arafat.
    Includes index.
    1. Munazzamat al-Tahrīr al-Filastīnīyah. 2. Arafat,
Yasir, 1929–   . 3. Jewish–Arab relations—1967–1973.
4. Jewish–Arab relations—1973–   . 5. West Bank—
International status. I. Title.
DS119.7.M56   1986   322.4'2'0899275694   86–9140
ISBN 0–300–03709–0 (alk. paper)

The paper in this book meets the guidelines for permanence and
durability of the Committee on Production Guidelines for Book
Longevity of the Council on Library Resources.

10   9   8   7   6   5   4   3   2   1

For Yeshai

CONTENTS

TABLES AND MAPS

PREFACE

Of all the aspects of PLO politics, the most salient is the contrast between the organization's diplomatic successes and its failure to translate these achievements into territorial gains. The successes have been impressive. After the 1967 Arab-Israeli war, the Palestine Liberation Organization enjoyed increasing support among Arab states and throughout the world; it came to be seen by the family of nations as an embryo state. Indeed, the PLO maintains a network of embassies throughout the world and is represented with sovereign status in a variety of international forums. Furthermore, the PLO gained broad legitimacy within the Arab world; certainly it exercised a growing influence over political developments concerning the future of the Palestinians.

In this respect, the PLO's success has been unprecedented in Palestinian political history. Since the emergence of Palestinian nationalism at the turn of the twentieth century, Palestinian groups and individuals have struggled first against the Jewish presence in Palestine, and later against Israel. Yet, until the mid–1960s, this struggle was assimilated into, and subordinated to, a general Arab setting—usually Nasserite or Baʿthist. The founding of the PLO in 1964 contributed to a process of differentiation between the Palestinian cause and the general Arab agenda and turned the former into an appealing rallying point for many Palestinians. Over the past two decades the PLO has successfully placed the Palestinian question at the forefront of Middle East and world attention. The notion that a peaceful settlement of the Arab-Israeli conflict requires a solution to the Palestinian problem has gathered wide support.

And yet the PLO has failed to make effective use of its achievements. It has been unable either militarily or politically to advance toward a settlement capable of satisfying even minimal Palestinian territorial aspirations. Its quest for a sovereign Palestinian state has remained unfulfilled.

This discrepancy has not escaped the notice of both students of and participants in the Middle East conflict. In the course of my research, I have come across two major explanations for the PLO's failure to translate its diplomatic successes into territorial gains. The first attributes the failure to the Arab states' attitude toward the organization. According to one interpretation of this argument, Arab attitudes after 1967 were equivocal. Publicly, Arab regimes provided the PLO with both diplomatic and material support, yet in more profound ways, the Arab states were less inclined to assist the Palestinians. Moreover, disputes and clashes among Arab regimes hampered their ability and desire to mobilize the pressure necessary to compel Israel's retreat from its anti-PLO position, permitting a mode of Palestinian independence in the West Bank and the Gaza Strip (occupied by Israel in 1967). A less benevolent interpretation maintains that the PLO served as a mere tool in inter-Arab struggles. Unwilling to subordinate their particular interests to those of the Palestinians, "none of the Arab leaders," as one PLO official has argued, "has ever been committed to an independent Palestinian state. . . . They do not see a need for a Palestinian state."[1]

A second explanation attributes the PLO failure to its refusal to recognize Israel publicly, to desist from armed struggle, and to renounce its ultimate goal of a Palestinian state in all of Palestine, that is, in Israel, the West Bank, and Gaza. True, following the 1973 war the PLO appeared to relent on this commitment by raising the option of a two-state solution: Israel and a Palestinian state in the West Bank and Gaza. In effect, however, PLO willingness to consider a political settlement has always been accompanied by a reluctance to accept the West Bank–Gaza state as a permanent

1. Shafiq al-Hut to the Saudi weekly *al-Sharq al-Awsat* (Riyadh), Oct. 21, 1983.

solution. Indeed, in the PLO's official publications and statements, the vision of a Greater Palestine to replace Israel and the notion of a mini-Palestinian state living in peace alongside Israel continue to appear hand in hand. PLO Chairman Yasir ʿArafat has thus been willing to reach a settlement through a peaceful process, but only so long as prior recognition of Israel is not the basis for political negotiations.

Both explanations of the PLO failure seem to be correct. There can be little doubt that both the Arab world's position regarding the PLO and the PLO's reluctance to alter its attitudes toward Israel have reduced its chances to participate in an eventual negotiated settlement. However, to the student of political behavior, both explanations share a common weakness: they focus on the reasons behind the PLO's failure to attain Palestinian statehood but not on its persistence in pursuing that path. They explain adequately enough how the PLO got to where it is, but they fail to explain why it remains there without being able to move ahead.

Certainly for ʿArafat and those PLO members who do not deny the possibility of a political settlement, it is nearly impossible to assure the PLO's effectiveness and survival and at the same time adopt a workable formula that guarantees simultaneously an unequivocal recognition of Israel, public renouncement of armed struggle, and a clearcut acceptance of a compromise territorial base for the Palestinians. Through its two decades of existence, the PLO has remained essentially an umbrella organization consisting of many rival factions. While strongly disagreeing on many issues, these factions are united around the goal of liberating all of Palestine through armed struggle. In view of this common denominator, the cessation of armed struggle, recognition of Israel, and acceptance of a mini-Palestinian state in the West Bank and Gaza as a permanent solution would almost certainly lead to the breakup of the organization, thus risking the position of ʿArafat and his supporters as representatives of the Palestinian people.

It is hard to believe that ʿArafat and his followers are unaware of the risks resulting from their position. After all, they are far from being a group of romantics or political suicides. They are well aware that the balance of power in the Middle East, both prior to and following the 1982 war in Lebanon, has clearly favored

Israel. Thus, the chance of a settlement under the PLO's favored conditions has little probability of success. Moreover, ʿArafat cannot remain indifferent in the face of continued Israeli occupation of the West Bank and the Gaza Strip. Expropriation of land, the massive settlement effort, and the tough Israeli policy against PLO supporters may yet present the PLO with a political fait accompli in the occupied territories. Under these circumstances, adherence to a policy of nonrecognition and to the doctrine of armed struggle might save the PLO from irreparable organizational damage but at the same time it could significantly reduce its chances of realizing Palestinian national aspirations in the foreseeable future.

In addition, ʿArafat's willingness to agree officially to a solution of a Palestinian state in the West Bank and Gaza as a final aim need not automatically affect either his role as leading spokesman of or his monopoly on Palestinian representation. It can be argued that ʿArafat's acceptance of such a solution would vastly increase his support among the West Bank and Gaza Palestinians who seek a speedy end to the Israeli occupation. As a result, he would stand a good chance of overcoming opposition within the PLO to a political settlement while still retaining his status as high priest of Palestinian nationalism. In the light of this analysis, one might argue that ʿArafat's persistent unwillingness to take a more overt posture of compromise has more to do with Israel's position toward the PLO than with internal constraints.

Since 1967 Israel's willingness to enter peace negotiations with the Arab nations on the political future of the occupied territories has always been accompanied by firm opposition to negotiations with the PLO. Both major Israeli political parties—the social democratic Maʿarakh (Alignment) and the rightist Likud (Unity)— claim that a PLO state in the West Bank and Gaza, no matter what the position of the PLO at any given time, could ultimately pose a threat to Israel. Both parties have sought to solve the Palestinian problem through direct negotiations either with Jordan or with the Palestinian local elite on the West Bank. Under these circumstances, it would be hard to assume that prior recognition of Israel and the renouncement of armed struggle would lead to a far-reaching change in the anti-PLO position of Israel. "If we recognize you and end the armed struggle," a senior PLO official told an Israeli reporter, "you will attempt to dictate to us who our representatives will be in the negotiations. Then you will demand that we accept recognized borders, a unified Jerusalem as [the Jewish people's] eternal capital, and so on. At the end we will be left with what we have today."[2]

However, 'Arafat and his followers follow political developments within Israel closely and are well aware of the bitter internal debate over the political and military cost Israel has been paying for the unresolved conflict with the Palestinians. Thus, it is hard to imagine that the PLO leaders have not considered the possibly favorable repercussions in Israel from the PLO's prior recognition of Israel and its readiness to accept a state in the West Bank and Gaza as a permanent solution. Such a statement would probably cause a political earthquake within Israeli public opinion similar to that which occurred following President Anwar Sadat's trip to Jerusalem in November 1977. It would place the Greater-Land-of-Israel camp on the defensive. It would generate an agonizing reassessment among Israeli decision makers and increase the chances for a new beginning in relations between Israel and the Palestinians.

Moreover, prior recognition, an end to armed struggle, and acceptance of a West Bank–Gaza state as a permanent solution would dramatically raise the PLO's international prestige and legitimacy in the United States and Western Europe. Prior recognition of Israel would also release the U.S. from the bonds of its 1975 memorandum of understanding with Israel, which committed the United States not to recognize or negotiate with the PLO unless it accepted United Nations Security Council Resolution 242 and Israel's right to exist. Also, recognition of Israel would undoubtedly lead the way to the formulation of new American and European peace plans more favorable to the PLO's demand for a state in the West Bank and Gaza Strip.

Still, 'Arafat has hesitated to adopt a new and daring strategy that would maximize his chance to participate in a negotiated settlement. To gain a better understanding of 'Arafat's reluctance to

2. Cited in Amnon Kapeliuk, "ba-Hazara le-Beirut" (Back to Beirut), *Koteret Rashit* (Jerusalem), Sept. 21, 1983.

take an innovative path, one must examine the nature of the PLO's internal and external political environment. Throughout this book I will elucidate 'Arafat's inability to assure control over developments in the two environments and his consequent fears that a daring strategy would not improve his chances of translating PLO diplomatic successes into territorial gains. Such an analysis should show how these fears have affected 'Arafat's decision to initiate or endorse only peace proposals that can be justified in the eyes of the PLO's rank and file. It should also clarify why he continues to rely simultaneously on a political process he does not trust and on an armed struggle whose outcome is increasingly doubtful.

ACKNOWLEDGMENTS

Many people at different times and in different ways helped in preparing this book. Gregory Kats, Michael Reich, Bruce Russett, James C. Scott, and Gladys Topkis were kind enough to read parts of the manuscript and contribute useful comments while I was at Yale in 1981–82. David Nachmias at the University of Wisconsin-Milwaukee, Michael Keren, Benny Temkin, Shimshon Zelniker at Tel Aviv University, Abraham Sela at the Hebrew University of Jerusalem, and several Israeli officials and Palestinians in the West Bank who prefer to remain anonymous were very helpful at a crucial point when I was preparing the final draft.

Shmuel Daniel, John Goldberg, Michal Sela, and Itai Sened were excellent research assistants, who helped me find my way through the vast amount of data available at the Dayan Center at Tel Aviv University and in the Truman Institute at the Hebrew University of Jerusalem. Good fortune has provided me with the help of Sylvia Weinberg, who carried the burden of typing patiently and efficiently and of Nancy Woodington, who edited the manuscript with insight and sensitivity.

I would not have been in a position to complete this volume had it not been for a grant from the Tel Aviv University Research Project on Peace and from the Social Science Faculty.

Finally, I wish to mention Marian Ash, Evelina and Ivan Kats, and my son Yeshai, who kept reminding me, each in a unique way, that dreams always require responsibilities.

ABBREVIATIONS

ALF	Arab Liberation Front (Jabhat al-tahrir al-ʿarabiyya)
DFLP	Democratic Front for the Liberation of Palestine (al-Jabha al-dimuqratiyya li-tahrir Filastin)
FLN	National Liberation Front (Front de Liberation Nationale)
IDF	Israel Defense Forces (Tsva haganah le-Yisraʾel)
NGC	National Guidance Committee (Lajnat al-tawjih al-watani)
PFLP	Popular Front for the Liberation of Palestine (al-Jabha al-shaʿbiyya li-tahrir Filastin)
PFLP-GC	Popular Front for the Liberation of Palestine—General Command (al-Jabha al-shaʿbiyya li-tahrir Filastin—al-qiyada al-ʿamma)
PLA	Palestine Liberation Army (Jaysh al-tahrir al-filastini)
PLF	Palestine Liberation Front (Jabhat al-tahrir al-filastiniyya)
PNC	Palestine National Council (al-Majlis al-watani al-filastini)
PNF	Palestine National Front (al-Jabha al-wataniyya al-filastiniyya)
PPSF	Palestine Popular Struggle Front (Jabhat al-nidal al-shaʿbiyya al-filastiniyya)
UNIFIL	United Nations Interim Force in Lebanon

CHAPTER 1

The Dilemma of the Disinherited

On November 13, 1974, Yasir ʿArafat, Chairman of the Palestine Liberation Organization (PLO), addressed the United Nations General Assembly. "Today," he ended his speech, "I have come bearing an olive branch and a freedom-fighter's gun. Do not let the olive branch fall from my hand. Do not let the olive branch fall from my hand. Do not let the olive branch fall from my hand."[1]

Much of PLO politics can be explained in terms of the tension between the dogmatic and the pragmatic approaches to the solution of the Palestinian problem, a tension between those who have seen armed resistance as the sole legitimate and effective way to "liberate" Palestine and those who have realized that the time has come for political initiatives in addition to arms. What are the origins of this tension? What has been its impact on the political behavior of the PLO?

Using guerrilla warfare to regain Palestine was not considered feasible in the 1950s. During these years Palestinian activists sought to fulfill their goals through a conventional military all-Arab effort. Some joined pan-Arab movements like the Arab Nationalists (al-Qawmiyyun al-ʿarab), which was associated with the Nasser regime, or the Baʿth Party, affiliated to Damascus. Others were active in the pan-Islam movements like the Muslim Brotherhood and the Muslim Liberation Party (Hizb al-tahrir al-islami). "Dur-

---

1. *Journal of Palestine Studies*, 4/2 (1975):192.

ing the 1950s," as one of the PLO leaders put it, "seldom was it possible to meet a young Palestinian who was not a member of a political party or movement, from the extreme right to the extreme left."[2]

Behind the activities of all these groups, no matter what they preached, lay the idea that Palestine could be restored through Arab unity; that is, through liquidation of the separate political states and concentration on the instrumental and ideological bonds of the Arab population in a single political entity. "Palestinian personalities and groups did not want to establish yet another border but to wipe out the existing ones."[3]

Participation in pan-Arab movements lessened the Palestinian feeling of political dependence, powerlessness, subordination, and patronage to the Arab regimes and created a sense of equality. It brought the Palestinians closer to the pan-Arab fundamental belief, to its powerful mysteries and its charismatic leadership.

The unification of Egypt and Syria as the United Arab Republic in 1958 raised high expectations. It was perceived as a step toward Arab unity and ultimately toward the reclamation of Palestine. President Nasser, as the high priest of Arab nationalism, was powerful enough to carry the message of unity to the Arab world. He was able to break ground through the union with Syria. But he was unable to overcome local sentiments, parochial interests, and the set of political symbols that prevailed in Arab society and limited the carrying out of the goals of pan-Arabism as expressed by Nasser and his followers.

The Syrian-Egyptian union came to an end in September 1961. The split, which occurred after three years of unity, and the failure in 1963 to establish a tripartite union of Syria, Egypt, and Iraq, renewed the sense, especially among the Palestinian younger generation, of grievance and anxiety, of alienation from their fellow

2. See Abu Iyad's interview with Lutfi al-Khuli, "Hiwar bayn Fatah wa al-Taliᶜa" (Dialogue between Fatah and al-Taliᶜa), *al-Taliᶜa* (Cairo) 6 (June 1969): 68.

3. Eliᶜezer Beʾeri, *ha-Falastinim tahat shilton Yarden: Shalosh sugiyyot* (The Palestinians under Jordanian rule: Three issues) (Jerusalem, Magnes Press, Hebrew University, 1978), 33–34.

Arabs. Nowhere was this sense more vividly expressed than in Fawaz Turki's *The Disinherited*:

> Living in Beirut as a stateless person . . . I did not feel I was living among my "Arab brothers." I did not feel I was an Arab, a Lebanese, or as some wretchedly pious writers claimed, a "Southern Syrian." I was a Palestinian. And that meant I was an outsider, an alien, a refugee and a burden. To be that, for us, for my generation of Palestinians, meant to look inward, to draw closer, to be part of a minority that had its own way of doing and seeing and feeling and reacting.[4]

The Palestinians, as Turki wrote, "were discriminated against on every level in Arab society. . . . Socially, Palestinians were despised, persecuted, or at least ignored. . . . I hated first the Arabs, then, in an inarticulate and vague manner, the world."[5]

The accusations and bitterness were directed also toward the Palestinian older generation, whose leadership was perceived as ready to acquiesce in political dependence on the Arab regimes. The emergence, therefore, of a traditional-style leader, Ahmad al-Shuqayri, the Palestinian delegate to the Arab League, as the first chairman of the PLO was hardly welcomed by young Palestinian militants in movements and organizations such as Fatah (Harakat al-tahrir al-watani al-filastini), the General Union of Palestinian Students, and al-Qawmiyyun al-ʿArab. These groups accepted al-Shuqayri's exploitation of the first Arab summit conference's resolution of January 1964—which authorized him to hold talks with Arab governments to enlarge the Palestinian role in an all-Arab effort at liberating Palestine[6]—in order to form the PLO and to approve the Palestinian National Charter four months later. However, they accused al-Shuqayri of turning the organization into an instrument in the hands of the Arab countries, especially Egypt and Jordan, ensuring Palestinian ineffectuality.[7] "Giving al-

4. Fawaz Turki, *The Disinherited: Journal of a Palestinian Exile* (New York: Monthly Review Press, 1972), 8.

5. Ibid., 40.

6. Ahmad al-Shuqayri, *Min al-qimma ila al-hazima maʿa al-muluk wa al-ruʾasaʾ* (From the summit to the defeat with the kings and rulers) (Beirut: al-ʿAwda, 1971), 61.

7. For more on this argument see *al-Muharrir* (Beirut) 12 and 16 (July 1965).

Shuqayri a free hand," argued al-Qawmiyyun, "far from creating effective popular control, raises a possibility of a return to the wretched manner in which the Arab Higher Committee conducted the struggle of the Palestinian people before the disaster [the 1948 Arab-Israeli war.]"[8] To them al-Shuqayri and the people around him represented the Palestinian old guard, who symbolized the Palestinian defeated generation—powerless opportunists who lacked political integrity.[9]

These new Palestinian groups shared the idea of guerrilla warfare as the alternative to conventional Arab military strategy against Israel, a way "to transform the distorted structure of reality"[10] that had increased their sense of inferiority and emphasized a status of inequality. By means of a contrary approach to conventional Arab military strategy, the militant Palestinian groups sought to play a more initiatory role in Arab politics in order to liberate Palestine. The Palestinians were searching for "an autonomous Palestinian action by which the Palestinian people will address themselves to their cause directly and not vicariously."[11]

The success of the National Liberation Front (FLN) in Algeria in July 1962 in achieving political independence through guerrilla warfare served as a living example. Although some of the Palestinian radicals were aware of the differences between the two cases, the FLN's accomplishment became, especially within Fatah, a source of hope for what might be accomplished through guerrilla activity. "The Palestinian youth sensed that they were not inferior

---

8. See "Clarification of the Palestine National Congress," al-Qawmiyyun al-ʿArab poster, June 1964 (archives, Jordanian Security Services, in Israel State Archives [Jerusalem], file 498–4). For similar arguments, see *al-Wathaʾiq al-filas-tiniyya al-ʿarabiyya li-ʿam 1965* (Palestine Arab documents for the year 1965) (Beirut: Institute for Palestine Studies, 1966), document 165, 476–78.

9. See, for instance, Naji ʿAlush, *al-Masira ila Filastin* (The way to Palestine) (Beirut: al-Taliʿa 1964), 189–91; also Yehoshafat Harkabi, *ha-Falastinim mi-tar-dema le-hitʿorerut* (The Palestinians from quiescence to awakening) (Jerusalem: Magnes Press, Hebrew University, 1979), 73.

10. Turki, *The Disinherited*, 99.

11. ʿIsam Sakhnini, "Tamthil al-shaʿb al-filastini wa munazamat al-tahrir al-filastiniyya" (The representation of the people of Palestine and the Palestine Lib-eration Organization), *Shuʾun Filastiniyya* (Beirut) (Nov. 1972): 27; Harkabi, *ha-Falastinim*, 56–57.

to their Algerian brothers and that they were capable of unfurling the banner of armed struggle and carrying it out."[12]

The idea of Palestinian armed resistance, however, was not so simple to carry out. The lack of territory and absence of independent political authority, as well as the shortage of material resources, forced the Palestinians to seek cooperation and certain commitments from the Arab world. Without such cooperation they might still have been able to carry guerrilla warfare from Arab territories into Israel, but they would have faced enormous obstacles. Cooperation, on the other hand, brought with it fears and suspicions. The inequality in power relations between the Palestinians and the Arab world meant dependence, which opened the door for Arab manipulation. Dependence could thus have undermined the Palestinians' ability to carry out guerrilla warfare successfully.

Young Palestinian activists, aware of this situation, strove for an operational formula that would enable them to act autonomously, without dependence on or subordination to the particular considerations of each Arab regime. Fatah, therefore, endeavored to construct its activity on the principle of practical cooperation with all Arab regimes, with the idea of mutual noninterference in internal affairs. The Palestinian organizations would autonomously initiate the first stage of the military struggle, leading eventually to a "comprehensive" war with Israel. By taking this position, Fatah sought to minimize the threat posed by Palestinian guerrilla warfare activity especially to the conservative Arab regimes like Jordan and Saudi Arabia. Fatah assumed that as it reduced this threat, the resistance of these regimes toward guerrilla operations would decrease, and the possibilities of activity without serious Arab intervention would increase.

The more radical organizations, most notably those led by Ahmad Jibril and George Habash, sought revolutionary changes within the political structure of the Arab regimes as a prior condition to the liberation of Palestine.[13] However, they too were

12. Abu Iyad, "Fatah wa al-Taliʿa."

13. The radical organizations included Ahmad Jibril and Ahmad Zaʿrour's Palestine Liberation Front (Jabhat al-tahrir al-filastiniyya), Ahmad al-Yamani and Shafiq al-Hut's Heroes of the Return (Abtal al-ʿawda), and George Habash's Youth

aware of the need to develop cooperative relations, at least with the radical Arab countries, in order to transmit their message successfully. They emphasized for this purpose their common ideological denominator and political goals with such radical regimes as those in Egypt under Nasser, Syria, or Iraq.

The radicals, as in the case of Fatah, tried to gain moral support and material assistance from Arab regimes. Like Fatah, they assumed that an all-Arab commitment to the military option as the sole way to liberate Palestine would enable them to develop enough bargaining power and maneuvering capability to overcome their dependence and create the proper conditions for cooperation with the idea of Palestinian guerrilla warfare.

One could argue that the rivalries and internal conflicts paralyzed any meaningful Arab action. The Palestinian organizations, however, relied on the vulnerability of the Arab regimes in crisis situations, where the discrepancy between commitments to orthodox pan-Arab beliefs and practical behavior is less tolerable, and there is less room for particular interpretations. Under these circumstances, the ability of the weaker party, the Palestinians, to reach an ideological consensus and mobilize material support was strengthened. Nowhere was this Palestinian ability to manipulate the Arab regimes more apparent than after the Arab-Israeli war of 1967.

GUERRILLA WARFARE AFTER THE 1967 WAR

Israel's occupation of the West Bank, the Gaza Strip, the Sinai Peninsula, and the Golan Heights during the 1967 war undermined belief in the effectiveness of a conventional Arab military struggle against Israel:

Prior to the June war a large percentage of their GNP was expended by Egypt, Jordan, and Syria on building up the armed forces. By the middle of the decade, the forces were widely regarded in the area as sufficiently strong to face a showdown with the Israelis. This situation was practically reversed following the June war. . . . The costly conventional war machine

---

of Vengeance (Shabab al-tha'r). After the 1967 war, some of these figures became leaders of major radical Palestinian organizations.

lay in ruins and all hopes for the restoration of Palestine in the foreseeable future were suddenly dashed. . . . The sudden defeat shattered the prestige and moral leadership of conservative and revolutionary regimes alike.

In this atmosphere . . . the renewed call of the Palestinian [organizations] to armed resistance at the beginning of October 1967 . . . was embraced . . . by most Arabs and particularly by the large augmented bulk of displaced Palestinians.[14]

The message of Palestinian armed resistance gained acceptance. Within a short period those Palestinian groups that espoused guerrilla warfare against Israel emerged as the new leaders of the PLO, replacing the old guard, changing its political structure, and redefining its operational goals and priorities. From an organization ready to follow the conventional Arab political and military approach, the PLO became an organization of militant groups that believed in their ability to mobilize enough support from the Palestinians and from the Arab world to conduct successfully an unconventional military struggle against Israel.

In December 1967 Ahmad al-Shuqayri, who "was held accountable among the Palestinians for his opposition to commando activities against Israel,"[15] was forced to resign and Yahya Hamuda became acting chairman of the PLO. In July 1968, at the fourth session of the Palestine National Council (PNC; the parliamentary body of the PLO), Fatah and the Popular Front for the Liberation of Palestine (PFLP) made substantial political gains.[16] Of the 100 seats on the council, Fatah and its supporters received 38 and the PFLP 10.[17] It took less than a year for Yasir ʿArafat, the head of Fatah, to succeed Hamuda as chairman of the PLO. Guerrilla warfare proponents celebrated their triumph.

14. Fuad Jabber, "The Palestinian Resistance and Inter-Arab Politics" in William B. Quandt et al., *The Politics of Palestinian Nationalism* (Berkeley: University of California Press, 1973), 176–78.

15. William B. Quandt, "Political and Military Dimensions of Contemporary Palestinian Nationalism," ibid., 68.

16. The PFLP was a new merger of radical organizations comprising the Palestine Liberation Front, the Heroes of the Return, and the Youth of Vengeance. All three organizations were established during the mid–1960s.

17. *New York Times*, July 14, 1968; *Arab Report and Record* (London), Oct. 1–15, 1968: 316; Bard E. O'Neill, *Armed Struggle in Palestine: A Political-Military Analysis* (Boulder, Colo: Westview Press, 1978), 127.

Nowhere is the dominance of this principle more apparent than in the 1968 amended version of the Palestinian National Charter. According to article 9, "Armed struggle is the only way to liberate Palestine and is therefore a strategy and not tactics." Guerrilla action, continued article 10, "forms the nucleus of the popular Palestinian war of liberation. This demands its promotion, extension, and protection, and the mobilization of all the masses . . . in the organization and involvement in the armed Palestinian revolution."[18]

The Palestinian organizations' efforts to implement the idea of armed resistance through a popular Palestinian war against Israel conducted from the occupied territories limited the maneuverability of the Arab regimes toward the Palestinian organizations. After the defeat of 1967 no regime in the Arab world could either question the legitimacy of the guerrilla operations or refuse moral support and material assistance to Palestinian guerrilla warfare. And as long as this activity was undertaken in the occupied territories without interference in the domestic politics of the Arab countries, no regime was ready to challenge it publicly.

GUERRILLA WARFARE THROUGH TERRITORIAL BASES

Since September 1967, the Palestinian organizations have tried to implement the idea of a popular Palestinian war, building territorial bases in the West Bank and Gaza Strip. The large and homogenous Palestinian Arab population in these territories and the mountainous terrain of the West Bank seemed to provide suitable conditions to carry out a popular armed revolution. ʿArafat, with several Fatah high commanders, left Damascus in July 1967 for the West Bank in order to build armed networks and direct their activities.[19]

From September 1967 to January 1968, numerous guerrilla operations were carried out in the occupied territories and within the pre–1967 Israeli borders. In September 1967, according to an Is-

18. See "The 1968 Palestinian National Covenant" in *Middle East Record* 1968, ed. Daniel Dishon (Jerusalem: Israel Universities Press, 1973), 433.
19. Ehud Yaʿari, *Strike Terror; The Story of Fatah* (New York: Sabra, 1970), 127.

raeli source, guerrilla operations against Israeli targets totaled 13, in October 10, in November 18 and in December 20.[20] Most of these activities were directed against civilian Israeli targets such as *kibbutzim*, apartment buildings, and factories. A movie theater in Jerusalem was also attacked. Other operations were directed against Israeli military personnel and headquarters, mostly in the occupied territories.[21]

By the end of 1967, however, the attempt to conduct a popular liberation war from territorial bases on the West Bank had been stymied by the Israeli security forces. Israeli military measures against Palestinian guerrilla operations were carried out along the Jordan River and within the occupied territories. In addition, reprisals against Palestinian inhabitants who had cooperated with the guerrillas led to the detection and elimination of the Fatah headquarters in Nablus and its guerrilla cells in Hebron, Tulkarm, Bethlehem, Qabatiya and East Jerusalem. About a thousand active guerrillas were arrested. Three years later Israeli authorities had achieved similar results in the Gaza Strip. Whatever role the Israeli military measures played in thwarting Palestinian attempts to build guerrilla bases inside the occupied territories, the fact remains that the Palestinian organizations failed to mobilize the population there into a popular armed revolution.[22] Neither the West Bank nor the Gaza Strip turned into an "Arab Hanoi" against an "Israeli Saigon."[23] At the end of 1967, it was clear that reaching this target had become an impossible mission, and by 1971 Palestinian military operations in the Gaza Strip had died out.

During the 1970s and 1980s, the PLO shifted its attention to political activities among the Palestinian inhabitants in the West

20. Ibid., 137.

21. For more details, see the *New York Times*, Sept. 25 and 26, 1967; also Ann M. Lesch, *Israel's Occupation of the West Bank: The First Two Years* (Santa Monica: Rand, 1970), 80–82.

22. For more details on the Palestinian organizations' obstacles to gaining local support, see Abraham Sela, "The PLO, the West Bank and Gaza Strip," *Jerusalem Quarterly* 8 (1978):66.

23. For more on these terms and what they represented, See "al-Istratijiyya al-siyasiyya lil-jabha al-sha'biyya" (The political strategy of the Popular Front), in *'Ala tariq al-thawra al-filastiniyya* (On the road of the Palestinian revolution) (Beirut: al-Tali'a, 1970), 10; *al-Hurriyya* (Beirut), Sept. 9, 1968.

Bank and Gaza. However, external and internal circumstances
have led the PLO to place a far greater emphasis on its activities
in the West Bank than in Gaza. At the same time, the scope and
intensity of local political activity is far less significant in the Gaza
Strip than in the West Bank.

Two major reasons appear to lie behind the PLO decision to
focus politically on the West Bank and deemphasize the Gaza Strip.
First, both Jordan and Israel see the West Bank as the key element
in any political solution of the Palestinian problem, yet their perceptions relating to the future political status of the West Bank
have clashed with those of the PLO. As a result, the organization
has intensified its activities in the West Bank in order to be able
to preempt any settlement contrary to its national goals. Second,
the West Bank is a more highly politicized society than that of the
Gaza Strip, because of significant differences in levels of economic
and social development. This higher level of development has led
to the crystallization of local West Bank interests that have, at
times, caused differences of opinion between the West Bank political elite and the PLO over ways to further a solution to the
Palestinian problem. PLO suspicions that under certain circumstances the West Bank leadership will opt for a solution unac-
ceptable to it has led the organization to devote most of its efforts
to the West Bank rather than to the Gaza Strip.

GUERRILLA WARFARE THROUGH EXTRATERRITORIAL BASES

The failure of the Palestinian organizations to build bases in the
occupied territories was compensated for by their success in establishing extraterritorial bases on the east side of the Jordan
River, that is to say, in Jordan. The new situation produced two
major constraints on the effective conduct of the organizations'
guerrilla operations. First, the undermining of their military presence in the occupied territories adversely affected their ability to
maintain direct contact with the Palestinian population under Israeli rule. This loss of direct contact could have lowered their
political status among the Palestinian inhabitants as well as among
the Arab countries. Second, conducting guerrilla operations from
Jordanian territory posed a threat to Jordan's political stability,

leading to conflict between the Jordanian authorities and the Palestinian organizations.

These potential problems did not immediately become realities. At the beginning of 1968, Palestinian attempts to combine intensive guerrilla operations with political resistance on the West Bank, and the continuing Arab adherence to the military option, allowed the Palestinian organizations to minimize the abovementioned problems.

The failure to establish territorial bases on the West Bank meant that the Palestinian organizations relied less on the direct support of the broad local Palestinian population. Instead they had to concentrate more on aid and assistance from small groups, especially students, young intellectuals, and white-collar professionals. The role of these groups was not just to conduct guerrilla operations. They also mobilized the local Palestinian population to participate in protest activities and hold school and business strikes, often on dates of national Palestinian significance, such as Israel's Independence Day (May 15) or the anniversary of the 1967 war (June 5).[24]

Toward the end of 1968, the Palestinian organizations tried to institutionalize the pattern of active protests. Members of al-Qawmiyyun al-ʿArab and later on the Communists took the initiative in establishing the Committees of National Unity in Nablus, Ramallah, and al-Bira. Behind this initiative lay the idea that the committees should first engage in a political struggle against the Israeli authorities and then proceed to a military struggle after consolidating their position.[25]

In spite of the importance of this activity the major efforts of the Palestinians focused on guerrilla operations in the occupied territories and within the pre–1967 Israeli borders. In the absence of territorial bases on the West Bank, guerrilla activities were carried out mainly by small units from extraterritorial bases and

24. For more details, see *Middle East Record* 1968, 450–51; Shaul Mishal, "Nationalism through Localism: Some Observations on the West Bank Political Elite," *Middle Eastern Studies* 17/4 (1981): 482–83.

25. See Elie Rekhess and Asher Susser, *Political Factors and Trends in the West Bank* (Tel Aviv: Shiloah Center for Middle Eastern and African Studies, Tel Aviv University, 1974), 5–6.

by some Palestinian local activists. At the beginning of 1968 most of these bases were located in the Jordan Valley along the cease-fire border with Israel, far from Jordanian cities. Karamah, a large Palestinian refugee camp in the Jordan Valley, became the central base and the area headquarters of Fatah. Palestinian guerrillas were sent from Karamah and other bases in the area to attack Israeli military and civilian targets. From thirty operations in March 1968 they reached a total of eighty a month at the beginning of 1970.[26]

Since 1968 the Palestinian organizations, especially Fatah and the PFLP, have succeeded in increasing the number of recruits to the organizations. In early 1968 Fatah had 2000 members; at the beginning of 1969 there were 5000, and in August 1970 the number had increased to 10,000, while the PFLP numbered 3000.[27] At the same time, a large number of Palestinians joined new organizations. These included the Syrian sponsored al-Saʿiqa, the pro-Iraqi Arab Liberation Front (ALF), the Democratic Front for the Liberation of Palestine (DFLP), the pro-Syrian Front for the Liberation of Palestine—General Command (PFLP-GC), and the Palestine Popular Struggle Front (PPSF). In September of 1970 al-Saʿiqa had reached 7000 members, the ALF 3000, the DFLP 1000, and the PFLP-GC 500.[28] By the summer of 1970, the total number of members in the different Palestinian organizations was approximately 25,000.[29]

This growth was due mainly to the heroic image that the guerrilla

26. From September 1967 up to the end of 1969 Palestinian organizations carried out 176 operations in the West Bank, 676 in the Gaza Strip, and 144 within the pre–1967 Israeli borders. In these activities 138 Israeli soldiers and 73 civilians were killed, and 575 soldiers and 523 civilians were wounded. For more details, see Yaʿari, *Strike Terror*, 366–71.

27. See the *Times* (London), Feb. 20, 1969; the *New York Times*, Aug. 15 and Sept. 19, 1970; Aryeh Y. Yodfat and Yuval Arnon-Ohanna, *PLO Strategy and Tactics* (London: Croom Helm, 1981), 47.

28. *New York Times*, Sept. 19, 1970. For more on these organizations see chapter 2.

29. It is worth mentioning that not all of the 25,000 members "were actually commandos. Some were support and political elements" (O'Neill, *Armed Struggle*, 253). Israeli intelligence estimated in early 1970 that the Palestinian guerrilla organizations could muster only 5000–6000 fighters. See the *New York Times*, Feb. 12, 1970.

organizations had gained among the Palestinian population and in Arab public opinion as a result of the Karamah battle on March 21, 1968. The battle involved a 1000-man Israeli raiding party and 600 Palestinians supported by 48 Jordanian tanks, 11 artillery batteries, and two brigades of infantry. The encounter ended, according to diverse sources, with between 70 and 150 casualties and 130 prisoners among the Palestinians, and 23 dead, 70 injured, and 3 missing in action on the Israeli side.[30] Although the Jordanian army fought alongside the Palestinians, the fifteen-hour battle was hailed as the first Palestinian military victory over the Israeli army since the war of 1948. The high number of Israeli casualties during one day's battle and the stiff resistance to superior Israeli equipment nourished the Palestinian self-image. "Karamah was responsible for restoring Arab self-esteem and for showing the Palestinians not only that they could face the Israelis' military but that only through armed struggle could they ever hope to defeat Zionism."[31]

After Karamah, Israeli operations from the air and on the ground forced the Palestinian organizations to transfer their headquarters and training camps from the Jordan Valley to the Palestinian refugee camps inside Jordan, close to such major cities as Amman, al-Salt, Jarash, and Irbid. The more guerrilla activities they launched against Israel, the more sympathy and cooperation they gained from the Palestinian population of Jordan. Under these circumstances the dispute between Fatah and the more radical organizations over the nature of the relations to be developed with conservative regimes like Jordan was reawakened.

Fatah leadership, guided by a more practical view, regarded Jordan as a strategic base for guerrilla warfare. After the failure of a popular revolution in the occupied territories, the launching

30. Ibid., March 23, 1968; also John Laffin, *Fedayeen: The Arab-Israeli Dilemma* (London: Cassell, 1973), 30–31; O'Neill, *Armed Struggle*, 77–79.

31. Hisham Sharabi (cited in Laffin, *Fedayeen*, 32); a similar argument was used by the PLO in August 1982 during the long Israeli siege of West Beirut. "We taught the Arabs how to fight. We proved that the Israelis were not invincible. We held them off longer than any Arab army in history." *Wikalat al-anaba' al-filastiniyya* (*WAFA*), (Palestinian news agency), Aug. 4, 1982; *New York Times*, Aug. 11, 1982.

of guerrilla operations from Jordan became the highest priority. Fatah therefore strove to build a relationship with Jordan that would lead to a modus vivendi. In contrast, the more radical factions, such as the PFLP and the DFLP, considered the pro-Western Jordanian regime as a threat and an obstacle to their struggle against Israel. They sought a military showdown with the Jordanian regime, believing in the probability of support from Syria and Iraq, as well as from Jordanian soldiers of Palestinian origin and Palestinians living in Jordan. That the Palestinian organizations in Jordan by the end of the 1960s ran welfare and health services inside the refugee camps and had formed their own police force and courts of justice served as additional proof of their ability to mobilize the Palestinian population against the central government in Amman and to threaten its political hegemony.[32]

Reviewing these political circumstances with optimistic eyes, the PFLP and the DFLP did not hesitate to initiate an open confrontation with the Jordanian army in the belief that Fatah would join them. Fatah, however, was more cautious. One can assume that from Fatah's point of view, no matter how the clash with the Jordanian army ended, it would carry the risk of undermining the PLO's position and its operational capabilities. Successful results might strengthen its independent status in Jordan, but at the same time could jeopardize its status among conservative Arab regimes, which would consider it an immediate threat to their existence. Failure, on the other hand, would have immediate negative effects on the PLO's ability to continue its guerrilla warfare against Israel.

Despite Fatah's reluctance, the more radical organizations were able to strengthen their position. Jordan's acceptance, following Egypt's, of the proposal to renew peace talks with Israel through the United Nations envoy Dr. Jarring in September 1970, and the response of the PFLP—hijacking Swissair, TWA, and BOAC airplanes to Jordan and forcing them to land near Zarqa'—intensified the conflict. Fatah's attempts to reach a modus vivendi with the

32. On the Palestinian organizations' activities inside the refugee camps and their impact on daily life, see the *Times*, Nov. 20, 1969; Yodfat and Arnon-Ohanna, *PLO Strategy and Tactics*, 30; Hisham Sharabi, *Palestine Guerrillas: Their Credibility and Effectiveness*, (Washington: Georgetown University Center for Strategic and International Studies, 1970), 28.

Jordanian authorities suffered a crucial setback. "Things cannot go on," announced King Hussein. "Every day Jordan is sinking a little further."[33] Jordan's sovereignty was in jeopardy.

While the hijacking negotiations were going on, the Palestinian organizations continued to undermine Jordanian sovereignty, increasing their control in Amman and Irbid and proclaiming the northern part of Jordan a liberated area. A clash with the Jordanian army became inevitable, and the ensuing war spelled disaster for the Palestinian forces in Jordan. Despite Syrian intervention on behalf of the Palestinians, the Jordanian army, enjoying indirect Israeli military support (a concentration of forces along the border) against Syria, was able to restore its control. On September 24, after nine days of fighting and 3500 casualties, the Palestinians accepted a cease-fire initiated by the Arab states. In July 1971, less than a year later, 3000 to 5000 guerrilla members were forced to leave the country and take refuge in Lebanon. Another 2300 had been taken prisoner.[34] "We completely rejected . . . any dialogue with those organizations," announced Amman Radio, "which represent nobody but themselves. They have become a fifth column."[35]

TOWARD A REASSESSMENT OF THE GUERRILLA STRATEGY

The PLO's loss of bases in the occupied territories at the end of 1967 and its loss of the extraterritorial military presence in Jordan in July 1971 had a critical impact on its ability to continue armed resistance. The loss of territorial continuity with the West Bank via the long Jordanian border with Israel limited the PLO's ability to conduct hit and run operations inside the occupied territories and within the pre-1967 Israeli borders. It also meant a decline in the capacity of the PLO to direct either passive or active resistance against the Israeli presence in the occupied territories.

The Palestinian population's participation in the first municipal elections held on the West Bank under Israeli rule in March and

33. *Le Figaro* (Paris), Sept. 15, 1970; Laffin, *Fedayeen*, 61.
34. *New York Times*, July 8, 14, and 21, 1971; *Arab Report and Record*, July 1–15, 1971: 349–50.
35. Aug. 18, 1971.

May 1972, despite PLO opposition, and the increasing willingness of some West Bank leaders to cooperate with the Israeli authorities on day-to-day issues, mirrored the changing political mood in the occupied territories after the civil war in Jordan. The growing cooperation between Israel and Jordan on welfare, education, and West Bank economic issues as well as King Hussein's 1972 federation plan for a political solution of the West Bank and Gaza Strip problem were interpreted by the PLO as an Israeli-Jordanian attempt to eliminate, or at least minimize, its role in any future political solution.[36]

The PLO's readiness in 1971 to redefine the role of armed struggle as a "principal" means rather than the "sole" means of liberating Palestine reflected its growing awareness of the limits of its ability to cope with these political developments by military methods.[37] Under these new circumstances, the PLO was ready to consider political and economic activities, working through local institutions in the occupied territories, as complementary to military ones.[38]

After the October War of 1973 the PLO became even more aware of its limitations. It became clear that the Arab countries were unable to force Israel to withdraw from the occupied territories by military means. Reflecting this new awareness, the Arab summit meetings in Algiers in November 1973 and in Rabat in October 1974 resolved to launch a diplomatic initiative to complement the military option. In addition, the January 1974 Egyptian-Israeli agreement on disengagement of forces, and the Israeli-Syrian agreement of March 1974, signaled a major shift toward acceptance of a moderate approach to resolving the Arab-Israeli conflict. The tenor of the once immovable zero-sum deadlock in

36. For more on these PLO fears and suspicions, see e.g., Abu Iyad, "Afkar wadiha amama marhala ghamida" (Clear thoughts on an obscure stage), *Shu'un Filastiniyya* (Jan. 1974):5–10. For more on the Israeli and Jordanian policies toward the West Bank in the post–1967 war period, see chapter 2.

37. See the March 1971 resolutions of the eighth session of the Palestine National Council, *al-Anwar* (Beirut), March 5, 1971.

38. For more details, see part 1 of "Aims of the Political Program of the Palestinian Revolution" adopted by the eleventh session of the Palestine National Council, Cairo, Jan. 12, 1973, published in *Journal of Palestine Studies* 2/1 (1972): 169–71.

the region was softened by this new give-and-take atmosphere adopted by the Arabs.

The new political reality made it unlikely that the PLO would continue to enjoy unequivocal commitments and material support from the Arab world, thereby increasing the concern of Palestinian leaders that if compromise were reached over the West Bank and the Gaza Strip, the PLO might "miss the train and be stranded in the station of oblivion."[39] PLO concern grew further after the second interim peace agreement between Egypt and Israel over Sinai in September 1975, and especially after the Camp David accords of September 1978 and the Egyptian-Israeli peace treaty of March 1979. The PLO's fear that a political settlement might be reached on the West Bank and the Gaza Strip without its participation became a more realistic possibility.

It was this fear of being bypassed that urged forces within Fatah, al-Sa'iqa, and the DFLP to advocate participation in the political process and face the here and now rather than adhere to a dogmatic doctrine that relied on an all-or-nothing approach. At the same time, they could not ignore the dangers entailed by this step. Considering the fragile balance between all PLO factions, could one then advocate a political solution without risking PLO symbolic and organizational hegemony and without downgrading its political status as the representative of the Palestinian people? Leaning toward a political solution was naturally tempting, but it carried risks and suspicions that had to be examined in order to understand the political dilemma PLO leaders faced whenever they considered the possibility of such a settlement.

NOTHING IS GIVEN, NOTHING IS FORGIVEN

The PLO's consideration of political means rather than exclusive reliance on armed struggle grew from beliefs that in light of the 1973 war a flexible policy is preferable to adamant adherence to a formal doctrine of armed struggle. In the dusty reality of the Middle East arena after the 1973 war, an exclusive reliance on

39. Hussein J. Agha, "What State for the Palestinians?" *Journal of Palestine Studies* 6/1 (1976):11.

armed resistance was an untenable policy, as the Arab states had
shown a readiness to negotiate a political settlement with Israel
over the occupied territories. "All [the Arab states] want," as a
member of the Fatah Central Committee put it, "is King Hussein,
and . . . through the Jordanian regime, a Palestinian government
should be established, conditional upon peace being made with
Israel."[40] If a political solution were reached, the argument continued, "The [PLO] resistance might be subjected to various pressures, local and international, that would lead to its eventual
liquidation. If Syria and Egypt had accepted peace with Israel, for
example, the decisive moves against the Palestinians in Lebanon
would be easier than otherwise. Alternatively, the movement itself
could split under the weight of a final settlement, which would be
presented to the people as an Arab victory. On both counts the
future seemed lonely and gloomy."[41]

PLO leaders who leaned toward the political process were very
skeptical about the PLO's ability to prevent such a settlement
despite its political achievements in the post–1973 era. It is worthwhile to examine these achievements for a better understanding
of the PLO's doubts that it would be able to play an influential
role in inter-Arab politics should there be a peace settlement.

The secret clauses of the resolutions reached at the November
1973 Arab summit in Algiers endowed the PLO with Arab recognition as the sole representative of the Palestinian people. All
Arab countries except Jordan ensured the PLO's right to veto any
political settlement proposal made by Arab countries: "The conference resolves that the objectives of the current stage of the joint
Arab Struggle are . . . commitment to the restoration of the national rights of the Palestinian people in the manner decided by
the Palestine Liberation Organization in its capacity as the sole
representative of the Palestinians."[42] At the Rabat Arab summit
of October 1974, all Arab countries, including Jordan, reaffirmed
publicly the status of the PLO as the sole legitimate representative

40. Abu Salih's speech in Sidon, Lebanon, as cited by *WAFA*, Jan. 18, 1974;
Journal of Palestine Studies 3/3 (1974): 192.
41. Agha, "What State for the Palestinians?" 12.
42. Article 3 of the Algiers Arab Summit Conference secret resolutions, *al-Nahar*
(Beirut), Dec. 4, 1973; Yodfat and Arnon-Ohanna, *PLO Strategy and Tactics*, 166.

of the Palestinian people, as well as secretly reassuring the PLO of veto power over any Arab peace proposal.[43]

Furthermore, in November 1974 the PLO gained the recognition of the United Nations as the representative of the Palestinian people, reaffirming its centrality in solving the Palestinian problem: "Having considered the question of Palestine," stated United Nations General Assembly Resolution 3236, [and] having heard the statement of the Palestine Liberation Organization, the representative of the Palestine people, [the General Assembly] . . . recognizes that the Palestinian people is a principal party in the establishment of a just and durable peace in the Middle East . . . [and] requests the Secretary-General to establish contacts with the Palestine Liberation Organization on all matters concerning the question of Palestine."[44] The U.N. demonstrated this recognition by inviting the PLO "to participate in the sessions and the work of the General Assembly in the capacity of observer [and] . . . in the session and the work of all international conferences convened under the auspices of other organs of the United Nations."[45] Moreover, in the years following these resolutions, the U.S.S.R., the Eastern European countries, and most of the Third World, and some Western countries established diplomatic relations with the PLO. By the beginning of the 1980s the PLO had representatives in more than eighty states.

While the PLO's political achievements limited the Arab states' ability to enter into peace negotiations with Israel over the West Bank and Gaza, they did not altogether preclude such a possibility. The fact that the Arab summit resolutions that gave the PLO veto power over any Arab peace proposal were made secretly is clear evidence of the Arab regimes' reluctance to relinquish the freedom to initiate policies serving particular national interests that might clash with PLO objectives.

Indeed, the Egyptian-Jordanian joint statement of July 1974

43. For more details on the secret clauses of the Rabat resolutions, see Musa Sabri's report in *Akhbar al-Yawm* (Cairo), Nov. 2, 1974.

44. See U.N. General Assembly Resolution 3236 (XXIX) on Palestinians' rights, Nov. 22, 1974. *United Nations Monthly Chronicle* 11/11 (Dec. 1974):36–37.

45. U.N. General Assembly Resolution 3237 (XXIX), Observer Status for the PLO, Nov. 22, 1974. Ibid., 37.

contradicted the 1973 Algiers resolution by defining the PLO as a "legitimate representative of the Palestinians, *except for* those Palestinians residing in the Hashemite Kingdom of Jordan"[46] (my emphasis). In addition, the March 1976 massacre suffered by the PLO at the Christians' hands and with Syrian backing in the Tal al-Za'atar Palestinian refugee camp in Lebanon, and the 1979–80 negotiations between Egypt and Israel over the autonomy plan for the West Bank and the Gaza Strip as part of the 1979 peace treaty between the two countries further testified to the vulnerability of PLO status in the Arab world. "The world," proclaimed Khalid al-Hasan, the head of the Palestine National Council's foreign affairs committee, "does not take Arab resolutions [with regard to the PLO] seriously, because there has been a lack of coherence, coordination, and solidarity. Arab leaders act contrary to their pronouncements."[47]

The emergence of the PLO as the sole representative of the Palestinian people after the 1973 war, therefore, neither assured its independent discretionary powers on Palestinian matters nor substituted the need for an innovative policy suitable to the new reality. Under these circumstances, total commitment to the doctrine of military struggle, at whatever cost, and willingness to defend dogmatic positions to the last man and last round "until we reach the sea,"[48] though perhaps heroic, clearly involved the risk of "losing an historical opportunity to regain part of Palestine."[49] On the other hand, readiness to participate in a negotiated settlement could significantly limit the Arab states' ability to reach a solution to the issue of the occupied territories by going over the PLO's head. And willingness to participate in a negotiated settlement would strengthen the PLO's political stand among the Palestinians under Israeli occupation and reduce the risk of an alternative Palestinian leadership there that might acquiesce in an Egyptian-Jordanian-Israeli solution. "The adoption of a stand

46. See "Sadat-Hussein Statement," July 18, 1974, *Voice of the Arabs* (Cairo), July 18, 1974. *Foreign Broadcast Information Service, Middle East*, July 19, 1974, D1–D2.

47. *al-Anba'* (Kuwait), Aug. 9, 1981.

48. See 'Arafat's speech in Kuwait, *Journal of Palestine Studies* 3/3 (1974):198.

49. Emmanuel Sivan, "ha-Dilemma shel Ashaf" (The PLO's dilemma), *Migvan* (July 1981):28.

based on negative . . . opposition," Na'if Hawatma, head of the DFLP, proclaimed, "will certainly not enable us to frustrate attempts to impose surrender and liquidation solutions. On the contrary, this will only add fuel to the flames."[50]

Fatah leader Abu Iyad, who was among the main supporters of the political process, followed the same argument: "The voice of the Palestinian people should be heard on their problems. If not, those problems will be left to others to deal with, others whom I believe to be historically responsible for the continuation of the [Palestinian] disaster, for the continued fettering of the Palestinian people, and for their being prevented from expressing themselves through the rejection of occupation by practical action."[51]

The message of the supporters of the political process was quite clear: There is no alternative but "the acceptance of what appeared to be the maximum that can be achieved in the context of settlement between the Arab regimes and Israel."[52] A settlement without PLO participation would be "the biggest defeat" for the organization.[53] The need to engage in a negotiated settlement to meet the political reality of the post–1973 war became inevitable.

However persuasive the argument to participate in the political process was, there was yet another consideration: taking into account both Israel's anti-PLO position and the Arab nations' unwillingness to subordinate their particular interests to those of the PLO, the outcome of negotiations could not be predicted. Furthermore, willingness to engage in a political process could mean upsetting the PLO's fragile unity. This was a risk no one dared to assume. In the absence of territory, sovereignty, and firm support from the Arab world, adherence to a formal doctrine of armed struggle and of no peace, no recognition, and no direct negotiations with Israel had served as a vital element in holding together the PLO factions. Disunity, therefore, could have severely threatened PLO existence and its ability to shape effectively the political future of the Palestinian people.

Even if the advocates of the political process were assured of territorial gains prior to the conclusion of the peace negotiations

50. *Journal of Palestine Studies* 3/3 (1974): 199–200.
51. Ibid., 204.
52. Agha, "What State for the Palestinians?" 11.
53. Hani al-Hasan's interview in *al-Nahar*, Jan. 29, 1979.

(in return for their willingness to participate in those negotiations), they would have still been hard-pressed to counter the argument raised by their critics. Bluntly stated, this criticism maintains that given the existing political and military balance of power in the Middle East, participation in peace negotiations could amount to no more than "Filastinistan"—a satellite Palestinian state—not "Filastin"—a free and independent Palestine.[54] George Habash, head of the PFLP, made this very clear:

> Will the balance of forces . . . allow us . . . to reach the goal of a Palestinian national democratic [regime], followed by total [Israeli] withdrawal from Arab territories without recognition, without peace [with Israel], without secure frontiers, without demilitarization zones, without international forces, without all these safeguards? My answer is certainly not. . . . An Israeli withdrawal from the West Bank is only possible in the event of there being established there a reactionary force or a force that is ready to surrender. Will Israel withdraw from the West Bank and just say good-bye? No, this is impossible.[55]

The argument went further. The new political climate "that will prevail in the area as a result of a peace treaty with Israel and the establishment of a West Bank state will make it difficult for the Palestinians to continue their struggle in a military way. A newly established state with a recently acquired network of international relations and communications will find it more difficult to recruit friends in the world to support military warfare against another state. This will make it easier for an Israel that is in a relative state of peace with the rest of the area and the world to hit harder at the Palestinians and get away with it."[56] The Palestinian revolution would lose its political vitality and raison d'être.

PLO leaders who were willing to pursue Palestinian national goals through political means thus found themselves in a dilemma: a negotiated settlement could not assure political and territorial benefits that justified risking PLO unity, while rigid adherence to armed struggle might maintain unity, but at the risk of losing the

54. For more on this argument, see the PFLP's organ *al-Hadaf* (Beirut), March 6, 1971.

55. *Journal of Palestine Studies* 3/3 (1974): 202–03.

56. Agha, "What State for the Palestinians?" 20.

chance to gain any part of Palestine in the foreseeable future. This dilemma dominated Palestinian politics in the 1970s and 1980s despite the fact that the political-settlement approach failed to emerge as a real alternative to the armed-struggle doctrine.

CHAPTER 2

The Fragmented Basis of Palestinian Nationalism

While Palestinians are unanimous in their desire for political rights and self-determination in Palestine, implementation of this desire varies from one Palestinian group to another according to local grievances, communal interests, ideological beliefs, and political experiences. Nowhere is the variety of meanings that infuse these national desires better seen than in the conflicting views and behavior found among the West Bank elite and the different factions of the PLO. And it is here one should seek to understand why PLO attempts to reach a consensus on policy to further Palestinian national interests through political means has caused intense debates and faced immense difficulties.

Palestinian Nationalism and West Bank Localism

As a result of the Arab-Israeli war of 1948 and the incorporation of the West Bank into the Hashemite Kingdom of Jordan, the West Bank Palestinian community became the largest concentration of Palestinians anywhere. It was the only Palestinian community that was not a minority, being twice as large as Jordan's original population. Half of the 900,000 Palestinians under Jordanian rule in 1948 were refugees.[1]

1. In 1950, the United Nations Economic Mission to the Middle East estimated the number of Palestinian refugees as 100,905 in the East Bank and 431,000 in the West Bank. The United Nations Relief and Works Agency estimated the total number of refugees in both banks on August 31, 1950, as 485,000. See United

The Palestinians on the West Bank differed from the other concentration of Palestinians in several respects. They were socially and economically more advanced than the predominantly Bedouin East Bank population.[2] Since there was no immigration into the West Bank from other Arab countries, the Palestinian community there remained homogenous until 1967, after which several thousand Israeli Jews settled in the area. And, finally, the West Bank Palestinians became the only Palestinian population in the Arab world to enjoy citizenship and the right to participate in political life.[3]

Despite their uniqueness, the West Bank Palestinian population has maintained a strong sense of identity with the larger Palestinian community. This, however, has not paralleled the political behavior of the West Bank elite. Under both Jordanian and Israeli rule, social and political conditions on the West Bank have enabled the elite to adopt pragmatic modes of behavior and at the same time to justify them in Arab or Palestinian terms. Radical leadership that sought to advance national interests primarily through violent means has not been widespread. In both Jordanian and Israeli periods moderate behavior has usually been presented as the optimal way to advance pan-Arab or Palestinian national interests. The elite have invariably bowed to national values, but not always in a radical posture.

Nations General Assembly, *Assistance to Palestine Refugees: Interim Report of the Director of the United Nations Relief and Works Agency for Palestine Refugees in the Near East*, Office Records: Fifth Session, Supplement 19 (A/1451/rev. 1), 1951, 4.

2. For more details on the Palestinian population of the West Bank, see Naseer Aruri, *Jordan: A Study in Political Development (1921–1965)* (The Hague: Martinus Nijhoff, 1972), 34–37; Shaul Mishal, *West Bank/East Bank: The Palestinians in Jordan, 1949–1967* (New Haven: Yale University Press, 1978), 3–5; Daniel Lerner, *The Passing of Traditional Society: Modernizing the Middle East* (New York: Free Press, 1958), 54–65.

3. Another Palestinian Arab community with the right to vote is the Arab minority in Israel (see J. M. Landau, *The Arabs in Israel: A Political Study* (London: Oxford University Press, 1969). However, this minority's influence on the political system in Israel and on the community at large is minimal. This was not the case in Jordan.

THE WEST BANK ELITE UNDER JORDANIAN RULE

Multi-Affiliation and Cooperation

The West Bank's annexation to the Jordanian kingdom in April 1950 engendered an ambivalence among its inhabitants with regard to their political allegiance. They were Palestinians, and yet at the same time they were also Jordanians who relied heavily on pan-Arab symbols. As Palestinians, their particular collective allegiance had its roots in such local institutions as the family, the clan, the village, or the town.[4] During the thirty years of the British Mandate in Palestine (1917–48), these ties were strengthened and received political importance largely in response to British policy and to Jewish activity. Many members of Palestinian Arab political groups considered these two elements a threat not only to the existence of an Arab majority in Palestine but even to the survival of the Arab community there.[5]

At the end of the 1948 Arab-Israeli war, the political boundary between Israel and the Kingdom of Jordan cut right through the territory inhabited by the Palestinian Arabs. This discord between social and political boundaries increased the desire of the Palestinian elite to restore Palestine as defined by the Mandate.[6] Pal-

4. On the structure of these institutions during the British Mandate period, see e.g., Yehoshua Porath, *The Emergence of the Palestinian Arab National Movement, 1918–1929* (London: Frank Cass, 1974), 287–88; Y. Shimoni, ʿ*Arvei Eretz-Yisraʾel* (The Arabs of Eretz-Yisraʾel) (Tel Aviv: ʿAm-Oved, 1947), 157–82, 206–11.

5. See, for instance, a statement issued by Palestinian Arabs in Ramlah and Lydda in which they argue: "Either us or the Zionists! There is no room for both elements struggling together in the same area. The laws of nature require that one side be defeated. We want life and they are striving for it, but life is indivisible. There is no escaping the fact that one of us must win" (Porath, *The Palestinian Arab National Movement*, 50).

6. One can point to Palestinian leaders in the West Bank like Shaykh Muhammad ʿAli al-Jaʿbari of Hebron and Wadiʿ Daʿmas of Bayt Jala, who supported King ʿAbdallah's goal of incorporating Palestinian territories into his kingdom. But many tended to make their support conditional on his willingness eventually to include all of Palestine in his kingdom and on the termination of the political independence of the Jewish community. This attitude was clearly articulated by the Jerusalem and Ramallah delegates to the Palestinian Congress (also known as the Jericho Conference) that was arranged by King ʿAbdallah and his Palestinian

estinian collective allegiance attached to land that was now part of Israel as well as to the West Bank. While Amman regarded itself as the government of both banks of the Jordan river, the West Bank elite's political desires were based on abolishing the territorial status quo, generally by military means.

During the period 1948–67 two major attempts to give real substance to an exclusively Palestinian option were initiated by Palestinian elements outside the West Bank. The first attempt was in September 1948, when the All-Palestine Government (*Hukumat 'umum Filastin*) was set up in the Gaza Strip to thwart King 'Abdallah's attempt to incorporate parts of Palestine into his kingdom.[7] The second attempt was in 1964 with the founding of the PLO. Since then the PLO has tried to focus attention on the idea of a Palestinian homeland and self-determination. Many groups within the West Bank elite did not perceive these attempts as realistic options because of Amman's monopoly over military and economic power.

The West Bank elite derived their political power from their economic position or family status. Since these power sources were for the most part local, West Bank leaders did not have a firm base of support if they sought to attain wider influence, either at the all–West Bank level or at the state level (Jordan). The fact that a majority of West Bank political leaders belonged to families with commercial and economic interests in Jordan further increased the dependence on Amman and made it difficult for them to take stands that might bring them into open conflict with the Jordanian authorities and damage their economic interests.[8]

---

supporters on December 1, 1948 in order to receive legitimation of his annexation of Palestinian territories to Jordan. For more details, see 'Arif al-'Arif, *al-Nakba: nakbat bayt al-maqdis wal-firdaus al-mafqud, 1947–1955* (The disaster: The calamity of the Holy Land and the loss of paradise, 1947–1955) (Beirut: al-Maktaba al-'asriyya lil-tiba'a wal-Nashr, n.d.), 877–78.

7. On the formation of the All-Palestine Government, see ibid., 89, 703–05; Aqil Abidi, *Jordan: A Political Study, 1948–1957* (New York: Asia Publishing, 1965), 49–52.

8. For further details, see Uriel Dann, "Regime and Opposition in Jordan since 1949," in *Society and Political Structure in the Arab World*, ed. Menahem Milson (New York: Humanities, 1973), 145–51.

Palestinian political activists, whether members of opposition parties or of pro-Jordanian parties, lacked the means to mobilize support on a large scale. For those in opposition parties, the Jordanian regime's restrictions prevented them from broad political activity at the all–West Bank or national level. For those in pro-Jordanian parties, it seems to have been largely their own lack of motivation that reduced their chances of deriving power through party office.[9]

Thus, despite the formal existence of political parties and elective institutions on both the parliamentary and the municipal level, power remained essentially a function of family position, property, and influence based on personal contacts among the local elite. The existing Palestinian power structure therefore lacked the authority to settle any all–West Bank conflicts, whether of social, economic, or ideological origin. As a result, most of the Palestinian political leaders on the West Bank tried to gloss over their differences with Amman by resorting to ambiguous formulas in defining their political goals. This kind of relationship was reflected in the growing readiness of the West Bank elite to affiliate itself with Jordan, although this affiliation was not sustained by the same political symbols and set of beliefs that engendered devotion to the idea of Palestinian allegiance. Their affiliation to Jordan was achieved mostly through participation in the political life of the kingdom and in the dependence on resources it allocated.[10] Amman in this sense served as a source of civil authority rather than as a focus of normative identification.

The elite's seemingly contradictory identification with both Palestinian and Jordanian interests was made possible by its pan-Arab leanings. According to the pan-Arab view, West Bank secession from Jordan was undesirable since it would mean increased fragmentation in the Arab world. Even those among the

9. On the structure and activities of the political parties in the West Bank under Jordanian rule, see Amnon Cohen, "Political Parties in the West Bank under the Hashemite Regime," in *Palestinian Arab Politics*, ed. Moshe Maʿoz (Jerusalem: Jerusalem Academic, 1975), 27–48.

10. See Mishal, *West Bank/East Bank*, 17.

elite who did not subscribe to pan-Arabism believed that the political redemption of Palestine could be achieved only through Arab unity.[11]

Within the West Bank elite, different groups related in different ways to each of the three sources of allegiance. Those who joined the Jordanian establishment as senior officials or who ran for election for Jordanian parliament tended to stress ties with Amman, or sometimes the pan-Arab allegiance. Opponents of the Jordanian monarchy, particularly those identified with opposition parties like al-Ba'th, al-Qawmiyyun al-'Arab, and the Communists, emphasized Palestinian and pan-Arab allegiances.[12] Individuals were not always consistent in their attitude toward the three sources of allegiance, veering in accordance with the Jordanian government's promises of personal benefits or with changes in Arab political attitudes toward Jordan and the West Bank issue.

The simultaneous affiliation of the West Bank elite to more than one source of allegiance enabled it to view the political arrangement between the two banks as temporary, pending the creation of political conditions that would lead to the realization of the ultimate goal. Thus, the local elite was able to agree with the definition of Palestinian national goals put forward by radical Arab or Palestinian bodies outside Jordan while reconciling themselves to accepting the existing situation until they could acquire the means for realizing their objectives. By regarding their political existence under Jordanian rule as temporary, West Bank leaders were able to justify their cooperation with Amman. This multiple affiliation enabled the West Bank elite to withstand the pressure to adopt a radical position.

Multi-Affiliation; National and Local Functions

As a result of their affiliation with three sources of political allegiance, the West Bank elite tended to concentrate on pragmatic activities at the local level, leaving the radical Arab regimes and Palestinian organizations to take on those activities expressive of

11. For more details, see Eli'ezer Be'eri, *ha-Falastinim tahat shilton Yarden: Shalosh sugiyyot* (Jerusalem: Magnes Press, Hebrew University, 1978), 33–34.
12. On these differences, see Mishal, *West Bank/East Bank*, chap. 4.

national solidarity and embodying Palestinian or pan-Arab values.[13] At first this role was filled primarily by Presidents Jamal
ʿAbd al-Nasser of Egypt and ʿAbd al-Karim Qasem of Iraq, and
later on by the leaders of the Palestinian organizations. The Arab
mass media made it possible to overcome the problem of distance
and to marshal West Bank inhabitants to the call of Arab solidarity.[14] Palestinian and pan-Arab leaders were active during spo-
radic periods of anti-Jordanian political unrest on the West Bank,
especially among the opposition political parties. Such unrest occurred in reaction to the Baghdad Pact of 1955, the establishment
of the United Arab Republic in 1958, and the tripartite unification
between Egypt, Syria, and Iraq in 1963. Activists from the opposition parties were ideologically articulate and inclined toward
political and social radicalism. In the main, however, they remained intermediaries for pan-Arab or radical Palestinian organizations outside Jordan and did not become leaders in their own
right.

The weakness of opposition activities stemmed not only from
the low level of political institutionalization in the West Bank,
which was maintained and perpetuated by Jordan in its own interest, but also from their poor socioeconomic position relative to
that of the pro-Jordanian political leaders. They were faced with
a choice: to desist from opposition activity and attempt to integrate
into the Jordanian establishment, thereby obtaining the conse-

13. This distinction between activity of "expressive" and "instrumental" meaning, to use Talcott Parsons's terms, should be considered one of degree rather than
categorical. In other words, while the West Bank political elite did concentrate
more on local activity of an instrumental nature, their activity acquired national-
symbolic meaning as well, especially under Israeli rule. Similarly, while the Palestinian organizations were primarily conceived as radical groups whose main activity was engendering nationalistic feelings, they also engaged in instrumental
activity. But the distinction helps to explain the ability of the West Bank elite to
adopt nonradical, pragmatic behavior. See Talcott Parsons, *The Social System*
(London: Free Press of Glencoe, 1951), 49.

14. For an example of Egyptian and Syrian use of propaganda broadcasts to
mobilize the West Bank population for political activity against the Jordanian
regime, see *Middle East Record 1960*, ed. Yitzhak Oron (London: Weidenfeld &
Nicolson, n.d.), 149–50.

quent benefits, or to continue their activities in Palestinian or other radical Arab frameworks, either from within Jordan or from outside. The existence of activity in political bodies outside the West Bank mitigated the pressure on the West Bank political elite to take a clearcut radical stand. They were therefore able to continue the pragmatic pattern of activity on the local level.

THE WEST BANK ELITE UNDER ISRAELI RULE

All–West Bank Activity

The nonradical, pragmatic mode of the local West Bank elite continued under Israeli rule. However, since the West Bank Arab population considered the Israeli rule a foreign administration, the Palestinian elite increased the national-solidarity content of its activities after the 1967 war.

The adaptation of the West Bank leadership to the situation created by the war of June 1967 had several stages. After the initial shock came the search for a way to function: collaborating with the Israeli authorities, continuing relations with the Jordanian government, or cooperating with the Palestinian organizations. This period, which continued until the end of 1971, was characterized by efforts to create an all–West Bank political framework around the idea of a Palestinian entity.

The activities of the adherents to the Palestinian entity idea took several forms. ʿAziz Shehada of Ramallah, a lawyer, Dr. Hamdi al-Taji al-Faruqi of al-Bira, and the political writer Muhammad Abu Shilbaya of Jerusalem proposed negotiating with Israel for the establishment of a Palestinian state on the West Bank that would precede a comprehensive settlement with the Arab states.[15] This approach was quashed by the negative responses of Israel,

15. ʿAziz Shehada stated the situation in these words: "The time has come for us to take the initiative in handling our own fate, even though we would have preferred that this initiative not be independent of the rest of the Arab world." See ʿAziz Shehada, "The Voice of the Forgotten Palestinian," *New Middle East* (December 1968): 14–15. See also the *Jerusalem Post*, September 7, 1967; *Haʾaretz* (Tel Aviv), Nov. 27, 1967, and Dec. 15, 1967; *Al-Quds* (Jerusalem), Nov. 9, 1969.

Jordan, and the PLO, and by the PLO attempt to assassinate al-Faruqi in December 1967.[16]

Shaykh Muhammad ʿAli al-Jaʿbari, then mayor of Hebron, took a rather different approach. On several occasions during 1969 and 1970 he tried to lay the foundations for a direct settlement between Israel and the Palestinian Arabs of the West Bank. He suggested the formation of a political body based on the existing West Bank leadership, principally the mayors.[17] This suggestion, which also met with Israeli, Jordanian, and PLO opposition, forced the local leaders to focus on day-to-day matters. The elite's contribution to national solidarity expressed itself mainly in declarations of readiness to view the PLO as its legitimate representative and as the spokesman of its political aspirations.

Israel, Jordan, and PLO Policy

Ironically, the policies of Israel, Jordan, and the PLO during the course of 1970 complemented each other at least in one sense: they were all less inclined to launch comprehensive political initiatives, preferring instrumental activity on the local level. This helped West Bank leaders to justify moderate behavior to some extent even under Israeli rule without being accused of taking an unpatriotic stand.

Israeli policy favored negotiation with Jordan regarding the future of the occupied territories while assuring the cooperation of the Palestinian leaders in day-to-day matters on the local level. The Israeli authorities remained indifferent to local political initiatives such as the move to establish a Palestinian entity on the West Bank. At the same time, they tolerated the nationalist declarations of West Bank leaders on condition that these declarations were not translated into subversive activity, for which the penalty was expulsion from the West Bank.[18]

16. On this attempt by Fatah to threaten supporters of the idea of a Palestinian entity, see *Middle East Record 1967*, ed. Daniel Dishon (Jerusalem: Israel University Press, 1971), 283.

17. For more details, see Elie Rekhess and Asher Susser, *Political Factors and Trends in the West Bank*, (Tel Aviv: Shiloah Center for Middle Eastern and African Studies, Tel Aviv University, 1974), 7–8, 11–13; See also David Farhi, "Hevra ve-politika bi-Yehuda ve-Shomron," (Society and politics in Judea and Samaria), Maʿarakhot 215 (June 1971): 16.

18. For a general survey of Israeli policy in the West Bank, see Mordechai Nisan,

Jordanian policy was also directed at preventing independent political initiative on the all–West Bank level as long as it was under Israeli control. In the absence of an independent Palestinian settlement with Israel, the key to a political settlement entailing Israeli evacuation of the West Bank would thus remain in the hands of the Jordanian government. This situation strengthened Jordan's position in its relationship with the West Bank Arabs and with other Arab countries. The Jordanian government therefore opposed attempts at political organization on the Israeli-occupied West Bank.

During the first months after June 1967, Jordan opposed West Bank cooperation with the Israeli authorities on the local level for fear of losing control over the local leadership and the Palestinian population in the occupied territories. Jordanian influence was directly ensured by the money the Jordanian authorities disbursed and by continuing family and economic ties, which were made possible by the Israeli policy of maintaining open bridges between the two banks of the Jordan.[19]

The Jordanian government twice sought the resignation of Hamdi Kan'an, then mayor of Nablus, on grounds of collaboration. It also expressed dissatisfaction with the mayor of Hebron, Muhammad 'Ali al-Ja'bari, because of his close ties with the Israeli authorities.[20] After the civil war in September 1970, Jordan's objection to West Bank collaboration with Israel gradually relaxed. The Jordanian government reconciled itself to the local activities of mayors and other West Bank dignitaries and confined itself to trying to prevent political initiatives encompassing the whole of the West Bank that were liable to influence the political future in

---

Israel and the Territories (Ramat Gan: Turtledove, 1978), 83–140; Shlomo Gazit, "ha-Shtahim ha-muhzaqim—Mediniyut ve-ma'as", (The administered territories—policy and practice), *Ma'arakhot* 204 (January 1970): 25–39; idem, "Israel's Occupation Politics," *New Outlook* 2/6 (1968): 47–55; and Nimrod Raphaeli, "Military Government in the Occupied Territories: An Israeli View," *Middle East Journal* 32 (1969): 177–90.

19. On Jordanian influence in the West Bank through the open-bridge policy, see Asher Susser, "Jordanian Influence in the West Bank," *Jerusalem Quarterly* 8 (1978): 57–61; on the flow of money from Jordan to the West Bank, see Raphaeli, "Military Government," 186; *Jerusalem Post*, Feb. 13, 1975.

20. See *al-Difa'* (Amman, Dec. 26, 1968, and Jan. 4, 1969.

a direction undesirable to Jordan. The PLO also opposed independent local initiatives with regard to the future of the West Bank. The PLO (and particularly Fatah) contended that it, and not the leaders living under Israeli rule, was the sole political advocate for the West Bank Palestinian Arabs.

Most West Bank leaders assumed that there was no way of solving the West Bank problem without PLO consent. They therefore held consultations on various issues with PLO representatives in Beirut, Damascus, and, until 1970, Amman. This created an anomaly whereby, until March 1972, the effect of PLO influence paralleled that of Israel and Jordan; it opposed independent political initiatives on the all–West Bank level and encouraged local leaders to concentrate on day-to-day activities.

As there was ideological justification for the elite's abstention from comprehensive initiatives after 1970 and for its concentration on more day-to-day local issues, the PLO's approach attained national significance. The ideological justification found its expression in the policy of *sumud* (steadfastness), meaning "passive resistance against any form of cooperation with the Israeli authorities, and the avoidance of any manifestation of acquiescence or agreement to their presence."[21] By 1970, West Bank Palestinian Arabs had created a rigid code with explicit definitions of behavior that would be considered as prohibited from a nationalist point of view. Such prohibitions included changes in local institutions; updating communal representation on various levels at elections held under the jurisdiction of the occupation authority; and banning formal contact between public bodies and the Israeli authorities beyond what was required by their day-to-day needs. Communal activity was legitimate only if approved by the Jordanian government, by the other Arab governments and the Arab League, and by the PLO.[22]

In 1970, when cooperation with the Israeli authorities on the local level became a way of life, sumud acquired a more positive

21. Abraham Sela, "The PLO, the West Bank and Gaza Strip," *Jerusalem Quarterly* 8 (1978): 68.

22. See David Farhi, "ʿAmadot politiyot bi-Yehudah ve-Shomron, 1972–1973," (Political attitudes in Judea and Samaria, 1972–1973), *Maʿarakhot* 231 (July 1973): 10.

connotation. "In 1967", said one West Bank leader, "we adopted sumud as a negative political motto, and on that basis we automatically rejected every Israeli proposal. Today our motto is positive sumud: we are prepared to consider every proposal for reform or development coming from the Israeli regime as long as it does not contradict our national interests as we understand them. Moreover, we are more inclined than in the past to rely on our own judgment in all that relates to our current communal interests, and not to accept dictates from without."[23] Participation in elections for chambers of commerce, support for the Israeli open-bridges policy, and willingness to permit the West Bank population to work in Israel are all expressions of this approach.

Positive sumud seems to represent an attempt on the part of the West Bank political elite to interpret the goals and national aspirations defined by other political forces, mainly the PLO, in a spirit coinciding with West Bank political interests and needs. Thus one can argue that the West Bank leaders were not just passive followers of political values formulated by others; they themselves have tried to have some impact on the values that guided their actions.

Since mid–1972, and especially after the Arab summit in Rabat (October 1974), which proclaimed the PLO "sole legitimate representative of the Palestinian people," West Bank political reality took a new direction. The PLO's growing involvement on the West Bank narrowed the local elite's impact. Moreover, the success of PLO supporters in the 1976 municipal elections—both in gaining new positions of power, as in Nablus and Hebron, and in strengthening their position, as in Tulkarm and Ramallah— raised expectations that the new West Bank leadership would be more likely to accept PLO dictates on every aspect of political action.

The new leaders were certainly more inclined toward political activity in the PLO spirit than their predecessors were, but this inclination did not mean the absolute subordination of local interests to those of the PLO. The considerations favoring a pragmatic policy that reflected local needs and interests continued to constitute an important element both in the reasoning of the new

23. Ibid., 9.

West Bank local leaders and in fashioning their relationship with Israel, Jordan, and especially with the PLO.

PALESTINISM AND PLO RADICALISM

The practice of interpreting national goals in a spirit coinciding with particular interests was not unique to the West Bank. It was followed by all PLO factions. All the Palestinian organizations sought to restore the Palestinians to a central position in the political and military struggle for Palestine. All the organizations shared the fundamental goal of liberating Palestine through armed struggle. Interpretations of this message, however, had different meanings. A dual Arab-Palestinian identity, a shared commitment to pan-Arab political unity, and exposure to both symbolic and material influences from different Arab regimes increased the tendency among the Palestinian organizations to endow their Palestinian national aspirations with an all-Arab meaning. No Palestinian could afford to be accused by fellow Arabs of preferring parochial Palestinian interests (*iqlimiyya*) over broad Arab nationalist ones.[24]

Coping with the burden of these combined, sometimes incompatible, commitments, the organizations adopted various political approaches. They searched for differing formulas to balance the demands of Arab nationalism and the requirements of Palestinian aspirations. These differences were mirrored by the variety of opinions on the operational goals of the Palestinian struggle, its priorities, and its political direction.

The Autonomous Approach: Fatah and the DFLP

Fatah, more than any other Palestinian organization, sought Palestinian political independence. This organization, which was formed in 1959 by young educated Palestinian refugees living in Egypt, "refused the confiscation of the Palestinian self and its

---

24. On the negative connotations of parochialism, or provincialism, in Arab nationalist thinking, see Sati‘ al-Husri, *Abhath mukhtara fil-qawmiyya al-‘arabiyya* (Selected studies on Arab nationalism) (Cairo: al-Ma‘arif, 1964).

melting in the wider circle, the circle of [Arab] nationalism."[25] Fatah awareness of the risk in focusing on particular Palestinian interests over all-Arab ones led it to emphasize the convergence of the two interests. It is, stated Fatah, a "serious mistake to link the Palestinian nature of the revolution to the area that imperialism called Palestine. We in Fatah view Palestine in terms of [Arab] national, not geographic, dimensions."[26] But in reality Fatah's strategy was to build an autonomous military capability in order to focus on the realization of Palestinian national interests first, and Arab unity second.

The liberation of Palestine through a Palestinian armed struggle, according to Fatah's interpretation, would lead to Arab unity, and not vice versa. By the same token, Arab assistance to Palestinian resistance meant supporting the campaign for Arab unity and participating in the central mission of Arab nationalism. The role of the Arab world in the first stage, according to this view, was to serve as a supporting front for the Palestinian resistance, backing it politically and materially. Later on, all Arabs would join the Palestinians in launching a comprehensive military campaign against Israel.

Establishment of a policy of reciprocal noninterference between the PLO and Arab states was aimed at facilitating PLO collaboration with all the Arab countries. "Since we do not interfere in the internal affairs of the Arab countries," stated ʿArafat, "since we have in common with them and with the Arab people the objective of ending the Israeli occupation, we see no reason for conflict between us."[27] Behind Fatah's approach of cooperating with the existing Arab regimes rather than espousing revolutionary changes lay the assumption that the fewer the ideological arguments over Arab national issues, the greater the chance to reach

25. Hani al-Hasan, "Fatah bayna al-nazariyya wal-tatbiq: al-itar al-nazari" (Fatah between theory and practice: The theoretical framework), *Shuʾun Filastiniyya* (March 1972): 17.

26. *Fatah* (Beirut), April 17, 1970: 10; William B. Quandt et al., *The Politics of Palestinian Nationalism* (Berkeley: University of California Press, 1973), 98.

27. *Jeune Afrique* (Paris), May 6–12, 1968: 494; Quandt, *Palestinian Nationalism*, 97.

a workable consensus and to mobilize broad support from fellow Arabs.

Fatah's desire to minimize the dispute over ideological issues was also reflected in its reluctance to define its social platform and its ideological position on the nature of the future Palestinian state. "We in the Palestine revolution aspire to the day we will begin our social revolution, but it is nonsense to insist that we wage both revolutions together, because if we do we will lose both."[28] ʿArafat put it in broader terms when he addressed the accusation that Fatah refused to define its social and ideological platforms:

I am a refugee. . . . Do you know what it means to be a refugee? . . . I have nothing, for I was banished and dispossessed of my homeland. What meaning does the left or the right have in the struggle for the liberation of my homeland? I want that homeland even if the devil is the one to liberate it for me. Am I in a position to reject the participation or assistance of any man? Can I be asked, for example, to refuse the financial aid of Saudi Arabia with the claim that it belongs to the right? After all, it is with the Saudi's money that I buy arms from China.

Are you demanding that I already define the type of government that will rule Palestine after its liberation? If I did so, I could be compared to the man who sells the bear's hide before hunting it down.

Must I publish a public statement to proclaim my belief in Marxism? Is this what I am required to do at this stage? Everybody asks what our social views are. Aren't we still in the phase of national liberation? If so, how can people demand that I forbid the whole Palestinian people from participating in the struggle for liberating their homeland?[29]

The Fatah tendency to blur the autonomous meaning of Palestinian national goals might be traced through the method it used to formulate the political objectives of its struggle. From the late 1950s to the 1967 war, Fatah defined its political objective in terms of a Palestinian entity (*kiyan filastini*) independent of Arab "custody" and with a Palestinian identity.[30] By choosing such vague terms, Fatah was able to stress the dominant role of the Palestinians

28. Hani al-Hasan interview in *al-Raʾy al-ʿAam* (Kuwait), April 23, 1970.

29. ʿArafat interview in *al-Sayyad* (Beirut), Jan. 23, 1969.

30. For more details, see Muhammad Y. Muslih, "Moderates and Rejectionists within the Palestine Liberation Organization," *Middle East Journal* 30/2 (1976): 128.

themselves in solving their problem without neglecting the Arab states' sensitivity toward the issue. The Palestinian struggle for Palestine, as 'Arafat described it, is "Palestinian in face, but Arab in heart."[31]

The decline of pan-Arabism as a driving power in the Arab world after the 1967 war encouraged the Fatah leadership to formulate its goal in more specific terms. In 1969 it adopted the DFLP's concept of a Palestinian democratic state where Christians, Jews, and Muslims would "enjoy the same rights and have the same duties, within the framework of the Arab nations' aspirations."[32] In 1974 Fatah adopted the formula of an "independent fighting national authority . . . over every part of Palestinian territory that is liberated" from Israel.[33] And in 1977 it announced the idea of a Palestinian state in the occupied territories "so that it can become a homeland to the people of Palestine."[34]

Although these proposals were presented as a transitional phase in the prolonged struggle "for the sake of completing the liberation of all Palestinian soil . . . as a step on the path of a comprehensive Arab unity,"[35] they reflected Fatah's preference for a more specific solution: that of reaching an independent territorial base rather than achieving a broader resolution through Arab unity. "What is important now," as a member of the Fatah Central Committee stated, "is to force Israel to withdraw from the occupied territories and to establish an independent Palestinian state. Only then will the Palestinian people determine their relations [with Arab countries], taking into consideration the Palestinian people's interests and those of the Arab nation at the same time."[36] Fatah's Palestinism and political pragmatism might explain its success in attracting members from various segments of Palestinian society and

31. *al-Muharrir* (Beirut), Nov. 19, 1968.

32. See resolutions of the eighth Palestine National Council in Cairo, Feb.–March, 1971, *Middle East News Agency*, March 4, 1971.

33. See "Political Program for the Present Stage of the Palestine Liberation Organization," drawn up by the Palestine National Council, Cairo, June 9, 1974, *WAFA*, June 9, 1974; *Journal of Palestine Studies* 3/4 (1974): 224.

34. Final Statement of the thirteenth Palestine National Council session, Cairo, March 1977, *Foreign Broadcast Information Service, Middle East*, March 21, 1977.

35. See "Political Program for the Present Stage," art. 8.

36. Mahmud 'Abbas to *Qatar News Agency*, Sept. 26, 1979; *Foreign Broadcast Information Service, Middle East*, Sept. 27, 1979, A1–A2.

its emergence as the largest and most influential faction within the PLO.

The closest organization to Fatah's autonomous view is the DFLP. The DFLP was formed in February 1969 by the left wing of the PFLP and was led by Na'if Hawatma, who had seceded from the PFLP after a power struggle with George Habash.[37] Like Fatah, the DFLP focused on an autonomous solution to the Palestinian problem through the establishment of an independent Palestinian state. However, the two organizations differed in their views on the proper political strategy for realizing this goal and on the nature of the future Palestinian state. These differences derived in part from the DFLP's Marxist-Leninist outlook. The restoration of Palestine, according to the DFLP, could be achieved only through the joint political and military efforts of all Arab states following a class struggle in Arab society. All Arab regimes, argued the DFLP, have demonstrated incompetence in solving the Palestinian issue. All regimes, whether progressive or reactionary, have to undergo political and social changes in order to restore Palestine to the Arabs.

Contrary to Fatah, the DFLP believed that interference in Arab internal affairs was inevitable. "The only ally of the Palestinian resistance movement [is] the progressive national forces that rejected in principle the regimes of their countries."[38] Adhering to this principle, the DFLP cultivated a close relationship with radical political elements in the Arab world, particularly with the leftist organizations and Communist parties in Iraq and Lebanon.[39]

The DFLP class orientation shaped its social and political perception of the nature of the future Palestinian state. Unlike Fatah, the DFLP saw the ultimate solution to the Palestinian problem in the establishment of a democratic, nonsectarian, secular state in

37. Up to 1975 the organization kept its original name—Popular Democratic Front for the Liberation of Palestine (PDFLP). The secession from the PFLP and the different political views of the PDFLP and the PFLP, which deepened after the 1973 war, induced the organization to emphasize these differences by changing its name to the Democratic Front for the Liberation of Palestine (DFLP).

38. Na'if Hawatma to the DFLP weekly *al-Hurriyya* (Beirut), May 19, 1969.

39. For more on the relationship between the DFLP and radical elements in the Arab world, see Aryeh Y. Yodfat and Yuval Arnon-Ohanna, *PLO Strategy and Tactics* (London: Croom Helm, 1981), 26–27.

place of Israel. In this state Jews who were ready to renounce their Zionist affiliation, Christians, and Muslims would live together sharing equal rights and having the same duties.[40] Leaving aside the vague formulation about the Jews' national rights in this stage, the DFLP solution was based on a proletarian class affiliation of the progressive elements of the three ethnic groups over parochial, religious, or national values.

Since mid-1971, and especially after the 1973 war, the DFLP has adopted a more flexible attitude toward cooperation with some Arab regimes, moving closer to the Fatah view. This revision resulted from DFLP military and political weakness after the Palestinian defeat in the 1970–71 civil war in Jordan. The need to reorganize its military units and rebuild its political power in the new refuge in Lebanon made it seem easier to reach a compromise between total rejection and full endorsement of the existing order in the Arab world. This compromise was reflected in the improvement of its relations with Syria and Iraq and in military and political cooperation with the Soviet Union, as the DFLP realized the vital role of those countries in the prosecution of Palestinian armed resistance.[41]

Although the DFLP continued to support the idea of a secular democratic state in Palestine, it advocated political means to reach a transitional solution by establishing an independent Palestinian state in the West Bank and Gaza Strip, a position later adopted by Fatah.[42] The rapprochement between the DFLP and Fatah on the pragmatic level, however, was contingent upon cooperation with reference to ad hoc interests. Changes in political circumstances carried the possibility of reassessment and adoption of a new position. Indeed, after the Camp David accords of 1978 and

40. For more details, see Muhammad Rashid, "Nahwa Filastin dimuqratiyya" (Toward a democratic Palestine) (Beirut, PLO Research Center, 1970); Muslih, "Moderates and Rejectionists," 130. On the Israeli interpretation of the democratic secular state idea, see Yehoshafat Harkabi, *Palestinians and Israel* (Jerusalem: Keter, 1974), chap. 4.

41. On U.S.S.R.-DFLP relations after 1973, see Galia Golan, *The Soviet Union and the Palestine Liberation Organization: An Uneasy Alliance* (New York: Praeger, 1980), 155–58.

42. See *The Transitional Program of the Palestine Liberation Organization* (New York: PLO Office, 1974).

the Egyptian-Israeli peace agreement of 1979, the DFLP opposed Fatah's pragmatism. Fatah's continued support of the option of a political settlement as well as its rapprochement with the pro-Western regime in Jordan exacerbated the conflict and sharpened the relations between the two organizations

The "Arab Revolution" Approach: The PFLP

The PFLP has presented an alternative political view to those of Fatah and the DFLP. The PFLP, contrary to the last two organizations, has subordinated the daily struggle over Palestine to the social and political interests of the whole Arab world. In its first statement, issued on December 11, 1967, the PFLP announced: "The struggle of the Palestinian masses in the occupied territories is an integral part of . . . the Arab revolution against world imperialism and its collaborating forces."[43] The theory of class struggle became the guideline for efforts to mobilize the Arab world into a political and social revolution. Class struggle therefore had to be carried out with equal force against Israel, Zionism, and what the PFLP called imperialism and Arab reactionism. Jordan, Saudi Arabia, and to a lesser degree Egypt and Syria were portrayed as agents of imperialism and enemies of the Arab people and the Palestinian revolution. The Popular Republic of South Yemen, Iraq, and to some extent Algeria and Libya were considered "positive" regimes who were closer to proletarian ideology and who adopted a hard line against Israel and imperialism.

The PFLP attitude toward the various groups within Palestinian society was also influenced by its class perception. The core of the Palestinian revolution is peasants and workers, whose role is to lead the class struggle and formulate its strategy. Because the PFLP attached importance to the numerical strength of the Palestinian petit bourgeoisie, it believed that bourgeois members should not be alienated from the revolution. However, the PFLP maintained that "because of the 'lax' and 'vacillatory' nature of this class, . . . it should neither lead the revolution nor draw up its political and military programs."[44] The PFLP allowed some groups among the

43. *al-Hurriyya*, Dec. 11, 1967.
44. Muslih, "Moderates and Rejectionists," 135.

Palestinian capitalist class to participate in the revolutionary process, although it was aware that these groups might do so only in order to support their own material interests.

Because of its affiliation to proletarian internationalism, the PFLP considered the Communist countries and national liberation movements in the Third World, as well as militant radical groups in the West, as close allies.[45] Indeed, the PFLP developed a close relationship with East European countries, Communist China, and North Korea, as well as with terrorist organizations in West Germany, Italy, and Japan. This policy was part of PFLP efforts to create a Palestinian-Arab front "that ripens, protects, and supports guerrilla action . . . to contain Israel from all sides as well as the enemy forces that provide it with support and protection."[46]

The October 1968 secession of Ahmad Jibril and Ahmad Zaʿrour from the PFLP, which led to the formation of the PFLP-GC, the later secession of Naʾif Hawatma, and finally the military defeats in the 1970–71 civil war in Jordan and then in Lebanon during 1975–76, weakened PFLP ability to carry out its revolutionary mission. Contrary to the DFLP, which adopted a flexible position and joined Fatah's political initiative to further particular Palestinian interests, the PFLP adhered dogmatically to its original position. The formal doctrine of launching a popular war against Israel through the Arab class revolution remained the basic guideline.

In September 1974 the PFLP seceded from the PLO Executive Committee and from the Palestine Central Council, accusing Fatah leadership and its supporters of risking reconciliation with Israel through political initiatives. The secession, which led to the formation of the Palestinian Rejection Front as a framework for Palestinian organizations sharing the PFLP view, is a clear example of the depth of the disagreement between the various PLO factions over the purpose and essential goals of the Palestinian armed resistance.

45. See the interview with George Habash in *al-Nahar* (Beirut), March 5, 1969.
46. See "al-Istratijiyya al-siyasiyya lil-jabha al-shaʿbiyya," in *ʿAla tariq al-thawra al-filastiniyya* (Beirut: al-Taliʿa, 1970), 55.

The Pro-Baʿthist Approach

A different interpretation of Palestinian desires and of the purpose of armed resistance is held by organizations affiliated with the Syrian and Iraqi Baʿthist regimes. Typical of these are the pro-Syrian al-Saʿiqa, the PFLP-GC and the pro-Iraqi Arab Liberation Front (ALF), the Palestine Popular Struggle Front, and Abu al-ʿAbbas's Palestine Liberation Front.

The Syrian-sponsored al-Saʿiqa (Thunderbolt) was formed in December 1968 by the Palestinian section of the Syrian Baʿth party. al-Saʿiqa defined the purpose of the Palestinian armed struggle in Syrian terms. "The Palestinian revolution," according to its political program, "is an integral part of the Arab revolution. . . . The destiny of Palestine is historically decided along with the future of conditions surrounding Palestine. . . . The [Palestinian] battle will create the revolutionary conditions necessary for the birth of an Arab region through a popular war of liberation that would . . . free Arab society."[47] Palestinian national aspirations would be fulfilled not through a separate solution but in a united Arab state under Syrian hegemony. "There are no differences," stated the former leader of al-Saʿiqa, Zuhayr Muhsin, "between Jordanians, Palestinians, Syrians, and Lebanese. We all constitute a part of one people. We speak about Palestinian identity only for political reasons."[48]

After the 1973 war, al-Saʿiqa, with Syrian backing, supported the political initiative of Fatah and the DFLP to establish in the occupied territories a "fighting Palestinian national authority," and later on a Palestinian state. This move, however, was considered a matter of tactics.

Insistence on the independence of the Palestinian state—as the Syrian Baʿth party organ proclaimed—is not a Palestinian rejection of Arab unity. . . . It . . . will be able . . . to claim the areas of Galilee, the Little Triangle, and the Negev; in other words over half of the territory of "Israel" before 1967. It will also be able to demand the return of a million Palestinian refugees to "Israel," namely more than the number of Zionists that are to be found on the soil of Palestine. . . .

47. *Arab World Weekly* (Beirut), Nov. 8, 1969.
48. Interview in *Trouw* (Amsterdam), April 3, 1977.

Hence . . . the creation of an independent and sovereign Palestinian state on the West Bank and Gaza does not mean a re-partition of the Arab homeland . . . and it should not be regarded as a step that is in opposition to the current Arab unity.[49]

Syrian ability to use al-Saʿiqa as an instrument to influence PLO internal affairs was made possible by complete Syrian control over its leadership, manpower, training, and facilities. Many of its members and officers were Palestinians who had grown up in Syria. Palestinian members of the Baʿth in Syria, according to one source, "are required to serve one month with al-Saʿiqa. In addition, members of groups affiliated to the party, and especially members of student groups, were asked to join al-Saʿiqa training courses."[50]

Syrian control over al-Saʿiqa was at its highest during Syrian intervention in the civil war in Lebanon in June 1976. In the first stages of the war al-Saʿiqa did not take part, although various PLO factions including the PFLP, DFLP, ALF and later on Fatah joined the left-wing Muslim Lebanese groups against the right-wing Christians. Later, however, with Syria's interference, al-Saʿiqa forces fought along with the regular Syrian units on behalf of the Christian right wing against the coalition of the leftist Lebanese groups and Palestinian organizations.[51] "al-Saʿiqa," as the Fatah leader Abu Iyad summarized it, "acted [first] as an agent of the Baʿth party [and] then as a part of the Palestinian movement."[52] Non-Palestinian considerations determined al-Saʿiqa's views and behavior.

Close relations with Syria, although of a more independent nature than al-Saʿiqa's, were also maintained by the PFLP-GC, led by Ahmad Jibril. PFLP-GC affiliation and cooperation with Syria were partly a result of the ties between its leadership and the Syrian regime. Ahmad Jibril is a Palestinian refugee from a village near Jaffa, who migrated to Syria in 1948. He joined the Syrian army,

49. *Sawt al-Taliʿa* (Damascus), Feb. 1978; Yodfat and Arnon-Ohanna, *PLO Strategy and Tactics*, 39.

50. John W. Amos II, *Palestinian Resistance: Organization of Nationalist Movement* (New York: Pergamon, 1980), 104.

51. For more details, see Michael Hudson, "The Palestinian Factor in the Lebanese Civil War," *Middle East Journal* 32/3 (1978): 270–73.

52. Interview in *Monday Morning* (Beirut), April 12, 1976.

where he became an engineering officer.[53] "Subsequently," as one source argues, "Jibril has been the subject of persistent rumors concerning his connections with the Syrian government . . . and it is said that he currently has personal ties with Syrian President al-Assad."[54] Other leaders, like Talal Naji and Fadhel Sharuru, were also Palestinian refugees who migrated to Syria during the Arab-Israeli war of 1948 and became active in Palestinian organizations during the sixties.

The attachment to Syria reached its peak during the course of the civil war in Lebanon. At the beginning of the war, the PFLP-GC supported the left-wing Muslim Lebanese groups. Syrian military intervention in June of 1976 on behalf of the Christian right wing changed Jibril's position. Unlike other PLO leaders, he withdrew his support from the left wing, seeking to avoid a confrontation with the Syrians. As a result, in 1977 Mahmud Ziadan (Abu al-ʿAbbas), one of the PFLP-GC leaders, seceded from the organization and formed the Palestine Liberation Front.

Despite his Syrian affiliation, after the 1973 war Jibril deviated from the Syrian political line on the Palestinian problem. Unlike al-Saʿiqa, which joined Fatah and the DFLP in adopting political means in addition to military ones to further a solution to the Palestinian problem, Jibril adhered to the idea of an all-Arab military struggle. Military struggle "against imperialism, Zionism, reactionism, and class oppression"— stated the PFLP-GC organ— "would ensure the unity of all factions of the Arab national liberation movement [and] liquidate the State of Israel."[55]

The Iraqi answer to the pro-Syrian organizations was to form the ALF in April 1969 and to sponsor several other organizations. Behind this Iraqi initiative lay the rivalry between the two Baʿthist regimes and the Iraqi desire to demonstrate that its commitment to the Palestinian cause was as great as that of the Syrians.

The ALF, like al-Saʿiqa, subordinated the liberation of Palestine to the broader goal of unification of the Arab world. Its immediate objective was an Arab democratic society in Palestine as part of a united Arab state under Iraqi hegemony. The varied origins of

53. *Arab World Weekly*, July 12, 1975.
54. Amos, *Palestinian Resistance*, 92.
55. *Ila al-Amam* (Beirut), May 17, 1974.

the ALF members reflect its pan-Arabist outlook. Most of its members are Iraqi, Lebanese, or Jordanian, with a few Palestinians from the refugee camps.

As an Iraqi-sponsored organization, the ALF adopted the Iraqi hard-line approach and rejected the notion of a political settlement to the Palestinian problem. "In the October War," stated the former leader of the ALF, ʿAbd al-Wahhab al-Kayyali, "the Arab people destroyed the wall of despair and surrender and regained their self-confidence and their determination to realize liberation. . . . But . . . the triumphs . . . [were] followed by certain concessions made by some Arab regimes. Our stand . . . is rejection of all bargains and rejection of the recognition of the Zionist enemy, . . . and refusal to have negotiations with the Zionist enemy."[56]

Similar views were expressed by the Palestine Popular Struggle Front (PPSF) and the Palestine Liberation Front (PLF). The two organizations have enjoyed political support and military assistance from Iraq. Simultaneously they have developed close ties with Libya. Their resistance to the PLO mainstream factions' (Fatah, al-Saʿiqa, and the DFLP) political approach to the Palestinian problem led them to join the Palestinian Rejection Front within the PLO, which also included the PFLP, ALF, and PFLP-GC.[57] The Front raised its voice against all political moves that might have been interpreted as a compromise with or acquiescence in Israel's existence.

Guided by a radical Arab vision, the rejectionist organizations viewed the 1975–76 civil war in Lebanon as a "war between the Lebanese progressive forces and Palestinian masses on the one hand and the reactionary imperialist-backed forces on the other."[58] They joined the Lebanese left against the Christian right-wing groups. Later on they fought along with the Muslim left wing against Syrian regular forces and the Syrian-sponsored al-Saʿiqa.

Syria's increasing military and political involvement in Lebanon weakened the rejectionist organizations' military position, also un-

56. *al-Hadaf* (Beirut), May 18, 1974.

57. The PFLP-GC was a member of the Rejection Front until 1977 when it was excluded because of its affiliation and military cooperation with Syria during the civil war in Lebanon.

58. George Habash interview in *Monday Morning*, April 5, 1976.

dermining their firm opposition to Fatah's idea of a transitional political solution. The 1979 Egyptian-Israeli peace treaty and the broad Arab opposition to it helped the Rejection Front to regain its power in the PLO and to emerge as a strong force within the organization.

FLEXIBILITY THROUGH CONFORMITY:
THE SEARCH FOR INNOVATIVE POLICY

The trend to approach Palestinian national desires in more attainable terms appeared among all PLO factions and widened the dispute over what course of action should be followed. As a result, those PLO factions that were willing to consider a political settlement on the West Bank and the Gaza Strip faced difficulties in taking such an innovative step. They were caught in an acute dilemma: political flexibility might help the PLO to mobilize the pressure necessary to compel Israel's retreat from its anti-PLO position and permit a mode of Palestinian independence in the occupied territories, but its inability to ensure such an outcome and the risk of disrupting the coexistence of PLO mainstream and rejectionist factions under a unified umbrella could have left the PLO empty-handed, without a state and without an organization. On the other hand, conformity to the PLO's stated doctrine at the price of renouncing any flexible policy would have led to stagnation and, in the end, to the loss of Palestine.

Conformity to doctrine, therefore, might have rescued the Palestinian boat for a while, but offered little chance to steer it to a safe shore. Political flexibility might improve the chances of success, but only at great risk. How could the mainstream factions' leadership further Palestinian national interests by political means without sacrificing PLO unity?

The principle that guided the mainstream response to this dilemma was based on the assumption that the more the concept of a political settlement could be justified in normative terms—that is to say, as the right thing to do—the less the possibility of being accused by the Palestinian rejectionists and radical Arab states of deviating from the ultimate PLO vision, and the less the risk of organizational disintegration.

How did the transition to the political route affect the mainstream factions' policy? To what extent did the leadership of these factions succeed in releasing themselves from the consequences of the dilemma inseparable from pursuing a policy that featured compromise? One can best follow the PLO mainstream's efforts to justify its position by analyzing the way in which the notions of a Palestinian national authority and the Palestinian state in the West Bank and Gaza Strip were formulated in the resolutions of the twelfth and the thirteenth sessions of the Palestine National Council, the parliament-in-exile. The resolutions combined new political ideas with old beliefs, emphasizing long-run goals and short-run requirements. They demonstrated conformity with the formal PLO doctrine while showing signs of political flexibility.

These resolutions, however, did not give equal weight to the new idea of a Palestinian state in the West Bank and Gaza and the old one of liberation of all Palestine and the establishment of a Palestinian democratic secular state in place of Israel. Rather, they subordinated the former to the latter by emphasizing the transitional nature and temporary status of any political settlement. "On the basis of the Palestinian National Covenant," stated the resolutions of the twelfth Palestine National Council in June 1974, "... the [Palestine] Liberation Organization will employ all means, and first and foremost armed struggle, to liberate Palestinian territory and to establish the *independent national fighting authority* for the people over every part of Palestinian territory that is liberated." At the same time, "any step taken toward liberation is a *step toward the realization of the Liberation Organization's strategy of establishing the democratic Palestinian state*" (my emphasis). Moreover, "it is impossible for a permanent and just peace to be established in the area unless our Palestinian people recover all their national rights and, first and foremost, their right to return and to self-determination on the whole of the soil of their homeland."[59]

The same pattern, although less sharply formulated, emerged from the political resolutions of the thirteenth Palestine National

59. See "Political Program for the Present Stage," introduction, arts. 1 and 2, p. 224.

Council of March 1977: "On the basis of the Palestine National Covenant and of the resolutions of the previous National Council . . . the Palestine National Council resolves to recover our people's national rights, and, first and foremost, their right to return [to Palestine], to exercise self-determination, and to establish an *independent national state* in their own land."[60] A state, rather than a national authority, in the occupied territories was mentioned for the first time. And the less specific "their own land" replaced the "whole of the soil of their homeland."

Furthermore, the resolutions of the thirteenth session of the Palestine National Council expressed a willingness "to participate, independently and on the basis of equality, in all international conferences, forums, and efforts relating to the Palestinian question . . . with the intention of realizing our non-negotiable national rights, which have been recognized by the United Nations General Assembly."[61] However, in the final statement the Palestine National Council "affirmed its adherence to the PLO's strategic objective, the liberation of Palestine from the racist Zionist occupation so that it can become a homeland to the people of Palestine in which a democratic state of Palestine can be established."[62]

By viewing any political agreement on the West Bank and Gaza Strip as temporary, the Palestine National Council achieved flexibility while avoiding the need for reciprocity. The PLO was ready to take territory without direct negotiation with or official recognition of Israel, to establish a Palestinian state without ending the state of war, and to receive rewards without renouncing its ultimate goals. In this way it hoped to maintain the organizational unity of diverse groups under the PLO umbrella. "The PLO," stated the twelfth Palestine National Council session, "will struggle against any proposal for a Palestine entity whose price is recognition [of Israel], peace, secure frontiers, renunciation of national rights, and the deprival of our people of their right to return [to the pre–1948

60. "Resolutions of the Thirteenth Palestine National Council, " art. 1, *WAFA* March 21, 1977; *Journal of Palestine Studies* 6/3 (1977): 189.

61. "Resolutions," art. 15; *Journal of Palestine Studies* 6/3:190.

62. *Foreign Broadcast Information Service, Middle East*, March 21, 1977, A11–A12.

Palestine borders.]"[63] The same idea was repeated in the thirteenth Palestine National Council Resolutions: "The Council resolves to intensify the Arab struggle for liberation of all occupied Arab territories . . . without peace or recognition of Israel."[64]

The decision of the Palestine National Council not to consider any political settlement as a final one minimized the conflict between the mainstream factions and the Rejection Front. At the same time, it set up constraints on a possible political initiative. However, despite these constraints, the 1974 and 1977 Palestine National Council resolutions left room for interpretation so that engagement of the mainstream factions in activities to advance a political settlement could be justified, to a limited degree, without entailing a serious threat to PLO unity.

This interpretation was made possible in part by a differentiation between short-term needs and a long-term commitment to Palestinian national goals. The perception of a political settlement as temporary demonstrated the mainstream factions' adherence to the ultimate Palestinian goal. At the same time, talk of a temporary settlement enabled them to emphasize the necessity of political achievements in the short run in order to realize ultimate goals in the long run. Political activity here and now had been justified in terms of hereafter. Acceptance of a political settlement for the short run was interpreted as complementary, not contradictory, to the long-run desires. "We believe," stated Faruq Qaddumi, head of the PLO political department, "that there is a state of interim peace (*salam marhali*) and a state of permanent peace (*salam da'im*). The permanent peace can only be achieved by the building of a democratic Palestinian state in which Muslims, Christians, and Jews coexist on a basis of equality. The permanent peace is in the building of this democratic state—that is, the long-term goal. The interim peace lies in the establishment of a Palestinian state in part of our territory. And there will certainly be one of these two kinds of peace in the area."[65]

After President Sadat's visit to Jerusalem in November 1977 and the Camp David accords of September 1978, the Fatah leadership

63. "Political Program for the Present Stage," art. 3, 224.
64. "Resolutions," art. 9, 190.
65. *Shu'un Filastiniyya* (June 1977): 40–41.

was able to continue justifying its willingness to accept a Palestinian state in the West Bank through political process by using the mechanism of differentiating between the short-term and the long-term in a more flexible manner. Fatah's fears that an agreement between Egypt, Israel, and Jordan would be concluded over the occupied territories without PLO participation persuaded it to belittle the long-term desire of a Palestinian democratic state in all of Palestine.

In a meeting with U.S. Congressman Paul Findley a few weeks after the Camp David accords, ʿArafat stated that "the PLO will accept an independent Palestinian state consisting of the West Bank and Gaza with a connecting corridor [and] in that circumstance will renounce any and all violent means to enlarge the territory of the state." But at the same time the ultimate goal was not diminished: "I would reserve the right, of course, to use non-violent means," continued ʿArafat, "to bring about the eventual unification of all Palestine."[66]

Fatah leader Abu Iyad, like ʿArafat, downplayed the practical meaning of a Palestinian democratic state, raising the possibility of coexistence and a mutual relationship between Israel and the Palestinian state-to-be. "I am convinced," Abu Iyad told Eric Rouleau, "that once we have a state to run . . . Palestinian subversive activities will vanish. Extremism will disappear from our ranks, even with the Rejection Front [and] . . . it will be very natural to have open borders between Israel and its Arab neighbor." The long-term goal, however, was not forgotten: "We remain faithful to our ideal—to our 'dream' as Yasir ʿArafat calls it—which provides for the reunification of Palestine in a secular and democratic state."[67]

The same pattern appears in statements made by ʿArafat after the peace treaty was signed between Egypt and Israel in March 1979. Although the positive statements reflected Fatah's efforts to minimize the importance of the Palestinian ultimate goal as an operational guideline for PLO activity, a clear renunciation of

66. *Journal of Palestine Studies* 8/2 (1979): 175.
67. Abu Iyad with Eric Rouleau, *My Home, My Land* (New York: Times Books, 1981), 225.

this goal did not occur: "I offered a democratic secular state but they [the Israelis] say we wanted to demolish and destroy Israel. We put it aside and said we will establish an independent state in any part of Palestine."[68]

In a meeting with former Austrian Chancellor Bruno Kreisky and Willy Brandt of West Germany in Vienna on July 6–8, 1979, ʿArafat went further by referring to the PLO's idea of a democratic secular state in Palestine as an old-fashioned notion. At the same meeting, ʿArafat also espoused a far-reaching interpretation of the anti-Israeli articles of the Palestinian National Covenant, interpreting them more as a symbolic expression of Palestinian national desires than as an actual guide to day-to-day politics. ʿArafat illustrated this point by comparing the Palestinian desire for all Palestine, as expressed in the Covenant, to West Germany's desire for unification with East Germany as stated in its constitution: both seem unrealistic dreams.[69]

However, putting aside the idea of a Palestinian democratic state and treating the anti-Israeli articles in the Palestinian National Covenant as symbolic indicates that ʿArafat is realistic enough to recognize the PLO's inability to attain its ultimate goals, at least for the time being. Positive statements provided a flexible interpretation to Palestinian desires, but did not indicate a desire to dismiss them completely.

This form of analysis can also be applied to the negative statements, which most strongly emphasize commitment to the ultimate goal and to an armed struggle, while leaving room to legitimize short-run political activities. This form is vividly expressed in the resolutions of Fatah's fourth congress, May 1980:

On the basis of unity . . . and in order to express the independent national will, for the complete success of the revolution, whereas the popular armed revolution is the only and inevitable way to the liberation of Palestine . . . the Fourth Congress of Fatah emphasizes: escalating all forms of Palestinian struggle. . . . Escalation of the armed struggle inside the occupied territories across the frontiers of confrontation with the Zionist enemy.

68. Transcript of "Face the Nation," CBS-TV, Dec. 3, 1979.
69. See *Shuʾun Filastiniyya* (Oct. 1979); *Haʾaretz*, Oct. 30, 1979.

. . . Strengthening of the steadfastness of our Palestinian masses in the land captured in 1948, to enable them to withstand plots aimed at impairing their unity and blurring their Arab identity.[70]

However, a statement by Fatah's Congress that the Palestine National Council resolutions had to be regarded as complementary to the PLO political program (article 7), and the fact that some of these resolutions raised the possibility of a political settlement, enabled Fatah to adopt political means as a legitimate path to further Palestinian national interests.

Differentiation between the commitment to the long-term Palestinian national vision and the short-term requirements made it possible for the PLO mainstream factions, and especially Fatah, to intensify both their diplomatic initiatives in the international arena and their political activities within the occupied territories. All of these activities were perceived as essential for the PLO in maintaining its control over the Palestinian issue. But the fact that all political activities had to be presented and justified in terms of the ultimate goal put restrictions on the ability to initiate, or to accept, far-reaching peace plans. The more that acceptance of these plans seemed to entail a clear deviation from the PLO's ultimate vision, the greater the hesitations and the search for safety measures. The fear among Fatah's leadership of disorder and disunity in its own movement and within the PLO, and the uncertain future of any peace plan, made concessions to Israel highly undesirable. But the keen awareness of the need to keep political channels open made it impossible to adopt a totally unyielding approach.

70. Filastin Radio (Beirut), June 1, 1980; *Middle East Review* 23/3–4 (1981): 74.

CHAPTER 3

Diplomacy in Chains

The PLO's professed willingness to accept a Palestinian state in the West Bank and Gaza Strip caught the world's imagination. It was perceived by many political observers as a breakthrough in the PLO's previous intransigence and seemed to indicate a PLO reappraisal of what was possible or reasonable and what was not. The idea of a Palestinian mini-state also strengthened the PLO's international status, raised its popularity, and enabled it to make further diplomatic achievements. By the early 1980s the PLO was granted official diplomatic recognition or some form of representation by more than eighty nations.[1] In many political circles the consideration of reaching a political settlement to the Palestinian problem without PLO participation has become inconceivable.

The PLO, however, has been unable to translate these diplomatic achievements into territorial ones; it has won the support of a large part of the public but is left without sovereignty over any part of Palestine. Although its willingness to consider a Palestinian state in the West Bank and Gaza has helped the organization to win many diplomatic battles, the Palestinians continue to lack a state of their own.

1. UPI release, Jan. 17, 1982; for more details, see Anis F. Kassim, "The Palestine Liberation Organization's Claim to Status: A Juridical Analysis under International Law," *Denver Journal of International Law and Policy* 9/1 (1980): 19–22, 29, 30.

DIPLOMACY IN THE SHADOW OF MAXIMAL GOALS

The idea of a Palestinian state in the West Bank and Gaza enabled the PLO to demonstrate its flexibility, but the restrictions the PLO set up on concessions to Israel limited its ability to pursue this goal through diplomatic means. Though willing to consider a political process and to participate in international forums, the PLO was not ready to pursue this goal at the price of publicly renouncing its commitment to a Palestinian state in all of Palestine or openly recognizing Israel's right to exist. "Israel," as Faruq Qaddumi says, "has occupied our country. . . . we shall be ready, within the framework of an international conference under the chairmanship of the United Nations, and with the attendance of all those involved in the conflict, to negotiate for a solution of the Middle East crisis. . . . [But] I shall make it perfectly clear. . . . We shall never recognize Israel."[2]

The PLO, under these circumstances, seemingly became a prisoner of its own policy. Signs of pragmatism were blocked by intransigence. Political realism was countered by dogmatism. Evidence of moderation was challenged by a mood of extremism. The organization, despite its achievements, remained vulnerable to continued manipulation by the Arab states and to the Israeli military and political campaign.

In pragmatic terms one might explain this lack of harmony between what seems to be a realistic redefinition of the PLO's political objectives and its uncompromising attitude toward Israel as the outcome of internal constraints and institutional anxieties. In view of the PLO's fragile structure, can the mainstream leadership publicly accept the solution of a Palestinian mini-state in the West Bank and Gaza as a final one? Can this leadership mobilize support for the idea of a Palestinian mini-state without maintaining its public commitment to the goal of a democratic state in all of Palestine? The answer to these questions is probably no. But one might ask different questions: with fewer institutional constraints and less fear of an internal split, could the Fatah leadership more easily recognize Israel and accept a mini-state as the final solution

2. *Stern* (Hamburg), July 30, 1981.

to the Palestinian problem? Could Fatah take this step without risking its symbolic and organizational hegemony? Are Fatah's difficulties in accepting the mini-state solution as the end to the PLO struggle against Israel only an outcome of organizational constraints, or do they also concern more fundamental obstacles?

In order to answer this question one must address the PLO's social structure and certain aspects of the Palestinian identity that make it almost impossible for the Fatah leadership publicly to accept the idea that Palestinian national goals will be fulfilled in less than the whole territory of Palestine. A full expression of these goals—better known as "national rights" and defined by the PLO after the October War of 1973—was included in the resolutions of the thirteenth session of the Palestine National Council in March 1977: "The Council resolves to pursue the struggle to recover our people's national rights, and, first and foremost, their right to return, to exercise self-determination, and to establish their independent national state on their own land."[3]

The fulfillment of the PLO demand for the right of return required a total change in the existing territorial reality: liberation of the whole of Palestine and the establishment of a Palestinian state in place of Israel. "We are marching through a dark tunnel," stated 'Arafat. "However, at the end we can already see the vast land with the mosques and churches of Jerusalem. Like the Vietnamese farmers who marched from Hanoi to Saigon, so will our people wave the flag first over Jerusalem, the West Bank, and Gaza, and then over Nazareth and the Negev."[4]

The Fatah leadership's difficulties in promulgating a less comprehensive interpretation of the right of return are rooted in the social origins of the PLO's personnel. Most of the organization's leadership and rank and file are Palestinian refugees who moved to Jordan, the Gaza Strip, Syria, and Lebanon after the 1948 Arab-Israeli war. Most came from cities, towns, and villages in the coastal plain and Galilee area of Palestine, which became part of Israel after 1948. Many were inhabitants, or children of inhabit-

3. "Resolutions of the Thirteenth Palestine National Council," art. 11, *Journal of Palestine Studies* 6/3 (1977): 189.
4. PLO Radio (Lebanon), Dec. 20, 1981; *Contemporary Mideast Background* (Jerusalem), March 14, 1982.

ants, of such places as Jaffa, Haifa, Ashkelon, Acre, Lydda, Ramlah and, to a much lesser extent, the western area of Palestine (the
West Bank). These last were incorporated into Jordan after 1948,
becoming Jordanian citizens.[5]

The right of return, therefore, had less to do with the 800,000
Palestinians of the West Bank than with the approximately 2.5
million Palestinian refugees who were located mostly in the East
Bank of Jordan, the Gaza Strip, Syria, and the Persian Gulf states
(see table 1). A Palestinian state occupying less than the whole
territory of Palestine might provide symbolic rewards, national
pride, and a name on earth, but it could hardly solve "the problem
of the refugees [and] the problem of the Palestinian territories that
are still occupied [namely, Israel]."[6] The 2200 square miles of the
West Bank are too small, too crowded, too poor, too traditional,
and too parochial to provide an adequate physical solution for the
Palestinian refugees.

Further, since most of the PLO's political and military activities
are carried out by the refugee segment of Palestinian society, acceptance of a territorial settlement of less than all Palestine would
be difficult to justify to the Palestinian fighting ranks. For "the
great popularity of the PLO among the Palestinian people is not
only due to its recognition by Arab states as the sole representative of the Palestinian people and to the wide support it re-

5. The West Bank's indigenous population differed socially from the Palestinian
refugees. During Ottoman rule and the British Mandate, such local institutions as
the family, the clan, the village, and the city played a stronger role among the
inhabitants of the western area (the West Bank) than among those of the coastal
plain and Galilee areas, from which the Palestinian refugees came. "The reason
for this difference," Yehoshua Porath has explained, "lay in social variance between
these regions. In the Judean mountains and Samaria [the West Bank] there was a
continuity of settlement from previous ages. The villages were organized in sub-
districts, at the head of which were the local sheiks. . . . On the other hand, the
villages in the coastal plain and in the valleys had been set up in later periods,
after the terror of the Bedouins had largely passed and after the latter had themselves begun to settle down in the empty regions of the country. In these villages
no social-administrative units had yet crystallized, nor did they have their own
leadership" (*The Emergence of the Palestinian Arab National Movement, 1918–
1929* [London: Frank Cass, 1974], 287). See also Joel S. Migdal, *Palestinian Society
and Politics* (Princeton: Princeton University Press, 1980), 9–31.

6. Faruq Qaddumi interview in *Journal of Palestine Studies* 6/4 (1977): 185.

Table 1   Distribution of the Palestinian Population, 1982

	Palestinians		Palestinians as percentage of total population (estimated)
	U.S. State Dept. estimate	PLO estimate	
Jordan	1,000,000	1,160,800	47–54
West Bank	700,000	818,300	99
Israel	500,000	530,600	13–14
Gaza Strip	450,000	476,700	99
Lebanon	400,000	600,000	15–22
Kuwait	320,000	278,800	25–22
Syria	250,000	215,500	3
Saudi Arabia	—	127,000	1
Iraq	120,000	20,000	1–0.2
Egypt	60,000	48,500	0.1
United Arab Emirates	40,000	34,700	4–3
Qatar	20,000	22,500	10–11
Libya	15,000	23,000	0.5–0.9
Oman	500	3,200	0.6–4
Other countries	424,500	283,300	—
Total	4,300,000	4,642,900	—

Source: *New York Times*, July 4, 1982.

ceives in the international arena, but also to the fact that among those claiming to represent the Palestinians it is the only body to identify at one and the same time with Palestinian sovereignty . . . and with the demand of 'return.' "[7] Acquiescence in a partial solution could imply a "renunciation of the right to return. It will . . . harm the PLO's status as the sole representative of the Palestinian people."[8] It could erode its popularity and undermine its raison d'être.

The same reasoning can be applied to the principle of self-determination. Implementation of Palestinian self-determination also

7. Matti Steinberg, "The PLO and the Mini-Settlement," *Jerusalem Quarterly* 21 (1981): 144.
8. Khalid al-Hasan interview in *al-Anba*ʾ (Kuwait), Aug. 31, 1981.

involves the liberation of the whole territory of Palestine. "The fulfillment of the right of self-determination and the establishment of an independent state" in the West Bank and Gaza Strip, Khalid al-Hasan has argued, "constitutes only one phase toward the final political goal, which is the establishment of a united Palestinian state over the whole of Palestine."[9] The PLO's difficulty in complying with a political solution that would fulfill Palestinian needs for self-determination in less than the whole of Palestine is largely due to "the centrality of the territorial principle in the definition of Palestinian identity."[10] One should examine the role of other components in shaping this identity in order to understand how the territorial principle became a key element in Palestinian self-definition and why this principle has had such a significant effect on the operational meaning of Palestinian self-determination.

Since the emergence of Palestinian nationalism at the beginning of the twentieth century, Palestinian individuals and groups, and later the guerrilla organizations, have been inclined to define their collective identity in pan-Arabist, pan-Islamic, and Palestinian terms. The name of the largest guerrilla organization, Fatah, for instance, means in Arabic a conquest for Islam gained in the holy war. The three brigades of the Palestinian Liberation Army— Quadisiyya, Hittin, and 'Ayn-Jalut—are named after great victories won by Muslim armies. "Yasir 'Arafat's *nom de guerre*, Abu 'Ammar, the father of 'Ammar," writes Bernard Lewis, "is an allusion to the historic figure of 'Ammar ibn-Yasir, the son of Yasir, a companion of the Prophet and a valiant fighter in all his battles."[11] 'Arafat's attachment to Islamic values was apparent when he referred to the idea of a Palestinian secular democratic state in Palestine as misleading. "al-Fatah," he stated, "had never used the term 'secular', nonreligious homeland."[12] In the PLO's basic documents, such as the Palestinian National Charter and the resolutions of the Palestinian National Council, as well as in Palestinian literature and poetry, the Palestinians refer to themselves

9. Interview in *al-Riyadh* (Riyadh), May 20, 1981.
10. Steinberg, "The PLO and the Mini-Settlement," 131.
11. Bernard Lewis, "The Return of Islam," *Commentary* 61 (1976): 43.
12. *al-Ra'y al-'Aam* (Kuwait), March 16, 1969; Aryeh Y. Yodfat and Yuval Arnon-Ohanna, *PLO Strategy and Tactics* (London: Croom Helm, 1981), 57.

simultaneously as the "Palestinian people" and the "Palestinian Arab people." "Filastin ʿarabiyya"—Palestine is Arab—has become the rallying cry of Palestinians everywhere.

As in other Arab communities, although to a lesser extent, the broad definition of a Palestinian identity is derived from simultaneous awareness of two primordial Arab allegiances.[13] One is *qawmiyya*, an abstract noun from *qawm*, meaning people, group, or tribe, used to express political allegiance and the commitment of social units to the realization of Arab nationalism through unity. The second is *wataniyya*, from *watan*, which means country or homeland and expresses patriotic attachment to a single country.[14]

Since the founding of the PLO in May 1964, and especially after the Arab-Israeli war of 1967, a consistent Palestinian effort has been made to emphasize the particular—that is to say, the wataniyya—element of Palestinian identity over the pan-Arab one. This effort is symbolized by the change of the title of the Palestinian National Charter of 1964, *al-mithaq al-qawmi al-filastini*, to *al-mithaq al-watani al-filastini* in the 1968 version. The shift implied a greater awareness of the national and political differences between the Palestinian people and the rest of the Arab nations. "The Palestinian Arab people," states article 28 of the 1968 charter, "insists on the originality and the independence of its national (wataniyya) revolution and rejects every manner of interference, guardianship, and subordination." Article 3 states fur-

13. A primordial allegiance or, "A primordial attachment," according to Geertz, "relates to the 'given' or more precisely . . . the assumed 'givens'—of social existence: immediate contiguity and kin connection mainly but beyond them the givenness that stems from being born into a particular religious community, speaking a particular language, or even a dialect of a language, and following particular social practices. These congruities of blood, speech, custom and so on, are seen to have an ineffable, and at times overpowering, coerciveness in and of themselves. . . . In modernizing societies where the tradition of civil politics is weak . . . primordial attachments tend . . . to be repeatedly, in some cases almost continually, proposed and widely acclaimed as preferred bases for the demarcation of autonomous political units." Clifford Geertz, *The Interpretation of Cultures* (New York: Basic, 1973), 259–60.

14. For more on these terms, see Satiʿ al-Husri, *al-ʿUruba awwalan* (Arabism first) (Beirut: al-ʿIlm lil-malayin, 1955), 13. For a detailed analysis, see Sylvia G. Haim, "Islam and the Theory of Arab Nationalism," in *The Middle East in Transition*, ed. Walter Z. Laquer (London: Routledge and Kegan Paul, 1958), 287–98.

ther, "The Palestinian Arab people possesses the legal right to its homeland, and when the liberation of its homeland is completed it will exercise self-determination solely according to its own will and choice."[15]

Since Palestinians share the same culture, historical roots, language, and religion as other Arab communities, it is logical to ask in what way Palestinians differ, and how this justifies separate self-determination. Clearly the Palestinians' territorial attachment to Palestine is the basis of the PLO's claim for Palestinian self-determination. This emphasis on the territorial component as a major factor in Palestinian national identity is clearly expressed in the Palestinian National Charter. "The Palestinians," states article 5, "are the Arab citizens who were living permanently in Palestine until 1947, whether they were expelled from there or remained."[16] The Palestinians, according to this definition, "are so called because they came from the territory of Palestine of which they claim to be the rightful owners. The fact that they do not rule Palestine . . . and that there are rivals and other claimants to it, such as Israel and Jordan, only makes them express their attachment to the territorial principle with redoubled emphasis."[17]

The justification for the claim of self-determination in terms of territorial identity limited the possibility of fulfilling this desire in less than the whole territory of Palestine. "To accept only part of their territory," as Matti Steinberg put it, "seemed to them to be a denial of the very essence of their existence and division of something which by nature cannot be divided. To agree to the territorial division of Palestine was in their eyes an irremediable defacement of the Palestinian identity."[18]

Against this background one should examine the Palestinian

15. See "The Palestinian National Covenant," in *Middle East Record 1968*, ed. Daniel Dishon (Jerusalem: Israel Universities Press, 1973), 432, 435.

16. Ibid., 432.

17. Steinberg, "The PLO and the Mini-Settlement," 130.

18. Ibid., 131; See also Faruq Qaddumi's description: "In 1947 we were like the mother who fought before King Solomon over her child. He suggested cutting the child in half. But the real mother said: 'Let us live, let us not be divided' " (*Stern*, July 30, 1981).

national right to establish a Palestinian independent state on the Palestinians' own land. The phrase "Palestinian state on Palestinian soil," instead of "a Palestinian democratic state in the whole of Palestine," was ambiguous enough to enable the PLO mainstream factions to advance the idea of a Palestinian state in the West Bank and Gaza. However, such activities could be interpreted by the PLO rejectionist factions or by the international community as a willingness to acquiesce in a partial territorial settlement to the Palestinian problem, denying rights to return and self-determination in the whole territory of Palestine.

The need to mitigate this tension led Fatah to join other PLO factions in a six-point program that emphasized the temporary status of the Palestinian mini-state solution in the West Bank and Gaza. The program was announced at the first conference of the Steadfastness and Confrontation Front composed of Libya, Algeria, Iraq, Southern Yemen, Syria, and the PLO, and held in Tripoli, Libya, after President Sadat's visit to Jerusalem in November 1977. "We, all factions of the PLO," stated the fifth point of the program, " . . . strive for the realization of the Palestinian people's right to return and self-determination within the context of an independent Palestinian national state on any part of Palestinian land without reconciliation or negotiations [with Israel] as an interim aim of the Palestinian revolution."[19]

The PLO's willingness to accept a Palestinian state on the West Bank and Gaza as an interim aim, without making concessions to Israel, became in F. G. Bailey's term an "unshifting guide for conduct,"[20] a normative rule for its behavior. Exercising the right to self-determination on part of the homeland was perceived as a stage "in creating the necessary conditions for the creation of a united democratic state in the whole of Palestine." It would serve to intensify the struggle for self-determination by Palestinians residing in Jordan. Moreover, it would activate the anti-Zionist Palestinian and Israeli forces in Israel itself. However, in the end, "the national struggle aimed at achieving the right of self-deter-

19. See *WAFA*, Dec. 5, 1977; *Journal of Palestine Studies* 7/3 (1978): 188.
20. F. G. Bailey, *Stratagems and Spoils: A Social Anthropology of Politics* (New York: Schocken, 1969), 22.

mination [could not] be achieved before the disintegration of Zionist institutions."[21]

Viewing the Palestinian mini-state as an interim phase limited the PLO's diplomatic maneuverability. Mainstream factions could engage in political activity to further the idea of a mini-state. But this activity could not preclude military or political options to fulfill Palestinian desires for return and self-determination within the framework of greater Palestine.

Aware of this territorial dimension of Palestinian identity and the PLO's organizational constraints, the mainstream factions, especially Fatah, preferred to maintain the delicate consensus that had been reached around the mini-state goal, even at the price of self-imposed restrictions: no negotiation that required recognition of Israel, no security guarantees to it, and no peace treaty with it. Conceding any one of these restrictions could have destroyed the legitimacy of the goal.

TOWARD SAFE DIPLOMACY

Fatah's effort to gain support for the idea of a Palestinian mini-state while still refusing concessions to Israel can be regarded as the least costly way to advance a new political idea without risking leadership position and hegemony. However, without more diplomatic flexibility, Fatah's chances of exerting sufficient diplomatic pressure to move Israel toward concessions and of reaching a compromise acceptable to both sides seemed very unlikely.

This fear of a political deadlock encouraged Fatah to search for diplomatic tactics that would enable the PLO to demonstrate flexibility without being accused of deviating from the official policy. Fatah leaders sought a course of action that would help them manipulate the formal restrictions of no recognition, no security guarantees, and no peace treaty with Israel. The more the organization could represent its diplomatic activity as contributing to, or at least not opposing, the PLO struggle for a Palestinian state in the whole of Palestine, the greater the possibility for a flexible interpretation of the restrictions on concessions toward Israel. The

---

21. As cited in *Contemporary Mideast Background*, June 8, 1982: 5.

question, thus, was not whether the PLO could achieve political
rewards without deviating from its official policy but rather whether
it could achieve these rewards at the price of calculated and controlled deviation that would not lead to structural disaster.
To what extent did Fatah succeed? One can follow Fatah's efforts
to minimize the meaning of the concessions made to Israel by
examining three proposals put forward in 1978 by Professor Walid
Khalidi, former head of the Institute of Palestine Studies in Beirut,
in 1980 by Khalid al-Hasan, Fatah leader and chairman of the
Palestinian National Council's Foreign Affairs Committee, and in
1982 by Dr. ʿIsam Sartawi, who served as a foreign affairs adviser
to Yasir ʿArafat. All three Palestinians were known to be close
to ʿArafat, and some observers believed that their proposals received ʿArafat's endorsement.

Khalidi's proposal, made public in *Foreign Affairs*,[22] called for
Israel's full withdrawal from Egyptian, Jordanian, and Syrian territories, which it had occupied during the 1967 war, and the establishment of an independent Palestinian state in East Jerusalem,
the West Bank, and the Gaza Strip prior to any negotiation. It
also asserted that the PLO "has to participate in the government
of the Palestinian state,"[23] that the state should have a national
armed force, that East Jerusalem should be the capital of Arab
Palestine, and that the settlement of the Palestinian problem
should be treated as part of an overall solution to the Arab-Israeli
dispute, especially the dispute between Israel and Egypt and Syria.

In return, "the new Palestinian government will . . . draw up the
constitution of the new state, to replace the [Palestinian] National
Charter." The Palestinian state would acquiesce in the idea of a
partition of Palestine, within the British Mandate boundaries, into
two states: Israel and Arab Palestine, "with minor and reciprocal
adjustments in the frontiers of 1967." The Palestinian refugees
"who cannot return to pre–1967 Israel (because of Israeli objections) or to the Palestinian state (because of lack of absorptive
capacity) will still have the options of compensation and Palestinian
citizenship." The Palestinian state would be nonaligned vis-à-vis

22. Walid Khalidi, "Thinking the Unthinkable: A Sovereign Palestinian State,"
Foreign Affairs 56/4 (1978):695–713.
23. Ibid., 707.

the superpowers "and other powers particularly in the defense and military field."[24] International and inter-Arab forums such as the U.N. Security Council and the Arab League could guarantee the arrangement.

Khalidi's plan entailed far-reaching concessions; the two-state solution is clearly a deviation from the Palestinian National Charter. "The partitioning of Palestine in 1947 and the establishment of Israel," stated article 19 of the charter, "is fundamentally null and void, whatever time has elapsed, because it was contrary to the wish of the people of Palestine and its natural right to its homeland, and contradicts the principles embodied in the Charter of the U.N., the first of which is the right of self-determination."[25]

Acceptance of a two-state solution could easily be interpreted as readiness to acquiesce to a Palestinian mini-state as a permanent solution and to renounce the PLO goal of right of return to the whole territory of Palestine. "With pan-Arab irredentism defused by a PLO endorsement of the Palestinian state," as Khalidi put it, "and Egyptian and Syrian irredentism defused by return to the 1967 frontiers, the stage will have been set for generation of an Arab consensus in favor of an overall settlement. Given its non-aligned status, it is difficult to see what expectation would promote a Palestinian regime to withdraw from such an arrangement."[26]

Moreover, the two-state solution, which implied recognition of and coexistence with Israel as well as acceptance of international and regional guarantees on security issues, can also be understood as a deviation from the resolution of the twelfth Palestine National Council, which vowed to "struggle against any proposal for a Palestinian entity whose price is recognition [of Israel], peace, secure frontiers, renunciation of national rights, and the deprival of our people of their right to return."[27]

Khalidi's proposal, however, entails elements that minimize this

24. Ibid., 707, 701, 709, 703.
25. *Middle East Record 1968*, 434.
26. Khalidi, "Thinking the Unthinkable," 711.
27. See article 3 of the "Political Program for the Present Stage of the Palestine Liberation Organization," *WAFA*, June 9, 1974; *Journal of Palestine Studies* 7/4 (1974): 224. More on this argument can be seen in an interview with the Palestinian leader Muhammad ʿIzzat Darwaza in *al-Qabas* (Kuwait), Sept. 14, 1977.

apparent deviation from the PLO's official policy. The fact that the Palestinian state in the West Bank and Gaza would be established prior to renunciation or amendment of the Palestinian National Charter, which calls for a Palestinian state instead of Israel, released the PLO from the burden of revising its basic national goal as a prerequisite to the establishment of the mini-state. True, the proposal stated that the Palestinian National Charter would be replaced after the establishment of the state. It did not, however, exclude the possibility that the new constitution would express the same political desires as the charter. By placing the establishment of the Palestinian state ahead of the renunciation or amendment of the charter, the proposal enabled the PLO to maintain its commitment to its ultimate goal—and at the same time demonstrate its willingness to accept a settlement based on two states in Palestine.

Khalidi also tried to minimize the meaning of concessions on the recognition and the guarantees issues. Khalidi's solution to the Palestinian problem, as has been mentioned, was presented as an integral part of a comprehensive Middle East settlement. The issue of recognition, therefore, had to be solved simultaneously between Israel and the Palestinian state and between Israel and the Arab world. "A different generation of Palestinian and Arab leaders in different circumstances today," stated Khalidi, "are prepared to say that they accept . . . Israeli-Palestinian and Israeli-Arab reciprocal recognition and coexistence."[28] The emphasis on multilateral recognition enabled Khalidi to make Palestinian recognition conditional on the willingness of other Arab countries, transferring part of the burden of recognition to the shoulders of third parties. By doing so, Khalidi's proposal enabled the PLO to avoid facing this issue alone.

As in the case of recognition, the issue of guarantees was presented in a way that enabled the PLO to demonstrate flexibility while avoiding an obvious deviation from the Palestine National Council resolutions. The proposal that the responsibility for guarantees to secure the boundaries of Israel be transferred to a third party—the superpowers, the United Nations, or the Arab na-

28. Khalidi, "Thinking the Unthinkable," 702.

tions—was intended to release the PLO from the need to confront this issue directly.[29] Guarantees by proxy made it possible for the PLO to interpret such a forbidden compromise in a pragmatic manner.

Khalid al-Hasan's proposal followed the same pattern. Put forward during his meeting with leaders of the nine states of the European Economic Community in April and May 1980, the proposal called for Israel's withdrawal without negotiations from the territories occupied in 1967, including East Jerusalem, and the stationing of U.N. forces in the evacuated areas for a transitional period not to exceed a year. During this period the United Nations would make arrangements for the self-determination of the Palestinian inhabitants of the West Bank and the Gaza Strip, leading to the establishment of a Palestinian state. A peace conference would then be held under the auspices of the United States and the Soviet Union, the European nations, and all parties in the Middle East, including Israel and the Palestinians, to discuss issues of frontiers and security guarantees. The U.N. resolutions on the Palestinians' rights and the U.N. Charter would guide these discussions.[30]

This proposal, like the previous one, is based on the assumption that in order to further the goal of a Palestinian state some concessions to Israel on issues of recognition and security guarantees are unavoidable. However, the price has to be kept as low as possible. Willingness to enter multilateral negotiation *after* the withdrawal of Israeli forces from the occupied territories and after the establishment of a Palestinian state serve this purpose, so that the PLO can bypass discussions over Israel's right "to live in peace within secure and recognized boundaries," as set forth in U.N. Security Council resolution 242 (1967). This resolution, which referred to the Palestinians as refugees, not as a people, is regarded by the PLO as a discriminatory statement that denies the Palestinians' rights to return and self-determination. While the PLO rejected

29. For more on these tactics, see Steinberg, "The PLO and the Mini-Settlement," 138.

30. See Khalid al-Hasan's interviews in *Shuʾun Filastiniyya* (July 1980): 50–52; and *al-Anbaʾ*, Aug. 31, 1981; see also Steinberg, "The PLO and the Mini-Settlement," 137.

the resolution as a basis for negotiation, its acceptance became an Israeli and American prerequisite for negotiation. Multilateral negotiations about frontiers and security guarantees also released the Palestinian state from committing itself solely and directly to the outcome of this negotiation. The door for maneuverability was left open.

'Isam Sartawi's 1982 peace proposal seems to be the most conciliatory of the three. It calls for mutual recognition of Israel and the Palestinian state after Israel's withdrawal from the occupied territories.[31] "The window for peace," said Sartawi, "will not remain open forever." Therefore, "the PLO and Arab governments should make fresh peace moves, looking toward a Palestinian state side by side with Israel . . . and also endorse talks with any Israelis who will recognize Palestinian national rights."[32] Sartawi also called for public talks with the Israeli "peace camp," meaning those "who accept the following principles: Israeli withdrawal to 1967 borders; recognition of the right of the Palestinian people to self-determination and a sovereign state, based on consent that the PLO is its sole legitimate representative."[33] The Palestinian failure to hold such talks, argued Sartawi, helps the Israeli Likud government's hawkish policy against the Palestinians.

In 1976 Sartawi participated in secret talks, authorized by the PLO, with members of the Israeli Council for Israeli-Palestinian Peace, including Uri Avneri and Aryeh Lova Eliav, former members of the Israeli Parliament, and Mattityahu Peled, a retired general. Reflecting on these talks, Sartawi stated that they "should have been publicly admitted, justified, and defended in the Arab world and to Israeli public opinion."[34] Furthermore, "we should have invited our Israeli interlocutors to Beirut for a direct exchange of views with Yasir 'Arafat. Or better yet, we should have invited them to address the Palestinian National Council, which held its

---

31. See 'Isam Sartawi's interview with Anthony Lewis, *New York Times*, March 4, 1982.

32. Ibid.

33. Sartawi interview with Eric Rouleau, *Le Monde* (Paris), Jan. 22, 1982.

34. Ibid.; for more details on these meetings see Mattityahu Peled, "Dialogue with Palestinians," *Ha'aretz*, Jan. 25, 1981, and Asher Susser, "The PLO: What Does It Say?" *Ha'aretz*, Feb. 20, 1981.

congress in Damascus last April [1981], two months before the Israeli [general] elections. In this way the PLO could demonstrate concretely its will to reach a just peace."[35]

During the 1982 Israeli invasion of Lebanon, Sartawi continued to support a political settlement based on mutual recognition. He welcomed a statement issued in Paris by Nahum Goldmann, president of the World Jewish Congress, Philip M. Klutznick, former U.S. secretary of commerce, and Pierre Mendès-France, former prime minister of France, which called on Israel to "lift its siege of [West] Beirut in order to facilitate negotiations with the PLO leading to a political settlement."[36] "Mutual recognition must be vigorously pursued," the statement continued, "and there should be negotiation with the aim of achieving coexistence between the Israeli and Palestinian peoples based on self-determination."

Sartawi's endorsement of mutual recognition and coexistence with Israel reflected greater readiness than the other two proposals for conciliatory gestures and showed the clearest deviation from the Palestine National Council's policy of not recognizing Israel. However, close examination of Sartawi's views on the issue of recognition will show that, like Walid Khalidi and Khalid al-Hasan, he too presented his conciliatory gestures in a way that could be justified to the Palestinian radicals.

As in the previous proposals, recognition is conditional upon the prior establishment of the Palestinian state. "A recognition like marriage cannot be unilaterally carried out; it calls for a reciprocating partner.... According to international law, recognition is a contractual agreement that is bilateral in nature; it is reached when outstanding problems have been solved satisfactorily; it has no meaning whatsoever as a precondition."[37] The suggestion that the Palestinian state-to-be should deal with the recognition issue released the PLO from dealing directly with it. In this sense Sartawi too sought to provide the PLO with a device

35. Interview, *Le Monde*; see also Anthony Lewis, "A PLO Voice for Peace," *New York Times*, March 9, 1982.

36. *Le Monde*, July 2, 1982; *New York Times*, July 3, 1982. On ʿArafat's positive response to the statement, see *Le Monde*, July 3, 1982.

37. ʿIsam A. Sartawi, "The Palestinian Dimension," *AEI Foreign Policy and Defence Review* 3/1 (1981):29.

that would enable it to show flexibility without shifting unequivocally from its uncompromising attitude toward Israel.

The search for a strategy to minimize the painful price of concessions to Israel can be seen also in Sartawi's attempt to interpret
the Palestinian National Charter in a way that would not require
its renunciation or amendment prior to or after the establishment
of the Palestinian state. "The Palestinian National Charter," wrote
Sartawi,

> is a statement of a set of general principles and definitions that reflect the
> Palestinians' understanding of their problem. . . . The Charter was never
> intended to be a day-to-day guide to political positions and attitudes.
> These are determined constitutionally by the PNC [Palestine National
> Council] resolutions . . . which are binding and enforceable. Without rec-
> ognition of this fact, the political position of the PLO cannot be under-
> stood. . . .
> The basic argument against the charter . . . is the assertion of the wish
> to liberate Palestine; this, it is felt, calls for the destruction of Israel.
> Assuming that this is the PLO's intention and discounting the [1977]
> resolution of the PNC calling for the establishment of a Palestinian state
> on part of Palestine, none of the proponents of this argument has shown
> how the PLO can destroy the militarily powerful Israel, or why the Israeli
> establishment is disturbed when Palestinian leaders deny that they want
> to or can destroy the state of Israel.[38]

Similarly, Sartawi's argument that his meetings in the late 1970s
with Israeli "peace camp" members should have been publicized
does not necessarily deviate from the PLO official line. During its
1977 session, the Palestine National Council stressed "the importance of relations and coordination with Jewish democratic and
progressive forces inside the occupied homeland, which are struggling against the ideology and practice of Zionism."[39] Indeed, the
refusal of the 1981 Palestine National Council session to reconfirm
this resolution brought the dialogue to a halt.[40] "I am a disciplined
fighter," stated Sartawi, "and I never acted contrary to the in-

38. Ibid., 30–31.
39. See "Resolutions," art. 14, *Journal of Palestine Studies* 6/3 (1977): 190.
40. On Sartawi's efforts to pass such a resolution, see *al-Nahar* (Beirut), April
18 and 19, 1981.

structions of the Palestinian people's representatives."[41] Sartawi's efforts to receive PLO approval "to resume the Palestinian-Israeli dialogue"[42] show the importance he placed on public adherence to the official PLO line, no matter what he believed deviation could contribute to the Palestinian cause.

All three proposals sought to provide the PLO with ways to balance its immediate political needs with its ultimate goals. Concessions to Israel in the form of conditional, hidden, or postponed recognition and guarantees through a third party seemed to serve this purpose. The assumption was that as long as these concessions would enable the PLO to further the idea of a mini-state through diplomatic means without clearly and publicly renouncing its commitment to the idea of a democratic state in the whole of Palestine, the deviations would probably be tolerated by Palestinian rejectionist factions.

The proposals, therefore, were intended to leave enough room for the PLO to continue describing the Palestinian state in the West Bank and Gaza as a stage in the Palestinian struggle. Khalid al-Hasan himself justified his proposal in these terms: "The final goal is the establishment of the Palestinian democratic state in the whole of Palestine. . . . After the 1973 war . . . the Palestinian leadership and the Palestine National Council adopted the idea of phasing (*marhaliyya*) the program of the Palestinian struggle, and thus agreed to establish a Palestinian independent state on any liberated part of the Palestinian land, provided that it would not contain any stipulation that would prevent the attainment of the final goal."[43]

That these proposals, as well as others following the same pattern, faced fierce opposition from most of the PLO factions and from leaders within Fatah demonstrated the difficulties of pursuing such political strategy, regardless of the rewards the PLO might gain.

41. Interview, *Le Monde.*
42. Ibid.
43. *Shu'un Filastiniyya*, (Jan.–Feb. 1982): 41–42.

CHAPTER 4

In the Web of International Diplomacy

While the PLO considered engagement in diplomatic activity essential to furthering the goal of a Palestinian state in the West Bank and Gaza, the need to pursue this goal with minimal deviation from its official line of zero concessions to Israel became a principal guide for conduct. In the previous chapter I examined three Palestinian peace proposals to show the effect of this operational guideline on shaping PLO diplomacy and the various strategies that have been used to minimize the price of concessions to Israel. In this chapter I examine the effect of this principle on the PLO's international behavior by analyzing its differing responses to five peace proposals.

These proposals were an outcome of diplomatic initiatives by the United States, the Soviet Union, the European Economic Community, Egypt, and Saudi Arabia. While the PLO responded positively to the 1977 joint U.S.-U.S.S.R. statement and to the 1981 initiative by Soviet President Leonid Brezhnev, as did Fatah in 1981 to the plan of King Fahd of Saudi Arabia (then crown prince), the PLO reaction to the 1978 Camp David agreements between Egypt and Israel and to the 1980 European Economic Community peace initiative was negative.

All five initiatives proposed a solution requiring some deviation from the official PLO policy of no concessions to Israel. However, the different responses to the five proposals, and especially within Fatah, reflected its wish to minimize ideological concessions toward Israel. The more a peace proposal succeeded (1) in gaining support

from Arab and non-Arab nations that recognize the PLO or maintain close relations with it, and (2) in indicating clear rewards—
that is, a willingness to accept the PLO as an equal partner in
peace negotiations and to affirm the right of the Palestinians to a
state—the greater the PLO's ability to disparage the concessions
to be made to Israel and the greater the chance for such a proposal
to win PLO endorsement. The less support the proposal received
from friendly nations and/or the less indication of clearcut rewards,
the less likely that the PLO would endorse it. The American-Soviet
statement, that of Brezhnev, and to a lesser extent that of Fahd
fall into the first category. The Egyptian-Israeli proposal and the
European one fall into the second.

THE JOINT U.S.-U.S.S.R. STATEMENT

The statement issued in 1977 by U.S. Secretary of State Cyrus
Vance and Soviet Minister for Foreign Affairs Andrei Gromyko
demonstrated an attempt by the two superpowers to reach a solution to the Palestinian problem in the framework of a comprehensive Middle East settlement. The Carter Administration's
willingness to join the Soviet Union in such an initiative symbolized
a far-reaching change in the American approach toward a solution
to the Palestinian problem.

Under the Nixon-Ford Administration, U.S. policy relied on a
step-by-step approach, on the assumption that any attempt to de-
fuse the Israeli-PLO conflict had to deal first with Arab-Israeli
issues. "Simply to get Israel into a conference room with a group
that had sworn its destruction and conducted a decade-long terrorist campaign against it," stated Henry Kissinger, "would be a
monumental assignment, consuming energy, emotion, and enormous amounts of time during which all progress would be frozen."[1]
Kissinger believed that a peace settlement to be reached step by
step through American mediation would decrease Soviet influence
in the area and contribute to political stability in the Middle East.

The Carter Administration, in contrast, felt that it would be

1. Henry Kissinger, *Years of Upheaval* (Boston: Little, Brown, 1982), 1138.

difficult, perhaps impossible, to solve the Arab-Israeli conflict without initially dealing with the Palestinian problem in the framework of a comprehensive peace settlement in which the Palestinians participated. The Palestinian issue "cannot be ignored if the others are to be solved. Moreover, to be lasting, a peace agreement must be positively supported by all the parties to the conflict, including the Palestinians. This means that the Palestinians must be involved in the peacemaking process."[2]

The Carter Administration also assumed that a solution to the Palestinian problem would decrease Soviet influence on the PLO and achieve stability in the region. "Saudi and American financial aid," according to this view, "would woo the PLO away from the U.S.S.R. . . . a Palestinian state with ties . . . [to] Jordan could not become a Soviet base and a source of trouble in the region."[3]

From this position, in the summer of 1977 the United States, supported by Egypt and Saudi Arabia, made an effort to persuade the PLO to accept, even if only partially, U.N. Security Council Resolution 242, which called for the sovereignty and security of all nations in the Middle East.[4] In return, the U.S. was willing both to support the idea of an "independent Palestinian entity" on the West Bank under U.N. supervision and to reassess its military aid policy toward Israel.[5] However, the American and Saudi assessment that 'Arafat could "deliver the goods" proved to be erroneous. The PLO's Central Council, a sixty-member consultative group, discussed the proposal and rejected it unequivocally.[6]

The failure to convince the PLO to move from its firm position against U.N. Security Council Resolution 242 played an important role in the shift of American policy toward seeking cooperation with the U.S.S.R. in order to bring the PLO to the negotiating

2. *U.S. Department of State Bulletin*, Oct. 10, 1977, 463.

3. Aryeh Y. Yodfat and Yuval Arnon-Ohanna, *PLO Strategy and Tactics* (London: Croom Helm, 1981), 111.

4. On these Egyptian efforts, see *al-Akhbar* (Cairo), Aug. 11, 1977. On Saudis' see *Guardian* (London), Aug. 9, 1977.

5. See *Al-Mustaqbal* (Paris), Aug. 27, 1977.

6. For more details, see the interview with Na'if Hawatma in the DFLP's *al-Hurriyya* (Beirut), Aug. 29, 1977.

table. The strong U.S.S.R.-PLO ties made the Carter Administration conclude that only through joint action with the Soviets could a solution to the Palestinian problem be found.

The joint Vance-Gromyko statement of October 1977 demonstrated an effort in this direction. "Both governments," declared the statement, "are convinced that the vital interests of the peoples of this area as well as the interests of strengthening peace and international security in general, urgently dictate the necessity of achieving as soon as possible a just and lasting settlement of the Arab-Israeli conflict. This settlement should be comprehensive, incorporating all parties concerned and all questions."[7]

A comprehensive settlement required the revival of the Geneva Conference, which met for two days in December 1973 after the October War of that year. The conference was to discuss and seek resolution of the issue of Israel's withdrawal "from territories occupied in the 1967 conflict; the resolution of the Palestinian question including ensuring the legitimate rights of the Palestinian people; termination of the state of war and establishment of normal peace relations on the basis of mutual recognition of the principles of sovereignty, territorial integrity, and political independence. The conference would also assure "the security of the borders with Israel and the neighboring Arab states . . . [with] demilitarized zones and the agreed stationing in them of U.N. troops or observers, . . . [as well as] international guarantees of such borders . . . should the contracting parties so desire. The United States and the Soviet Union are ready to participate in these guarantees."[8]

Seemingly the U.S.-U.S.S.R. initiative required far-reaching changes in the PLO position, asking it to recognize Israel and establish normal peace relations. The PLO also had to participate in an agreement to secure Israel's borders. Moreover, the joint statement did not recognize the PLO as the sole representative of the Palestinian people and did not mention a Palestinian state as part of the comprehensive settlement.[9]

7. "Joint U.S.-U.S.S.R. Statement on the Middle East, Oct. 1, 1977," art. 1, U.S. State Department Release, Oct. 2, 1977.

8. Ibid.

9. For more on these arguments, see Khalid al-Hasan's interview in *al-Anba'*

Nevertheless, Fatah's first response and to some extent the al-Sa'iqa and the DFLP responses to the initiative were positive. "The American-Soviet statement," stated 'Arafat, "is a basis for a realistic settlement in the Middle East."[10] The statement, according to Faruq Qaddumi, represented an international effort to recognize the legitimate right of the Palestinians for self-determination. It also provided a basis for a new United Nations Council resolution to replace 242.[11] Former al-Sa'iqa leader Zuhayr Muhsin, although criticizing what he described as the statement's ambiguous and general language, saw it as an indication of "a slight and partial change in the American position toward official recognition of the PLO and of the political rights of the Palestinian people."[12] The DFLP followed the same line. Although the organization expressed fear that the initiative would strengthen the pro-American elements in the region, it welcomed Soviet participation in a comprehensive settlement.

Behind this positive response was the PLO's realization of the political benefits that endorsement of such a proposal could bring. Public recognition by the Americans, for the first time, of the legitimate rights of the Palestinian people, instead of just the "legitimate interests," as well as America's acceptance of Palestinian participation in the negotiations for a comprehensive Middle East peace settlement, was perceived by the PLO as an indication of increasing American acceptance of the organization as a partner in a direct political dialogue.[13]

The absence of direct reference to U.N. Security Council Resolution 242 in the joint U.S.-U.S.S.R. statement, the multilateral framework of negotiations, with the participation of the U.S.S.R.—which officially recognized the PLO and supported its

(Kuwait), Aug. 31, 1981; Matti Steinberg, "The PLO and the Mini-Settlement," *Jerusalem Quarterly* 21 (1981): 137.

10. *New York Times*, May 1, 1978; See also 'Arafat's interview with ABC News, April 2, 1978; and *Guardian*, Jan. 3, 1978.

11. See Faruq Qaddumi's interview in *Journal of Palestine Studies* 7/2 (1978): 175.

12. *al-Watan* (Kuwait), Oct. 18, 1977.

13. For more on this argument, see e.g., Qaddumi interview, *Journal of Palestine Studies* 7/2, 175–76.

desire for a Palestinian state—as a counterpart to the U.S., and
the international guarantees for secure boundaries all enabled the
PLO to minimize the symbolic meaning of the concessions to be
made to Israel. The possibility of sharing or transferring the responsibility for such concessions with the U.S., the U.S.S.R., and
the U.N. also allowed the mainstream leadership to justify the
apparent deviation from the official PLO line.

However, Israeli criticism led the U.S. to reassess its position
and to institute better coordination with Israel over the implementation of its Middle East policy. The American move, which
elicited a harsh response from the PLO, limited the prospects that
the joint peace initiative would lead to a solution acceptable to
both the PLO and Israel. The visit of Egypt's President Sadat to
Jerusalem in November 1977 precluded possible further steps.

FAHD'S PLAN AND BREZHNEV'S INITIATIVE

The eight-point peace plan of King Fahd was first proposed on
August 7, 1981, in an interview with the Saudi News Agency. The
plan provided clearer rewards to the PLO and better ways to
minimize the value of concessions to Israel than the U.S.-U.S.S.R.
proposal had. Fahd's plan was far more explicit on the Palestinian
right to sovereignty and less explicit on the issue of recognition.

The Saudi plan called for "the withdrawal of Israel from all
Arab lands occupied in 1967, including Arab Jerusalem, and the
removal of settlements established by Israel in Arab lands after
1967." It also called for the subjection of the West Bank and Gaza
Strip "to a transitional period, under the supervision of the United
Nations, for a period not exceeding a few months." After the
transitional period, a Palestinian independent state would be established "with Jerusalem as its capital." The plan also confirmed
"the rights of the Palestinian people to return [to Palestine] and
compensation for those who opt not to do so." In return, "the
right of the countries of the region to live in peace" would be
affirmed, and "the United Nations or some of its members [would]
guarantee the implementation of these principles."[14]

14. See Fahd's eight points as presented at the United Nations General Assembly

Fahd's plan enabled the PLO to bypass all critical issues. Like the U.S.-U.S.S.R. initiative, it did not mention Resolution 242. And like the Khalidi and al-Hasan plans, Fahd's plan called for turning over the West Bank and Gaza Strip to the supervision of the United Nations for a brief period prior to the establishment of a Palestinian state. As such it suited the PLO's interest in avoiding direct negotiation with Israel.

On the recognition issue, the reference to the right of the countries of the region to live in peace allowed the PLO to omit any official recognition of Israel. "The Saudi plan mentions only the right of all countries to live in peace [and not] . . . the sovereignty of all countries," said Khalid al-Hasan. "Anyone versed in diplomacy and in international law should understand the significant difference between the two. . . . The Fahd plan does not call for an official recognition of Israel."[15]

The ambiguity of subsequent Saudi comments contributed to this interpretation. On November 15, 1981, the chief Saudi envoy to the United Nations, Ja'far al-Laghany, stated that the Fahd plan did recognize Israel. "You cannot negotiate without sitting together, and that means recognition. . . . It does recognize Israel. It says 'all states.' We are not afraid to say that it does recognize Israel. We are not shying away from the word 'Israel' in any sense."[16] Two days later these comments were disavowed by a Saudi official source. "Mr. al-Laghany," stated the Saudi government press, "was expressing his personal views. The eight points were clear and did not need interpretation . . . Mr. al-Laghany . . . had not been authorized to talk about the plan."[17]

By suggesting international security guarantees to be given "either by the United Nations or some of its members," the plan enabled the PLO to avoid facing this issue directly. The Saudis, who were aware of the importance of such a mechanism for the PLO, made it clear that "the intention of the . . . peace plan is not

---

by the Saudi Foreign Minister Saud al-Faysal on Oct. 5, 1981, arts. 1 and 2, 5, 6, 4, and 7 and 8.

15. *al-Anba³*, Aug. 31, 1981.

16. *New York Times*, Nov. 15, 1981.

17. Ibid., Nov. 17, 1981.

to communicate with the enemy, but rather with the international community, and especially with the United States and Western Europe."[18] It is against this background that one should understand ʿArafat's initial endorsement of Fahd's plan. Almost from the moment the plan was announced, he began praising it as "a good beginning for a lasting peace in the Middle East,"[19] although he expressed reservations about the seventh point of the proposal, which affirmed the right of all countries in the region to live in peace. In a statement made during his visit to Japan in October 1981, ʿArafat described the plan as positive because "it calls for coexistence between Israel and the Arabs"—which he later corrected to "coexistence between Jews and Arabs."[20] This correction coincides with the official PLO stance, defining Judaism as a religion and not as "a nationality with an independent existence."[21]

Other Fatah leaders such as Abu Iyad and Mahmud ʿAbbas (Abu Mazin), both members of the Palestine Executive Council, followed ʿArafat's lead. "Abu ʿAmmar [ʿArafat]," stated Abu Mazin, "declared several times that the organization welcomes the [Fahd] plan as a proper basis for a comprehensive and just peace in the Middle East. This is the real PLO position. The organization has criticisms of some points in the Saudis' plan, and Yasir ʿArafat has discussed these with the Saudi leaders."[22] Abu Iyad followed the same line: "There is no doubt that the Fahd plan includes positive points that do not contradict the PLO's political platform except for the seventh point, which deals with coexistence with Israel."[23]

The denunciation of the plan by all PLO factions except Fatah caused ʿArafat to soften his position. After the PLO factions attacked the plan both as implying tacit recognition of Israel and as

18. *al-ʿUkkaz* (Jedda), Aug. 24, 1981.

19. *New York Times*, Aug. 17, 1981.

20. Ibid., Oct. 31, 1981.

21. See "The Palestinian National Covenant," art. 20, in *Middle East Record 1968*, ed. Daniel Dishon (Jerusalem: Israel Universities Press, 1973): 435.

22. *al-Mustaqbal*, Nov. 21, 1981.

23. *al-Watan*, Nov. 25, 1981.

an American dictate,[24] ʿArafat raised more reservations. "The plan," he claimed, "does not specifically recognize the PLO; it is limited to lands Israel has occupied since 1967; the Soviet Union must play a role in any international conference on the Middle East."[25]

Further criticism came from other members of the Steadfastness and Confrontation Front—Algeria, Libya, Syria, and Southern Yemen—as well as from Iraq and Yemen. The hard-line Arab nations attacked the plan as an American proposal and "ridiculed it, referring to the Camp David accords as 'Camp Fahd.' "[26] This opposition culminated in the refusal of presidents Hafiz al-Asad of Syria, Saddam Hussein of Iraq, and Colonel Muʿammar Qadhafi of Libya to attend the Fez Arab summit meeting of November 1981 to discuss the plan. This opposition within the PLO and among the Arab nations lay behind the reversal in Fatah's position and led to open rejection of the plan. Although the Fahd plan coincided with Fatah's political interests, the Saudi failure to prevent its rejection by Arab and non-Arab "progressive" political elements restricted Fatah's ability to continue justifying the price of such a solution.

Soviet President Leonid Brezhnev's 1981 peace proposal clearly demonstrated the importance of such progressive support for Fatah's ability to manipulate the cardinal rule of no concessions to Israel in a pragmatic fashion. Addressing the twenty-sixth congress of the Communist Party of the Soviet Union on February 23, 1981, President Brezhnev criticized the U.S. for embarking "on the path of the Camp David policy . . . splitting the Arab world and organizing a separate deal between Egypt and Israel," which caused a deadlock. Instead, Brezhnev suggested "collective searching for a comprehensive settlement on a just and realistic basis . . . [to] be done . . . within the framework of a specially convened international conference." In such an effort, the Soviet Union was "prepared to take part in conjunction with other interested parties—

24. For more details, see interviews with PLO leaders in *al-Hurriyya*, Nov. 9, 16, and 20, 1981.
25. *New York Times*, Nov. 22, 1981.
26. Ibid., Nov. 25, 1981.

the Arabs (including the Palestine Liberation Organization, of course) and Israel,"[27] in addition to the United States, the European states, and the United Nations.

Referring to the principles that would guide the Soviet Union's position in such a conference, Brezhnev stated that "if there is to be genuine peace in the Middle East, there must be an end to the Israeli occupation of all Arab territories seized in 1967. The inalienable rights of the Arab people of Palestine, up to and including the creation of their own state, must be realized. It is necessary to ensure the security and sovereignty of all states in this region, including Israel."[28]

The demands for total Israeli withdrawal from all occupied territories and the establishment of a Palestinian state mark the similarities between Soviet and Saudi peace plans. However, the Brezhnev initiative, like the Vance-Gromyko statement of 1977, was far more explicit on the issue of recognition of Israel. While Fahd spoke about the right of the countries of the Middle East to live in peace, Brezhnev clearly called for a settlement that would assure the sovereignty of all states, including Israel.

Despite this clause, the PLO radical factions joined Fatah in endorsing the Brezhnev plan. During the fifteenth session of the Palestine National Council in April 1981, the PLO Political Committee, composed mostly of leftists, agreed upon the following recommendation:

The Council declares that it welcomes Comrade Brezhnev's declaration ... on the Middle East crisis and the Palestine question as providing a sound basis for a just settlement. It also welcomes his affirmation of the basic role the PLO should play in the solution of the Middle East crisis and the Palestine question and of the need for the enforcement of the inalienable national rights of the Palestinian people, including their right to establish their independent national state in conformity with the U.N. resolutions on the Palestine question, and also affirmation that the U.N. has a part to play in solving this question.[29]

27. *Current Digest of the Soviet Press* 23/3 (March 25, 1981): 8.
28. Ibid.
29. See Bilal al-Hasan, "The Palestine National Council in Session," *Shu'un Filastiniyya* (June 1981); *Journal of Palestine Studies* 11/4 (1981): 177–78.

The PLO Political Committee was aware of the risk inherent in endorsing a proposal which called for, among other things, the security and sovereignty of Israel. Acceptance of a plan that included such a statement meant a retreat from the PLO's declared policy of not accepting any political solution that required recognition of and a peace treaty with Israel. This can be interpreted as acquiescence to a Palestinian state in the West Bank and Gaza as a permanent solution, and not as a transitional settlement looking toward the establishment of a Palestinian democratic state in the whole of Palestine.

Indeed, Brezhnev's reference to Israel's sovereignty and security brought the PLO Political Committee to discuss the possibility of rejecting the Soviet initiative in its entirety or, alternatively, responding positively but with clearcut reservations about the security and sovereignty issues. The committee, however, preferred not to express its reservations explicitly. Rather, its resolution "provided agreement of views and recorded a positive position to the initiative, without committing itself to the articles on which reservations were expressed. [The resolution] also indicated that agreement was reached on the general political position, with precise information as to how it should be understood and formulated."[30] The fifteenth session of the Palestine National Council adopted this approach, though its resolution on the Brezhnev initiative was slightly different from the recommended resolution of the PLO Political Committee.[31]

The Palestinian left, although raising careful reservations, endorsed Brezhnev's proposal. But later it sharply criticized Fatah's positive response to Fahd's proposal, which was much less explicit

30. Ibid.

31. "The Council," stated the resolution, "welcomed President Brezhnev's statement on the Middle East crisis at the 26th Conference of the Soviet Communist Party, in which he stressed the importance of the role of the PLO in reaching a just solution of the crisis and the need for the implementation of the inalienable national rights of the Palestinian people, including their right to establish their independent national state as affirmed by the UN resolutions on the Palestine question, and the importance of the UN playing a role in the solution of this problem." See "Final Political Statement of the Fifteenth Session of the Palestine National Council, Meeting in Damascus, April 11–19, 1981, *Journal of Palestine Studies* 10/4 (1981): 186.

in recognizing Israel than the Brezhnev proposal. As in the case of the joint Vance-Gromyko statement, the very fact that the Soviet Union stood behind this proposal played a key role in shaping the PLO left's positive response. The Soviet Union, as Na'if Hawatma, head of the Marxist DFLP, explained, is a friendly state that recognizes the PLO as the legitimate representative of the Palestinian people, supporting its desire for a sovereign state and its participation in negotiations to achieve this goal. Nevertheless, the Soviet Union is not "a fraternal Arab state but a foreign state [with] its own policy on this or that international issue. Therefore, one should not expect Moscow to see eye-to-eye with the Arabs on every issue and, in any case, its position on recognition of Israel was not binding on the Arabs."[32]

King Fahd's plan, on the other hand, deserved a negative response because Saudi Arabia, as an Arab state, should not be "defining for the Arabs and the PLO the upper limit of patriotic Arab and Palestinian rights."[33] According to Hawatma, by seeking Arab and PLO approval to a proposal that implied recognition of Israel and at the same time failing to mention the PLO as the sole legitimate representative of the Palestinians, the Saudis' plan violated the "Arab consensus adopted at post–1973 summits from Algiers to Baghdad" on these two issues.

For the PLO left it was easier to endorse a peace proposal made by a friendly foreign state, even though it entailed clearer concessions to Israel than an Arab initiative that proposed concessions in vaguer terms. Such endorsement did not commit the PLO and the Arab world to accept all aspects of the proposal, as would have been the case had the Saudi plan won the approval of the Fez Arab summit. Therefore, endorsement of Brezhnev's proposal, with reservations on the article that called for the security and sovereignty of Israel as well as of other nations in the Middle East, enabled the PLO to maintain its commitment, or at least minimize the violation of its commitment, to the establishment of a Palestinian state on the West Bank and Gaza without concessions

32. *al-Ra'y al-ʿAam* (Kuwait), Nov. 23, 1981; cited in George E. Gruen, "The Palestinians and Regional Rivalries," in *The Palestinians in Perspective*, ed. George E. Gruen (New York: Institute of Human Relations, 1982), 42.
33. Ibid., 43.

to Israel. The reservations on the security and sovereignty issues paved the road for the PLO to accept the proposal as a basis for negotiation while continuing to demonstrate its adherence to the ultimate Palestinian goals.

During the Israeli military operations in Lebanon in June–August 1982 and in the course of the indirect negotiations held between the American special envoy to the Middle East, Philip Habib, and the PLO over its withdrawal from West Beirut, the conditional endorsement of Brezhnev's proposal, as well as the PLO's positive response to the Vance-Gromyko statement, was exploited by Fatah to show the PLO's readiness to move toward political accommodation with Israel and to reach a peaceful solution to the Palestinian problem. In a response to a comment that the "PLO does not really want peace" by Uri Avneri, editor of the Israeli weekly *Ha'olam Hazeh* and one of the leaders of the Israeli Council for Israeli-Palestinian Peace, 'Arafat said:

We have declared our approval for the American-Soviet communiqué in October 1977. We have declared our approval and appreciation for President Brezhnev's initiative. . . . When we said O.K. to this initiative, this meant that we accepted all its items. We said that it is a good platform for a peaceful settlement, for a just solution in the Middle East. And you remember that I myself declared that the Fahd proposals are a very good platform for a solution in the Middle East. So we gave many signals that we are looking for peace.[34]

'Isam Sartawi, 'Arafat's political adviser, also interpreted the PLO's partial endorsement of the American-Russian statement and of Brezhnev's proposal as a sign of its willingness to recognize Israel and as a way to meet one of the American conditions for direct contact with the PLO. In a speech to the French Institute of International Relations on July 13, 1982, Sartawi said that "the PLO was prepared to recognize Israel . . . the PLO has formally conceded to Israel in the most unequivocal manner the right to exist on a reciprocal basis. . . . I therefore call upon the government of the United States to extend to the PLO formal recognition and to establish formal contact with it."[35]

34. See 'Arafat's full interview in *Ha'olam Hazeh* (Tel Aviv), July 7, 1982; and excerpts in *New York Times*, July 13, 1982.
35. *New York Times*, July 14, 1982. For more on this argument, see Sartawi's

Behind this Fatah campaign lay an attempt to convince the Reagan Administration to shift from indirect negotiation with the PLO over its withdrawal from Lebanon to direct talks about the political fate of the Palestinians as part of the overall Middle East question.[36] Nevertheless, the fact that ʿArafat's and Sartawi's signals of readiness to move toward political accommodation with Israel relied on formulas for peace that had won partial support from the radical PLO factions supplied enough ammunition to diminish the value of ʿArafat and Sartawi's declarations in the eyes of Palestinian extremists, so that Fatah leaders could demonstrate flexibility and goodwill toward Israel while at the same time adhering to the official PLO stand. In this respect, the Vance-Gromyko statement, and particularly Brezhnev's proposal, permitted Fatah leaders to make a pragmatic use of the PLO rule of no concessions, justifying their moderate statements to their followers as a way to improve the PLO's bargaining position and not as a shift from the PLO official line.

THE CAMP DAVID AGREEMENTS
AND THE VENICE DECLARATION

The 1978 Camp David agreements, and the June 1980 Venice Declaration of the European Economic Community, unlike the Vance-Gromyko statement, Brezhnev's initiative, and the Fahd proposal, offered the PLO fewer rewards and gave Fatah less opportunity to justify deviation from official PLO policy. Both proposals tried to provide such rewards and such an opportunity. However, an analysis of the two proposals will show that these efforts were not sufficient.

The Camp David agreement recognized "the legitimate right of the Palestinian people and their just requirements." It sought to reach a "resolution of the Palestinian problem in all its aspects" through negotiations between "Egypt, Israel, Jordan, and the rep-

---

joint press conference with Uri Avneri and Mattityahu Peled in London, *Haʾaretz*, July 16, 1982.

36. Thomas L. Friedman, "PLO Political Aims," *New York Times*, July 22, 1982.

resentative of the Palestinian people." The agreement would provide full autonomy to the inhabitants of the West Bank and Gaza Strip for a transitional period not exceeding five years. It also included a withdrawal of the "Israeli military government and its civilian administration" and the establishment of "self-governing authority . . . freely elected by the inhabitants of these areas to replace the existing military government." The Palestinian representatives from the West Bank and Gaza or other Palestinians as mutually agreed were to participate in the negotiations to define the responsibilities of the self-governing authority, as well as in the negotiations over "arrangements for assuring internal and external security and public order." After Palestinian self-government, or the administrative council, was formed, "but not later than the third year after its establishment, negotiations [would] take place to determine the final status of the West Bank and Gaza and its relationship with its neighbors. . . . These negotiations [would] be conducted among Egypt, Israel, Jordan, and the elected representatives of the inhabitants of the West Bank and Gaza."[37]

Egyptian and American interpretation of "the legitimate rights of the Palestinian people" seems intended to encourage the PLO not to reject totally some form of participation in the peace process. The Egyptian and American position in this sense suited the PLO's interests. Contrary to the Israeli view, implementation of the legitimate rights of the Palestinians, according to Egypt, means a Palestinian state. President Sadat argued that "the Israelis are opposed to any Palestinian entity . . . to an independent state. . . . I am sure that after a year of autonomy and after the agreement with us is signed, the Israelis will feel secure enough to agree to the establishment of a Palestinian state."[38] The Egyptian minister of state for foreign affairs, Butrus Ghali, went into more detail. "The realization of autonomy in the West Bank and Gaza . . . is a first step. . . . in the second stage, in accordance with the spirit of

37. See "A Framework for Peace in the Middle East Agreed at Camp David," signed by President A. Sadat for the Government of the Arab Republic of Egypt and Prime Minister M. Begin for the Government of Israel. Witnessed by President J. Carter of the United States of America. *U.S. Department of State Publication* 8954, *Near East and South Asian Series* 88 (September 1978), art. 1.

38. Interviewed in *Ma'ariv* (Tel Aviv), Nov. 21, 1978.

the Camp David agreement, a Palestinian entity will evolve, that is, a Palestinian state."[39]

The Carter Administration opposed the idea of an independent Palestinian state "because ... this would be a destabilizing factor in the Middle East and certainly would not serve United States interests."[40] However, the administration, like Egypt, saw autonomy "as a transitional solution which would lead to a Palestinian entity ... tied to Jordan in federation or confederation."[41]

Egyptian attempts to maintain contact with the PLO and American efforts to initiate such contact—mainly through the Palestinian leadership in the West Bank and Gaza—further reflected their desire to leave the door open for a political dialogue. Both countries assumed that this dialogue could lead to PLO participation in the autonomy talks. After approval of the Camp David agreements, Egypt did not withdraw its recognition of the PLO nor freeze its diplomatic ties with the organization as it did with other Arab nations who rejected the agreements. Despite President Sadat's appeal "to the Palestinians to disassociate themselves from the PLO,"[42] Egypt continued to inform the PLO through its representative in Cairo, Saʿid Kamal, of developments in the autonomy talks.

American comments and deeds left the same impression. "Obviously, as is well known by Israel," stated President Carter, "there are members of the PLO, individual members, who are mayors of major cities, for instance, in the West Bank and the Gaza Strip, and both we and the Israelis deal with them as Palestinians, not, however, in their capacity as members of the PLO."[43] Later on, this statement was followed by three meetings of the U.S. ambassador to Austria, Milton Wolf, with ʿIsam Sartawi in July 1979 and of the U.S. ambassador to the United Nations, Andrew

---

39. *Middle East News Agency*, Jan. 6, 1979; for more details on Egypt's position, see Aryeh Shalev, *The Autonomy—Problems and Possible Solutions* (Tel Aviv: Tel Aviv University, Center for Strategic Studies, 1981), 26–29.

40. *Baltimore Sun*, Feb. 26, 1980.

41. Shalev, *Autonomy*, 51; See also Mark Heller, "Begin's False Autonomy," *Foreign Policy* 37 (1979–80): 114.

42. Yodfat and Arnon-Ohanna, *PLO Strategy and Tactics*, 4.

43. *Weekly Compilation of Presidential Documents*, May 18, 1979, 907–08.

Young, with the PLO observer at the U.N., Labib Tarazi, to discuss possibilities of reducing the PLO's opposition to the Camp David agreements.[44]

However, Egyptian and American efforts to encourage some form of PLO participation in the peace talks failed. Despite their attempts to give a pro-Palestinian interpretation to the autonomy agreement, several articles in the agreement were so contradictory to official PLO policy that participation in any form was considered impossible. The most controversial article stated that negotiations over Palestinian autonomy and over the final status of the West Bank and Gaza should be based on the acceptance by all parties of Resolution 242. This resolution, as previously mentioned, was perceived by the PLO as discriminatory, denying Palestinians political rights. To engage in the autonomy talks might, therefore, have been interpreted as a renunciation of one of the fundamental PLO political principles.[45]

American officials were aware that their position "not to negotiate with or recognize the PLO unless it first recognizes Israel's right to exist and accepts United Nations Security Council Resolution 242"[46] contradicted PLO policy. This awareness lay behind the American initiative to discuss secretly with PLO officials, in Vienna and at the U.N. in July 1979, the possibility of amending or replacing Resolution 242 to permit PLO participation in the peace talks.[47] The Egyptian and American attempt to bring the PLO into the autonomy talks or to win its approval for the participation of West Bank and Gaza leadership was also weakened by Israel's firm position against such a move, as well as by its insistence that Palestinian autonomy should apply to people, not territory, that institutions of autonomy can have administrative without legislative functions, that laws governing land and water

---

44. For more details on these meetings, see *Ha' aretz*, Aug. 16, 1979; *Newsweek*, Aug. 20 and 27, 1979; *Time*, Aug. 27, 1979.

45. For more on this issue, see Faysal Hourani, "A Political Reading of the Camp David Documents," *Shu'un Filastiniyya* (Nov. 1978).

46. See President Carter's statement in the *Baltimore Sun*, Feb. 26, 1980.

47. On such a possibility, see Moshe Dayan's Comments in the *Economist* (London), Aug. 11, 1979, 49; also see Yodfat and Arnon-Ohanna, *PLO Strategy and Tactics*, 116.

must be Israeli, that Palestinians in Jerusalem can have no part in
the autonomy rule, and that autonomy would not lead to a Palestinian state.[48]

In consideration of the Egyptian and American interpretations
of the Camp David agreements, one might argue that despite Israel's position in the autonomy talks, the PLO could still have
gained politically through indirect participation, without confronting the issue of Resolution 242. Participation by proxy, that is to
say, through Palestinian representatives from the West Bank and
Gaza, could have improved the PLO's political image as a moderate organization, enhancing its status in the occupied territories
and further diminishing the possibility that it would be excluded
from a solution.

However, the rejection of the Camp David agreements by the
Soviet Union and all the Arab nations except Egypt, Sudan, Oman,
and Morocco made it difficult for those inside the PLO who usually
favored political means to further the Palestinian cause to consider
indirect participation. The omission from the Camp David agreements of any reference to the PLO as the legitimate representative
of the Palestinians and partner in the autonomy talks and a lack
of discussion of the Palestinians' right to a state made the backing
of friendly nations crucial for direct or indirect participation in the
talks. Without this, Fatah's ability to justify participation to the
radical PLO factions would have been weak.

The lack of friendly nations' support influenced Fatah's decision
to join other PLO factions in a unilateral rejection of the Camp
David agreements. According to the fourteenth session of the Palestine National Council in 1979,

The U.S. settlement of the Arab-Zionist conflict embodied in the Camp
David agreements poses grave threats to the cause of Palestine and Arab
national liberation. The settlement condones the Zionist enemy's continued usurpation of the national soil of Palestine, abrogates the inalienable
right of the Palestinian Arab people to their homeland, Palestine, as well
as their right to self-determination and to the exercise of their national
independence on their soil. It dissipates [the unity of] other Arab territories and overrides the PLO, the leader of our people's national struggle

48. For more details on the Israeli position, see Shalev, *Autonomy*, 54–56, 166–
68.

and their sole legitimate representative and spokesman expressing their will.

... we reject all resolutions, agreements, and settlements that do not recognize or that impinge upon the inalienable rights of our people to their homeland, Palestine, including their right to return, to self-determination, and to the establishment of their independent national state. This applies in particular to Security Council Resolution 242.[49]

Fifteen months later, in its next meeting, the Palestine National Council confirmed this resolution: "The Council expressed the view that no initiative can be valid if it regards the Camp David agreements and methods as the basis for a solution and does not recognize the PLO as the sole legitimate representative of the Palestinian people and the right of our people to return, to self-determination, and to establish their independent state on the soil of their homeland."[50]

Aware of the Palestinians' inability to participate in the Camp David autonomy talks, the nine member states of the European Economic Community initiated a proposal, which was summed up in the Venice Declaration of June 1980. The declaration was based on the assumption that a solution to the Palestinian problem could not be achieved without PLO participation in an overall settlement and that the more a peace proposal refers clearly and positively to the political desires of the Palestinian people and recognizes the central role of the PLO in the fulfillment of these desires, the better the chance for PLO participation.

In this regard, while the Camp David agreements defined the meaning of Palestinian rights in vague terms, the Venice Declaration in part adopted the PLO definition. "The Palestinian people," stated the European Economic Community, "must be placed in a position, by an appropriate process defined within the framework of the comprehensive peace settlement, to exercise fully its right to self-determination."[51]

---

49. See "Political and Organizational Program Approved by the Palestine National Council at its Fourteenth Session, Held in Damascus, Jan. 15–23, 1979," *WAFA*, Jan. 18, 1979; *Journal of Palestine Studies* 8/3 (1979): 165–67.

50. See "Final Political Statement," 187.

51. "European Community, Venice Declaration, June 13, 1980," art. 6 (AP release).

Although the declaration mentioned Security Council resolutions 242 and 338 as a basis for a comprehensive settlement, it also emphasized that "a just solution must finally be found to the Palestinian problem, which is not simply one of refugees." This statement implied a willingness to amend Resolution 242 and to recognize the PLO as an equal partner "that will have to be associated with the negotiation."[52]

The European Economic Community, in order to encourage PLO participation in the peace process, was also ready to take part, "within the framework of a comprehensive settlement in a system of concrete and binding international guarantees." Furthermore, the declaration "stress[ed] the need for Israel to put an end to the territorial occupation that it has maintained since the conflict of 1967" and criticized Israel's settlement policy in the West Bank and Gaza as "a serious obstacle to the peace process."[53]

The willingness to recognize Palestinians' right to self-determination, the idea of a multilateral negotiation to be conducted in the framework of an overall settlement, the international guarantees to be provided by the United Nations and the European Economic Community all seemed to clear the way for PLO participation in the political process. However, the PLO felt that the price for participation in the political process under these conditions was higher than the political rewards.

Like the U.S.-U.S.S.R. and Brezhnev initiatives, the E.E.C. plan asked the PLO to accept "the right of existence and security of all the states in the region including Israel" and the right of all "countries in the area . . . to live in peace."[54] But the Venice Declaration did not affirm the Palestinians' right to a state as Brezhnev's proposal had, nor did it inspire hope in this direction, as had the U.S.-U.S.S.R. statement. Thus "the European statement. . . . gives substance to the expectations of the pessimistic Arabs inasmuch as it complements the Camp David agreements."[55]

The European declaration, according to this view,

52. Ibid., art. 7.
53. Ibid., arts. 5 and 9.
54. Ibid., arts. 4 and 5.
55. Michel Abu Jawdeh, "Nothing New from Venice," *al-Nahar* (Beirut), June 14, 1980; *Journal of Palestine Studies* 10/1 (1980): 167.

does no more than call for PLO participation in any negotiations on the solution to the Middle East crises. Egypt called for this when the Camp David agreements were signed, and is still doing so, without any opposition on the part of the U.S. . . . The Venice statement mentions the legitimate rights of the Palestinian people and their right to self-determination, and says that the question is not just a question of refugees . . . with reservations on the status of Jerusalem and settlement policy. This is the sort of talk that even the U.S. cannot object to, the sort of talk in general terms that might be heard even in Israel.[56]

In sum, "the Venice statement, which Mr. Yasir 'Arafat described in advance as 'a bone intended to distract us,' is slightly better—better, that is, in its wording—than the American position. But it is certainly not up to the positions of some European countries, such as France . . . [and] Austria."[57] The PLO Executive Committee added that the European initiative was "merely as a step that must be developed, and that the European countries must be urged to take up more positive and more effective positions."[58] The Palestine National Council in its meeting in April 1981 was more specific: "no initiative can be valid if it . . . does not recognize the PLO as the sole legitimate representative of the Palestinian people, and the right of our people to return [to Palestine], to self-determination, and to establish their independent state on the soil of their homeland."[59]

The PLO response to the Venice Declaration and other diplomatic peace proposals can be seen as a continuation of the PLO diplomatic practices and activities of the 1970s and 1980s. The cultivation and maintenance of the idea of a Palestinian mini-state in the West Bank and Gaza without renouncing or weakening the commitment to the goal of a state in the whole of Palestine had become the central mission of PLO diplomacy.

The PLO's growing awareness of the need to conduct diplomatic activity to advance the idea of the Palestinian mini-state while maintaining adherence to the maximal goal stemmed from the new sense of political reality that emerged in the Middle East in the

56. Ibid.
57. Ibid.
58. See *Journal of Palestine Studies* 11/4 (1981): 176.
59. "Final Political Statement," 187.

post-October War era, and from social and organizational circumstances within the PLO. The readiness of Egypt, Jordan, and Syria
to launch a diplomatic initiative to regain the occupied territories
from Israel increased the PLO's concern about a political settlement in the West Bank and Gaza without its participation and
encouraged it to consider adopting political means to regain these
areas of Palestine. At the same time, the social structure of the
PLO, its ideological diversities and organizational frictions, narrowed the possibility of launching this political and diplomatic
activity without demonstrating firm adherence to the use of military
means to liberate all of Palestine.

The need to combine ad hoc calculations and "hereafter" considerations lay behind the PLO's growing involvement in diplomatic activities that enabled it to further its short-term interests,
maximizing the immediate rewards while minimizing the ideological price. Thus the PLO, in particular Fatah, was ready to endorse
diplomatic proposals for a Palestinian mini-state as long as these
initiatives assured it of tangible political rewards such as participation as a full partner in peace negotiations and affirmation of
the right of the Palestinian people to an independent state, and as
long as they did not reduce its ability to demonstrate adherence
to its ultimate goals. This rule of conduct helps explain the PLO's
distinction between the two categories of peace proposals. The
first category included proposals that entailed concessions to Israel,
received backing from friendly nations that recognize the PLO or
maintain close relations with it, and granted considerable rewards.
The second included proposals that entailed concessions but failed
both to receive backing from friendly nations and to grant clear
rewards.

The Vance-Gromyko statement and Brezhnev initiative met the
requirements of the first category. Both proposals were initiated
or supported by the Soviet Union. Neither was rejected by other
friendly nations, and both provided considerable rewards to the
PLO. They therefore won a positive response and enabled Fatah
to demonstrate to the world the PLO's willingness to accept political negotiation. The Fahd plan also provided the PLO with
considerable rewards and a device to minimize its concessions to
Israel in future negotiations. But the plan failed to receive backing

Table 2   Peace Proposals and PLO Response

	Support from friendly nations	Rewards		PLO response
		PLO accepted as partner	Palestinian state affirmed	
Vance-Gromyko	positive	moving toward	moving toward	positive
Brezhnev	positive	positive	positive	positive
Fahd	negative	positive	positive	negative
Camp David	negative	negative	negative	negative
Venice	positive	positive	negative	negative

from other friendly Arab nations and their followers within the PLO. Fatah was reluctant to commit the PLO to political negotiations based solely on the Saudi plan's terms.

Both the Camp David and the European peace proposals fall into the second category. The Camp David proposal failed to gain the support of most of the Arab nations and of the Soviet Union. At the same time, it could not assure the PLO of clear rewards at the end of the autonomy talks between Egypt and Israel. Under these circumstances, mechanisms to minimize concessions to Israel were very weak, making endorsement unlikely. The European proposal, on the other hand, came from nations sympathetic to the PLO and to the idea of Palestinian self-determination. But the proposal failed to provide sufficient rewards and thus limited Fatah's ability to interpret concessions to Israel pragmatically, and so forfeited the support of other PLO factions. Table 2 summarizes the features of the five peace proposals and the PLO response to them.

The same principles which determined the PLO's response to the five proposals lay behind its diplomatic activity in the course of the negotiations over PLO withdrawal from West Beirut in the summer of 1982. The PLO tried to link discussions over withdrawal to the issue of a Palestinian state on the West Bank and Gaza. It was ready to initiate proposals to obtain political achievements in this direction without committing itself to concessions regarding the PLO's ultimate goals. This thinking lay behind Arafat's two-state solution, mentioned in his interview on July 3, 1982 with Uri-

Avneri of *Ha'olam Hazeh*. It also directed 'Arafat's written statement to the five-member delegation of the U.S. Congress headed
by Paul N. McCloskey on July 25, 1982, in which he "accepts all
U.N. resolutions relevant to the Palestinian question."[60] In both
statements 'Arafat was very careful not to contradict the idea of
a Palestinian state in the whole of Palestine and not to affirm
Israel's right to exist.

But statements of this nature, combined with the PLO endorsement of certain peace proposals, convinced many statesmen and
international political leaders that the PLO's public acceptance of
Israel's right to exist and its agreeing to a settlement on the West
Bank and Gaza as a permanent solution were matters of cost and
time rather than principle. However, such an assessment, whatever
role it played in the PLO's diplomatic success, did not shake the
Israeli government's belief that the organization remained faithful
to its ultimate vision of a Palestinian state in place of Israel. Guided
by such a belief, Israel took political and military measures in the
occupied territories to reduce the chances of the establishment of
a Palestinian state, perceiving this as a first step toward the fulfillment of the PLO's original goal—Israel's destruction. It is the
PLO's fears of losing the West Bank that led the organization to
increase its political activity among the Palestinian inhabitants in
the occupied territories in addition to its diplomatic moves in the
international arena.

---

60. See *New York Times*, July 26, 1982. "After the meeting with Mr. 'Arafat,"
added the *Times*, Mr. McCloskey said the Palestinian leader "signed for us his
acceptance of all United Nations resolutions which include the right of Israel to
exist. . . . When he finished speaking, Mr. 'Arafat corrected him, saying, 'All UN
resolutions concerning the Palestinian question . . . .United Nations Resolution
242, adopted after the 1967 Middle East War, and 338, adopted after the 1973 war,
make no reference to the Palestinians or the Palestinian question, which is why
the Palestine Liberation Organization has always resisted accepting them.' "

CHAPTER 5

The PLO and the West Bank:
An Uneasy Alliance

LOCAL LEADERSHIP AND NATIONAL ASPIRATIONS

Although most of the West Bank leadership shared the PLO's goals of Palestinian statehood and self-determination, their particular concerns, local aspirations, and motives made for an uneasy relationship. Broad segments of the local elite preferred to focus on the immediate, close-to-home issue of how to achieve an end to the Israeli occupation in the near future rather than engage in a long-term political and military struggle to fulfill the PLO's goal of a Palestinian state encompassing all of Palestine.

This tension between the PLO and West Bank political leaders over the proper meaning, content, and practice of Palestinian goals and strategy was most evident between 1967 and 1974, the first years of the Israeli occupation. While the PLO emphasized a militant solution, most West Bank political groups, both conservative and more radical, sought a peaceful solution that would lead to Palestinian-Israeli coexistence. "If we must wait for the [PLO's] military solution . . . the land will no longer be a land, the homeland no longer a homeland, and no trace of the people of this land will be seen."[1]

The activity in 1967 through 1970 of the supporters of the Palestinian entity was led by ʿAziz Shehada of Ramallah, Dr. Hamdi al-Taji al-Faruqi of al-Bira, Muhammad Abu Shilbaya of Jerusalem, and Shaykh Muhammad ʿAli al-Jaʿbari of Hebron. This

1. *al-Quds* (East Jerusalem), Oct. 25, 1974.

activity presumed that Israel was a fact in the Middle East and that there was no hope of defeating it militarily; the only way to solve the Palestinian issue, according to this logic, was through political negotiations with Israel to establish a "Palestinian entity" in the West Bank and Gaza. This entity would sign a peace treaty with Israel and would serve as a political and economic bridge between Israel and the Arab states.[2]

The idea of a narrow territorial solution ran counter to the PLO's ultimate goal of Palestinian independence and self-determination in all of Palestine. The more limited option was intended to serve the immediate interests of the West Bank and Gaza inhabitants— liberation from Israeli occupation—rather than to provide a home for Palestinian refugees who wished to return to Palestine.

Although the idea of a Palestinian entity evoked broad opposition from both conservative and radical West Bank circles, objections were not concentrated against reaching a political solution to the Palestinian problem through accommodation with Israel, but rather against the notion of reaching a solution through negotiations independent of the Arab world. According to this view, no solution reached in this way would be viable. The state-to-be would be too weak economically, dependent on Israel, and too politically controversial in the eyes of the Arab world and Palestinians elsewhere. It would carry the stigma of an Israeli satellite, risking cultural, political, and economic boycott by the Arab world.[3] Instead, during the first seven years of Israeli occupation most of the West Bank political leaders favored a two-bank solution—West and East—although they differed over the content and the form of this solution.

Local organizations and individuals who enjoyed high political and social status because of their close ties with the Hashemite regime in Amman (before and after the 1967 war) preferred a political settlement based on the unity of the two banks, with Hashemite rule over the West Bank such as existed before the

2. For more details see *Middle East Record 1968*, ed. Daniel Dishon (Jerusalem: Israel Universities Press, 1973): 449–50; *Middle East Record 1969–70*, 375–78.

3. For more on this argument, see Elie Rekhess and Asher Susser, *Political Factors and Trends in the West Bank*, (Tel Aviv: Shiloah Center for Middle Eastern and African Studies, Tel Aviv University, 1974), 8.

1967 war. The Supreme Muslim Council and the Chamber of Commerce, among other groups, followed this line. Prominent West Bank figures who supported this solution included the former governor of the Jerusalem district, Anwar al-Khatib; the former governor of the Nablus district, ʿAbd al-Rahman al-Sharif; former Jordanian defense minister Anwar Nusayba; former Jordanian foreign minister Qadri Tuqan; and former speaker of the Jordanian Parliament, Hikmat al-Masri.[4]

Fears among pro-Hashemite circles that a political solution to the West Bank problem excluding Amman could weaken their political status and economic privileges appear to have played an important role in shaping their political views. It is here one should look to understand why during the first years of Israeli occupation the adherents of the pro-Hashemite solution rejected both the Palestinian-entity proposal and the PLO's more ambitious formula of a Palestinian democratic state in all of Palestine. Both solutions required far-reaching changes in the existing power structure, and both risked sacrificing relatively safe political status and economic benefits for an uncertain future and unpredictable results.

After 1973 the position of many pro-Hashemite figures underwent a gradual change. This was in response to the improvement in the PLO's international and inter-Arab status after the 1973 Arab-Israeli war, which was followed by the 1974 PNC decision to consider the establishment of a "national authority" in any part of the occupied territories of 1967 to be evacuated by Israel as a first-step solution. This stance further evolved with the PNC's 1977 resolution to establish a Palestinian state in the West Bank and Gaza, also as a transitional settlement. The change was expressed by the willingness of these leaders to declare their recognition of the PLO as the legitimate representative of the Palestinian people and to welcome "any positive move that comes from the Palestinian National Council to find a political solution to the Palestinian problem."[5] Though willing to support the PLO's idea of a Palestinian state in the West Bank and Gaza, pro-Hashemite leaders sought

4. Clinton Bailey, "Changing Attitudes toward Jordan in the West Bank," *Middle East Journal* 32/2 (1978): 156.

5. *al-Quds*, March 21, 1977; *Middle East Contemporary Survey* 1 (1976–77), ed. Colin Legum (New York: Holmes & Meier, 1978), 212.

ways to maintain the link with Jordan. They proposed a federation between the West Bank and Amman, maintaining that the majority of West Bank inhabitants would support such a solution. According to Mayor Elias Freij of Bethlehem, "Jordan is our country, the people of Jordan are our people, and setting up such a federation will serve the interests of all."[6] Thus the pro-Hashemite leaders tried to balance PLO dominance in the state-to-be through the federative formula suggested by King Hussein in March 1972.[7]

Critics and opponents of the Jordanian regime including Mayor Hamdi Kan'an of Nablus and members of the Communist Party on the West Bank also strove for the liberation of the area from Israeli occupation through a two-bank solution. In contrast to the pro-Hashemites, however, they sought to "guarantee the emancipation of the Palestinians from specific Hashemite control"[8] prior to the reunification of the two banks. The demand for revision in the power relationship that existed between the two banks until 1967 differed from one group to another. Hamdi Kan'an, who was mayor of Nablus during the first two years of the Israeli occupation, Walid al-Shak'a, a Nablus leader, and Taysir Kan'an, a lawyer from East Jerusalem, advocated a reunification based on incremental changes in the existing political order in Amman. They called for "immediate constitutional changes providing for Palestinian autonomy in the West Bank, which would then be united with the East Bank on an equal basis. This would be implemented after Israel's evacuation and the return of the West Bank to Jordan, in compliance with Security Council Resolution 242."[9]

During and immediately after the civil war in Jordan in September 1970, Hamdi Kan'an and his followers radicalized their position. They now sought "the overthrow of the Hashemite regime"[10]

6. *al-Quds*, Jan. 24, 1977; *Middle East Contemporary Survey* 1 (1976–77): 211.

7. On King Hussein's federation plan to include the West Bank, the East Bank, and the Gaza Strip see Zvi Alpeleg, "Tokhnit ha-federatzyya shel Hussein: Gormim ve-tguvot" (Hussein's federation scheme: Factors and reactions) (Tel Aviv: Shiloah Center for Middle Eastern and African Studies, Tel Aviv University, 1977); Asher Susser, "Jordanian Influence in the West Bank," *Jerusalem Quarterly* 8 (1978): 53–65.

8. Bailey, "Changing Attitudes toward Jordan in the West Bank," 159.

9. Ibid., 160; for more on this position, see *al-Quds*, Jan. 2, 1969.

10. Rekhess and Susser, *Political Factors and Trends in the West Bank*, 15.

in Amman and the establishment of a Palestinian state on both banks that would negotiate a peace treaty with Israel. According to Hamdi Kan'an, the PLO formula of a Palestinian state replacing Israel was not practical and did not favor the Palestinians socially and economically. He further argued that Israel would never agree to renounce voluntarily the Zionist idea of an independent Jewish state. With Jews and Arabs together within one state, the Arab citizens would inevitably become second-class citizens, since the more populous Jews would be better educated and would have the economic strength to control the Palestinian population. On the other hand, argued Hamdi Kan'an, "A separate Palestinian state in the West Bank and Gaza is also not a desirable solution. Confronting a strong and advanced Israel, such a state would turn into an Israeli satellite. The optimal solution, therefore, is the establishment of a Palestinian state in the East Bank, the West Bank, and the Gaza Strip alongside Israel. The two states, Israel and Palestine, can maintain federative relations or any kind of association."[11]

Hamdi Kan'an's ability to advance his ideas was limited by the character of his supporters, mostly young, educated Palestinians in Nablus and East Jerusalem who lacked political and economic power and were not as influential as the pro-Hashemite leaders. Kan'an's difficulties led him gradually to withdraw from his radical position toward the regime in Amman and instead to search for a common denominator with local traditional leadership, a search that brought him back to his pre–1970 formula of a two-bank solution based on constitutional amendments.

Against this background one can understand Kan'an's initially positive response to King Hussein's 1972 federation plan, which called for two autonomous provinces:

If we find this federation plan acceptable, it is not out of love for the King or his regime. The unity of the two banks gives expression to a natural connection between the two populations. This connection is not merely historical, but since 1948 has been familial as well, as many of our relatives now live on the East Bank. Moreover, the unity of the two banks is a

---

11. Based on author's interview with Hamdi Kan'an, Oct. 28, 1970.

step toward the greater unity of the Arab world in which we grew up believing and still believe. And let us not forget that the West Bank was conquered from Jordan, and that Security Council Resolution 242 calls for its return to Jordan.[12]

The shift from Hamdi Kanʿan's radical views back to a solution based on incremental changes in the existing political order in Amman left the Jordanian Communist Party and its branch in the West Bank—the Palestine Communist Organization—almost the only organized bodies advocating a two-bank solution conditional upon prior radical changes in the Jordanian political system. The Communists' preference for such a solution rather than a separate Palestinian state, either in the West Bank and Gaza or in all of Palestine, was itself a result of a change in the Communist attitude toward Jordanian rule in the West Bank in the early 1950s, a change that lasted until the summer of 1973.

From the time that Jordan took control over the West Bank in 1948 up to mid–1951 the Communists had expounded a clear and consistent separatist line. Their position was determined by their support of the 1947 United Nations plan to partition Palestine into two states—Jewish and Arab—and by their opposition to Jordanian activity on the West Bank. During the first years of Jordan's rule the Communists still hoped that the partition plan could be put into effect and that "alongside the state of Israel there would arise a Palestinian Arab state on the West Bank of the Jordan, linked, one way or another, to Israel . . . [and] separated from the British-dominated Hashemite Kingdom."[13]

In 1951 the Communist endorsement of separatism began to give way to a call for "solidarity of the Palestinian and Jordanian peoples" and for a struggle within the Jordanian system to bring about fundamental changes in the existing political order in Amman. The Party even called for Palestinian participation in the elections to the Jordanian parliament set for August 29, 1951.[14]

Thus, from mid–1951 until the 1967 war, Communist groups on

12. al-Quds, March 14, 1973.
13. Eliʿezer Beʾeri, ha-Falastinim tahat shilton Yarden: Shalosh sugiyyot (The Palestinians under Jordanian rule: Three issues) (Jerusalem: Magnes Press, Hebrew University, 1978), 36–37.
14. Ibid., 40.

the West Bank tended to align themselves clearly with the union of the two banks. After the official annexation of the West Bank by Jordan in April 1950, the Communists changed their name from the League for National Liberation to the Jordanian Communist Party, indicating their newfound willingness to see the West Bank as part of the Kingdom of Jordan.[15]

The shift in the Palestinian Communists' position resulted in part from the Soviet position, which regarded the Palestinian issue more as a refugee problem to be settled between Israel and the Arab states than as an issue of national rights to be fulfilled in a separate state. The U.S.S.R.'s approach to the Palestinian problem in the 1950s and 1960s

was part of the Soviets' overall interpretation of the 1948 [Arab-Israeli] War, which until 1955 was portrayed by Moscow as nothing more than a British-U.S. provocation in which each power assisted its own puppets, setting them against each other. With the post-Stalin change in the Soviet attitude toward the Arab regimes and, in consequence, the change in approach to the Arab-Israeli conflict, the more extreme view of Palestinian refugees was gradually revised. By the time of 'Abd al-Nasser's visit to the Soviet Union, Moscow was willing to include a phrase in the final communiqué acknowledging the "legitimate rights of the Palestinian Arabs," and during his 1964 visit to Egypt, Nikita Khrushchev spoke of the "inalienable and lawful rights of the Palestinian Arabs." Nonetheless, the approach was still one of the plight of refugees rather than of a national liberation movement.[16]

Guided by this approach, the Soviet Union responded indifferently to the establishment of the PLO in 1964, and later it ignored the PLO quest for self-determination and the establishment of a separate Palestinian state.[17] The solution to the Palestinian problem, according to the Soviet point of view in the 1960s, had to be found within the existing Middle East political framework, not through radical changes in the territorial status quo.

15. See Amnon Cohen, "The Jordanian Communist Party in the West Bank, 1950–1960," in *The USSR and the Middle East*, ed. Michael Confino and Shimon Shamir (New York: John Wiley and Sons, 1973), 420.

16. Galia Golan, *The Soviet Union and the Palestine Liberation Organization: An Uneasy Alliance* (New York: Praeger, 1980), 6.

17. Ibid., 6–7.

As long as the Soviet attitude toward the PLO and the idea of Palestinian self-determination continued to be negative, the position of the Palestinian Communists did not change. During the first three years after the 1967 war, the Communists continued to advocate a solution based on reunification of the West and East Banks, refusing to support either the PLO vision of a Palestinian democratic state in all of Palestine or its strategy of armed struggle.

Certainly at this period Communist activists on the West Bank were ready to engage in anti-Israeli activities together with Ba'th and al-Qawmiyyun al-'Arab members. The Communists, however, restricted themselves to what they called "aggressive political struggle," refusing to participate in armed resistance against Israeli rule in the occupied territories. "So far," elaborated a Communist sympathizer in early 1969, "there is no strong revolutionary party in the West Bank able to lead the public into armed struggle. Thus, the Communists are struggling in accordance with the possibilities of the current historical phase. They assume that riots, demonstrations, strikes, and other forms of passive political resistance are preferable at this time to military means."[18] Whatever the Communist reason for not following the PLO's call for popular armed resistance against Israeli occupation after the 1967 war, its refusal reflected reluctance to participate in the PLO's military struggle to further a political goal that contradicted their own preference for a two-bank solution.

The change in the Soviet attitude toward the PLO at the end of 1969, granting the organization the status of a legitimate national liberation movement and considering its struggle "for the liquidation of the consequences of Israeli aggression as a just anti-imperialist national struggle of liberation" resulted in a reassessment of the Communist position.[19] A communiqué issued in March 1970 by the Arab Communist parties proclaimed their willingness to join the "PLO struggle against Israel involving the use of arms as well as other stratagems."[20] This resolution led the Arab Com-

18. Interview with an anonymous ex-member of the Jordanian Communist Party, March 15, 1969.

19. *Trud* (Moscow), October 21, 1969; Golan, *The Soviet Union*, 10.

20. Amnon Cohen, "The Changing Patterns of West Bank Politics," *Jerusalem Quarterly* 5 (1977): 109.

munist parties to authorize the Jordanian Communist Party to form, in the same year, a Palestinian guerrilla organization, al-Ansar. The organization's goal was to operate militarily in the occupied territories and to gain political influence within the PLO through membership in the PLO's principal representative bodies: the Palestinian National Council, the Central Council, and the Executive Committee.

The Communists' willingness to take part in PLO political and military activities seemed to imply full support for independence and the PLO's radical version of fulfilling this desire in a Palestinian democratic state that would replace Israel. However, close examination shows that the Communists' readiness to accept the PLO formula of armed struggle was motivated not so much by the wish to further Palestinian self-determination through the annihilation of Israel as by the desire to force Israel to evacuate territories occupied in the 1967 war.

This intention was summed up clearly in the clandestine publication of the Palestinian Communist Organization in the West Bank, *al-Watan*, in October 1970. According to this publication the Palestinian Communist struggle against Israel aimed to

(1) strengthen [Palestinian] resistance to the Zionist occupation and reject all its surrounding plans such as a Palestinian entity and self-rule, (2) emphasize the two-bank unity, which is based on "unity of struggle" and common destiny, (3) condemn the crimes of Amman's rulers during the civil war in Jordan [September 1970] and strive to overthrow the traitor government in Amman, (4) demand the establishment of a democratic national regime in the East Bank that would represent all the progressive and national elements on the two banks and that would cut off Jordan's connection with imperialism, granting freedom to the people and turning Jordan into a main front in the liberation campaign against the [Zionist] enemy.[21]

Instead of mirroring a fundamental policy shift, the Communists' collaboration with the PLO in the early 1970s was an attempt to reinterpret the PLO's ultimate goals in a way that would enable the Communists to advance their two-bank solution.

The PLO's awareness of the gap between its goals and those of

21. *al-Watan* (The West Bank), 343 (Oct. 1970).

the Communists led most of the PLO factions except the Marxist PFLP and DFLP, to refuse to grant al-Ansar the status of a Palestinian organization and membership in the PLO representative bodies. This PLO rejection of al-Ansar, as well as intensive Israeli operations against the organization, led to its failure to become effective in the West Bank, and finally to its disbanding in 1972.

After the 1973 October War, the gap between the Communists and the PLO regarding the future of the occupied territories narrowed. The Soviet position toward an independent Palestinian state in the occupied territories changed in 1973; the change became more evident in the fall of 1974, when Soviet leaders referred publicly for the first time to the Palestinians' right to establish a Palestinian state in the West Bank and Gaza.[22] Consequently, the Palestinian Communist Organization shifted from endorsement of two banks toward an independent Palestinian state solution. This shift led to the establishment of the Palestine National Front (PNF) in mid–1973. The PNF was presented as a nonpartisan national movement that was intended to serve as the PLO's principal political instrument inside the occupied territories. However, although the rapprochement between the PLO and the Palestinian Communist Organization narrowed their areas of disagreement, it did not eliminate them completely. While the PLO publicly adhered to the idea of a Palestinian state in all of Palestine, the Communists continued to emphasize a solution based upon a Palestinian state in the occupied territories, beside Israel.[23]

On the eve of the October War there were only two political groups in the West Bank and Gaza that fully supported the PLO's definition of the ultimate solution to be achieved through armed struggle. These were activists of the Ba'th party, associated with al-Sa'iqa, and supporters of al-Qawmiyyun al-'Arab, who maintained a close relationship with George Habash's PFLP. Certainly not all West Bank political groups who supported a short-term strategy categorically rejected the PLO idea of armed struggle against Israel. Even key adherents of the Palestinian entity, such

22. On the change in the Soviet position, see e.g., *Pravda*, Sept. 9, 1974; Golan, *The Soviet Union*, 55–56.

23. See e.g., "Interview with the Palestine National Front," *Palestine Digest* (Washington) (Oct. 1976): 21.

as Hamdi al-Taji al-Faruqi, manifested sympathy toward, or even support of, the PLO military campaign. It is clear, however, that most of these groups viewed armed struggle as a *tactical* instrument to enhance a political solution. They tended to see a PLO armed struggle as an additional tool to strengthen Palestinian bargaining power in political negotiations with Israel over the future of the West Bank rather than as a substitute means to further the goal of a Palestinian state in all of Palestine.[24]

THE PLO, LOCAL LEADERSHIP, AND THE WEST BANK POLITICAL VISION

Because of the success of the traditional West Bank social structure in sustaining power under Israeli occupation, values of patronage, kinship, and traditional difference continued to dominate the West Bank public's world view and to shape its behavior. These values, as well as the conflicting views of Israel, Jordan, and the PLO regarding the West Bank, enabled the leading local conservative element—the extended families (*hamulas*)—to persist in seeing Palestinian interests in a local context and to mobilize support from broad segments of the West Bank population for this position and against the PLO's pressure. The hamulas maintained their influence by offering the local population an effective way of coping and even identifying with PLO radicalism while maintaining its conservative views and behavior.

Given these social circumstances it is not surprising that the PLO's attempts to strengthen its position in the West Bank met with difficulties, since the policy was to cultivate a substitute leadership that would be willing to subordinate local interests and concerns to the PLO's broader goals. The PLO's difficulties in challenging existing West Bank localism can be readily shown by an analysis of the voters' response to external pressures in two municipal elections for West Bank local councils in 1972 and 1976.

In the absence of district echelons or all–West Bank political organizations under Israeli occupation, municipal institutions

24. For more on this distinction as a central theme in a process of revolution in traditional societies see James C. Scott, "Revolution in the Revolution: Peasants and Commissars," *Theory and Society* 7/1–2 (1979): 97–134.

gained substantial status. They became the sole representative local bodies, enjoying considerable recognition from Israel, Jordan,
the local population, and later on even from the PLO. The importance attached to municipal councils was further increased because the Israeli authorities refrained from direct intervention in
their composition, although the Jordanian Municipal Elections
Law of 1955 empowered the central government to select a mayor
and to appoint two council members in addition to those elected.[25]
Finally, two amendments to this law, introduced by Israel before
the 1976 elections, enfranchised women and changed the municipal
taxpayers' registration.[26] The extension of the franchise increased
the importance of municipal institutions in comparison to what
they had possessed under Jordanian rule in the West Bank before
1967. The growing importance of the West Bank municipal bodies
led Jordan and later the PLO to try to influence the municipal
elections through persuasive or coercive means in order to further
their interests and minimize the effect of Israeli activities on West
Bank political behavior.

Municipal elections were in principle personal. Though candidates were officially forbidden to organize themselves into lists,
they frequently joined forces unofficially on the same list in order
to make their campaigns more manageable. The elections were
thus generally contested by two such lists as well as by single
candidates. The single candidates were usually either the strongest

25. See the *Jordanian Official Gazette* May 1, 1955. It is worth noting that during
the Jordanian rule on the West Bank the government kept several options for
control over the elections and the composition of the municipal councils. Electoral
zones were determined by the minister of the interior. Usually the entire municipal
area formed a single zone, but it was the minister's prerogative to subdivide it.
The central government also determined the eligibility of voters and candidates.
All this, together with the right to appoint two additional council members and to
select the mayor, gave the government considerable influence. See Ori Standel,
ha-Behirot la-ᶜiriyot ba-Gada ha-Maᶜaravit, 1951–1967 (The municipal elections in
the West Bank, 1951–1967), mimeo. (Judea and Samaria Area Command, 1968),
2–3; also Allen Gerson, *Israel, the West Bank and International Law* (London:
Frank Cass, 1978), 119–20.

26. For more details see Moshe Drori, "Second Municipal Elections in Judea
and Samaria under Israeli Administration: Legislative Change," *Israel Law Review*
12 (1977): 526–31.

or those who were thought to have no chance and who, therefore, did not attract partners. Although in some cases the lists had a clear political character, they generally centered around strictly apolitical platforms and often included candidates representing different ideological leanings. The lists were usually formed for purely pragmatic purposes just before the elections and dissolved immediately afterwards.

Voting procedure required each voter to write on a ballot the names of his preferred candidates, whose number was not to exceed the number of seats (surplus names were erased from the bottom of the list). The representatives were appointed according to the number of times their names appeared on valid ballot slips. However, from time to time, the validity of the elections was questioned. For instance, in 1951 a case became known wherein one voter from Hebron complained that when, being illiterate, he had asked the election official to help him write down his candidates, the official wrote down other names on his slip—a complaint that caused the cessation of elections in the city. (See Standel, *ha-Behirot*, 10.)

When the number of candidates was identical to the number of seats, all candidates were appointed as council members without elections. Such settlement (*tazkiya*) was usually the result of negotiations among candidates in order to limit their number. Ignoring settlements of this type made in the small communities, tazkiya has been achieved only three times since 1948: in Hebron in 1955, in Nablus in 1959, and again in Hebron in 1972. Hebron's ex-mayor Muhammad ʿAli al-Jaʿbari's efforts to prevent elections through tazkiya in 1976 failed, causing his withdrawal as a candidate and the nonparticipation of his followers in the elections. Although one may argue that tazkiya reflects the influence of traditional politics within the hamula framework, its infrequency permits us to exclude it from the analysis of voting behavior.

In dealing with the election results I have chosen to rely on an aggregative analysis of fluctuations in voting patterns in municipal elections rather than on public opinion polls. I did so because of the difficulties of conducting reliable polls under military occupation. Sources include election results published by the Israeli military government and by the Jordanian government, personal interviews with candidates, local dignitaries, and Israeli officials in contact with the West Bank population and press reports.

The analysis focuses on voting behavior in the West Bank's eleven largest towns: Bayt Jala, Bayt Sahur, Bethlehem, al-Bira, Hebron, Jenin, Jericho, Qalqilya, Nablus, Ramallah, and Tulkarm. The remaining thirteen smaller towns are excluded. In the two election campaigns analyzed, these eleven towns accounted for almost 80 percent of the urban population and 40 percent of the entire population of the West Bank. In 1972 they accounted for 85.3 percent and in 1976 for 81.4 percent of the eligible voters.[27]

Participation in the municipal elections was rather high: 62.8 percent of those eligible voted in 1972 and 69.3 percent in 1976. It should be pointed out, however, that in 1972 only slightly more than 10 percent of the urban population was eligible to vote. In 1976, following the amendments to the Municipal Elections Law of 1955, the proportion of the eligible population increased to 27.3 percent. Due to their enfranchisement, women constituted 36.8 percent of the electorate in 1976, while the number of eligible males had increased by 76 percent.

Under section 7 of the Municipal Elections Law, the number of council members varied between seven and twelve, irrespective of the size of the electorate or the population. Although in 1976, for example, Hebron's population was only 45,000 and Nablus's 80,000, of whom 11,244 and 19,447 respectively were eligible to vote, each city elected an equal number of members, ten, to its municipal council.

The total number who actually voted in the towns studied was 18,331 in 1972 and 49,918 in 1976. To calculate the proportion of the votes given to each candidate, the number of votes for each

27. Data on population, voting participation, and the division of voters is based on official publications by Israel's Central Bureau of Statistics, on reports by the military government concerning the occupied territories, and on data that appeared in the Arabic newspapers *al-Quds* and *al-Anba*', published in Jerusalem. The data were analyzed in collaboration with Abraham Diskin. For more details see Shaul Mishal and Abraham Diskin, "Palestinian Voting in the West Bank: Electoral Behavior in a Traditional Community without Sovereignty," *Journal of Politics* 44/2 (1982): 547–58.

Table 3   Palestinian Votes by Candidates' Social Origins
(% of votes cast)

	1972	1976
Hamulas	83.9	85.7
Non-hamulas	16.1	14.3
Muslims	70.4	79.9
Christians	29.6	20.1
N	7,945	22,152

candidate in each town was divided by the number of the town's council members. However, since voters did not always vote for all council members, N in table 3 is smaller than the total number of voters.

Analysis of the election results points to two seemingly contradictory tendencies: electoral stability, reflecting a tendency to maintain loyalty to candidates of veteran hamulas, and voting mobility, reflecting a readiness to support candidates who had not been part of the outgoing councils. The tendency toward electoral stability is clearly apparent (Table 3).

It should be noted that although members of the leading veteran hamulas sometimes ran for office as independent rather than hamula candidates, most of the independent candidates were from refugee families who arrived in the West Bank after the 1948 Arab-Israeli war. The votes given to hamula members who did not enjoy the support of hamula leaders are included with the non-hamula votes in the table. The hamulas accounted for a much smaller proportion of the population than the support for their candidates would suggest. In other words,.hamula candidates gained massive support from a voting community outside the extended family. The stability indicated by the consistent support given to hamula candidates is especially remarkable in light of the fact that hamulas frequently introduced new candidates.

The religious vote (Christian or Muslim) does not reflect the proportion of the two groups within the population either. Christian candidates were never elected in cities with a Muslim majority,

Table 4   Voting Mobility and Sociodemography (Cramer's V)

	1972	1976
Voters' religion (Muslims vs. Christians)	0.41	0.02
Support for hamula candidates	0.08	0.16
Regional affiliation of the voters	0.39	0.65

like Hebron or Nablus, and Muslims were only rarely elected in cities with a Christian majority, such as Bethlehem or Ramallah. In predominantly Christian towns Muslims received 2.8 percent of the votes in 1972 and 4.9 percent in 1976, despite the fact that in some of those towns the religious minorities constituted a considerable proportion of the population. Thus, in Christian Ramallah the proportion of Muslims after the 1967 war was about 45 percent;[28] yet only two of the nine council members elected in 1976 were Muslims. This reflects once again the tendency of the West Bank voter to support members of the elite. That the proportion of total votes given to Muslim candidates in 1972 was less than in 1976 is probably because no elections were held in Muslim Hebron that year.

The voting pattern shows, then, two related tendencies: (1) a preference for hamula candidates, showing support for local traditional power foci; and (2) support for the locally dominant religion. At the same time, voting mobility—that is, the tendency to support candidates who had not been part of the outgoing council—was extremely strong. In 1972, 49.3 percent of the votes went to new candidates, and in 1976 support for new candidates reached 82.5 percent. Table 4 shows the relationship between sociodemographic characteristics of the population and voting mobility calculated according to Cramer's V coefficient.[29]

28. See Binyamin Shidlovsky, *Ramallah-al-Bira: Skira he-vratit-politit* (Ramallah-al-Bira: Sociopolitical survey), mimeo. (Judea and Samaria Area Command, 1970), 8.

29. Cramer's V is a coefficient that indicates the strength of the correlation between the explained phenomenon and the explaining factor. That is to say, how much of the variance of the dependent variable (e.g., voting behavior) is explained

The relationship between voting mobility and the voters' religion declines in strength but maintains its direction: Muslim voters show a greater tendency to support veteran candidates. The decline in our V coefficient may perhaps be attributed to the fact that exposure to growing political pressures from outside, especially after 1972, had a greater effect on the originally more traditional Muslim groups than on the more modern Christians. Another finding is the tendency to support veteran candidates among those voting for hamulas. The tendency to support hamula candidates thus coincides with the tendency to support veteran candidates.

The strongest relationship is found between voting mobility and geographical location. Although Israeli authorities divided the West Bank into seven administrative regions, it is politically more meaningful to relate here to two main areas: the northern part, where political leadership usually comes from Nablus, and the southern part, most of whose leadership comes from Hebron. Voters in the more developed northern region showed a stronger tendency to support veteran candidates than voters in the south. Yet hamula voting was more frequent in the south than in the north (Cramer's coefficients of 0.20 in 1972 and 0.22 in 1976). Thus, although generally conservatism in the sense of hamula loyalty ties in with loyalty to veteran candidates, hamula affiliation was clearly stronger in the south, while support for veteran candidates was stronger in the north. This may be explained by the differing levels of sociopolitical development in the two regions: voters in the more developed north compensate for their lost sense of loyalty toward

---

by the independent variable (e.g., voters' religion). The coefficient is based on the X^2 (chi square) test. Its range goes from 0 to 1, and its formal definition is:

$$V^2 = \frac{X^2}{N \cdot \min(\text{rows}-1; \text{columns}-1)}$$

The value of chi square is divided by the N of the sample multiplied by the smaller of the two: number of categories of the dependent variable (rows) minus one, or number of categories of the independent variable (columns) minus one. Unlike Cramer's V, X^2 denotes the significance of the correlation—how sure we are that the sample findings hold for the whole relevant population. It is unnecessary to present the X^2 results in our case since we deal with the whole population. See Hubert M. Blalock, *Social Statistics* (New York: McGraw-Hill, 1960), 230.

Table 5   *Political Affiliation of the Palestinian Voter (%)*

	1972	1976
Prosystem	69.8	27.6
Antisystem	11.7	39.8
"Fence-sitters"	18.5	32.6
N	7,945	22,152

the hamula by consistent electoral support for veteran candidates, while the hamula commitment of the more traditional southern voters has not yet been undermined.

Table 5 presents findings on the interdependence between election results and the directions of political affiliation in the two elections. Analysis of these findings helps clarify how voters responded to external pressure and how the traditional local leadership maintained its influence among the voting population despite this pressure.

Prosystem voters are the supporters of candidates sympathizing with the Jordanian regime. Antisystem voters, those who supported candidates identified with expatriate elements, refers to supporters of candidates affiliated with the PLO, while fence-sitters support uncommitted candidates. In the 1972 election the candidates who gained most support were those identified with the Jordanian regime. The support for pro-Jordanian candidates, and even their participation in the elections, reflected a clearcut deviation from the official PLO stand. The PLO at the time called for armed struggle against Israel and made no significant attempt to promote radical candidates, demanding that the population abstain from voting as an act of passive resistance.[30] However, the weakness of the PLO after the September 1970 civil war in Jordan, Jordan's withdrawal of its opposition to the 1972 election, and Israel's attempt to discourage voters from supporting antisystem candidates all helped voters to disobey the PLO's call.

During the 1976 elections the PLO was able to effect a radical

30. Abraham Sela, "The PLO, the West Bank and Gaza Strip," *The Jerusalem Quarterly* 8 (1978): 73–74.

change in voting trends. For the first time in the political history of the West Bank, the antisystem voters, although failing to gain an absolute majority, emerged as the largest single group. The new trend can be attributed to political developments after 1972. In March 1972 King Hussein suggested a political solution to the West Bank issue: the West Bank, the East Bank, and the Gaza Strip would become autonomous districts in a federative framework with Jordan. This proposal intensified the competition between Jordan and the PLO for control of the West Bank, leading the PLO, which had until then considered armed struggle the key element in its strategy, to view political action as a way to counteract the Jordanian proposal. Developments following the October 1973 war provided further inducement to the PLO to think in terms of a political solution. Political bargaining, followed by the agreements signed by Israel with Egypt and Syria during 1974 and 1975, which provided for Israeli withdrawal from some territories, fed PLO hopes that Israel might withdraw from territories on the West Bank, too. Hence the decision reached at the session of the Palestinian National Council in June 1974, whereby a "fighting Palestinian national authority" would be established in any area liberated from Israel. Though explained as a tactical change, it marked a real shift in the PLO position toward the occupied territories; unequivocal support for military struggle has ever since been supplemented by a willingness to consider political means as well.

This change made a modification in the PLO's attitude toward the activities of the West Bank population necessary. Although it had originally called for passive resistance and the reduction of contacts with the Israeli authorities to a minimum, the PLO now realized the need for political involvement in the West Bank in order to ensure the loyalty of its population in future developments. Indeed the PLO's new approach, the decisions of the Arab summit meetings in Algeria (November 1973) and Rabat (October 1974) to recognize the PLO as the sole representative of the Palestinian people, and the PLO's success in the international arena further strengthened its position among West Bank residents and brought about a decline in Jordanian and Israeli prestige.

So far, I have discussed separately the questions of political

Table 6   Political Affiliation, Voting Mobility, and Sociodemography (Cramer's V)

	1972	1976
Voting mobility	0.32	0.13
Voters' religion (Muslims vs. Christians)	0.26	0.30
Support for hamula candidates	0.14	0.06
Regional affiliation of the voters	0.33	0.20

affiliation on the one hand, and voting mobility and sociodemographic characteristics of the population on the other hand. In table 6 I analyze the directions of political affiliation in the two elections and their relation to voting mobility, voters' religion, support for hamula candidates, and regional voting patterns.

There is a positive relationship between the tendency to vote for new rather than veteran candidates and support for the prevalent political trend. In 1972, when prosystem voting was the dominant trend in the West Bank, 82.6 percent of support for new candidates came from prosystem voters, who accounted for only 57.4 percent of the support for veteran candidates. In 1976, when antisystem sentiment became preeminent in West Bank voting, the antisystem voters accounted for 43 percent of the support for new candidates as against 24.5 percent of the support for veteran candidates. These percentages indicate that, although the supporters of veteran candidates also changed their voting in the direction of the overall shift (see table 5), they did so to a lesser degree than those who supported new candidates.

In both campaigns prosystem voters supported non-hamula rather than hamula candidates: 84 versus 67 percent in 1972; 33 versus 27 percent in 1976. These percentages may have resulted from the fact that in order to attract votes non-hamula candidates had to demonstrate control over material resources, which necessitated some affiliation with Israeli or Jordanian authorities. Hamula candidates, on the other hand, already controlled such resources simply because they represented a hamula. Consequently hamulas could afford to put up radical candidates, counting on the voters' confidence that support of a hamula-based radical candidate would not be likely to hurt their material interests.

Analysis of the relationship between political affiliation and voters' religion reveals that Muslim voters tend to be fence-sitters. The tendency of the Christian voters to take a more committed stand is probably a sign of their being less conservative than the Muslims. The higher level of sociopolitical development among the Christians, due to their greater exposure to Western cultural influences, explains this tendency. Moreover, Christian political radicalism may be related, in the Palestinian case as well as throughout the Arab world, to their minority status in a Muslim environment. Perpetually driven to prove their loyalty, they tend to identify with secular national causes rather than with religious groups.[31]

Analysis of regional voting trends in 1976 indicates that more conservative voters tended to continue fence-sitting. In the southern region, considered more traditional, 34.8 percent voted for uncommitted candidates, as against 25.5 percent in the northern region. However, in the 1972 elections, southern voters showed a stronger tendency to vote for prosystem candidates than did voters from the northern region: 93.8 versus 61.3 percent. The decline in support for prosystem candidates may be due to the increased political pressures on West Bank voters. Fence-sitting, then, enabled tradition-bound voters in the southern region to cope with these pressures by postponing their decisions.

The voting patterns that emerged in the 1972 and 1976 elections showed the ability of the hamulas, a local and traditional element, to retain their status and to gain support from different voting groups for their moderate political views and local preferences. In spite of the PLO's efforts to achieve significant control of and maximum obedience from the population, the hamulas, through a careful selection of candidates, were able to offer the local pop-

31. See D. Tsimhoni, "The Christian Communities in Jerusalem and the West Bank, 1948–1967," *Middle East Review* 9/1 (1976): 44–45; also idem, "The Arab Christians and the Palestinian Arab Movement during the Formative Stage," in G. Ben-Dor, ed., *The Palestinians and the Middle East Conflict* (Ramat Gan: Turtledove, 1978), 73–90.

ulation a way of easing this pressure. The hamulas selected people who reflected the balance of power between Jordan and the PLO as perceived by the voting population. When this balance leaned toward prosystem candidates, the number of hamula candidates with a pro-Jordanian orientation grew. When the influence of the PLO increased, the hamulas put up more candidates sharing the antisystem orientation. Palestinian voters, therefore, were able to reconcile the conflict between old forms of localism and current trends of patriotism; to integrate social conservatism with political radicalism; to bridge concrete and immediate grievances and long-term national desires. They were able to maintain their loyalty and obligations to the hamula's framework while supporting even anti-system, pro-PLO candidates.

Thus the West Bank's growing identification with the PLO since mid–1970 did not so much replace local forms of beliefs and behavior with new ones as it added new dimensions to these forms. It meant not a movement from local interests and parochial loyalties to a complete identity with the PLO's national goals but rather the pursuit of these goals and means in a local context.

The West Bank's local interests were not always at odds with those of the PLO; Israel's occupation, settlements, and land expropriation emphasized a common destiny. Yet the West Bank's unwillingness to renounce its local interests and embrace the PLO's political goals clearly demonstrated the persistence of divergent views. This divergence found expression in the tendency to interpret the PLO's goal of Palestinian independence according to local spirit. On the practical level, this divergence was expressed by noncompliance with PLO demands when they did not coincide with the goals of local politics. As a result, despite the growing collaboration between the West Bank and the PLO, relations between the two parties remained tenuous.

CHAPTER 6

The PLO and the West Bank: A Bridge over Troubled Water

Following President Sadat's 1977 peace initiative, West Bank leaders felt freer than at any time since 1967 to take political stands that deviated from the PLO line. Since most of the West Bank mayors who came to power in the 1976 municipal elections were involved in extramunicipal political activity corresponding more with local needs than with PLO interests, the PLO feared that it would lose its ability to play a leading role in determining political developments in the West Bank. In order to understand how, and how successfully, local West Bank leaders challenged the PLO's positions, we must first examine the influence of the Camp David peace agreements on the West Bank policies of the various PLO factions, policies that enabled the local leadership to lay the groundwork for more independent activity.

WHO SHOULD LEAD THE STRUGGLE ON THE WEST BANK?

The 1978 Camp David agreements led the PLO factions to reassess their position toward the occupied territories. Israel's willingness to negotiate with a Jordanian-Palestinian delegation on the future of the occupied areas intensified PLO suspicions that, under certain conditions, Jordan, together with West Bank and Gaza leaders, might find a way to join the peace negotiations.

The PLO's fear that the autonomy plan for the West Bank as concluded at Camp David might pave the way to a settlement without its participation was not farfetched. Leaders in the West

Bank and Gaza Strip, especially those who maintained close ties with Jordan, viewed the autonomy plan as a positive step. They argued publicly that the plan could eventually lead to an independent Palestinian state on the West Bank, Gaza, and East Jerusalem. Two pro-Jordanian mayors, Elias Freij of Bethlehem and Rashad al-Shawwa of Gaza, were the leading proponents of this position. In mid-1980, al-Shawwa visited Amman and Beirut and met with Jordanian and PLO officials in an effort to convince them that "Palestinians from the [occupied] territories and from the Arab States [should] participate in the autonomy talks."[1]

This position was not held only by the pro-Jordanian local leaders. Pro-PLO activists also supported Palestinian participation in the talks, although they preferred to raise the issue with PLO leaders behind the scenes "for fear of being labeled 'traitors' by anti-autonomy forces, who soon dominated public opinion in the occupied territories."[2]

The rejection of the autonomy plan by the PLO and the majority of the Arab world, including Jordan, significantly hampered the West Bank leaders' efforts to convince the PLO to agree to their participation in the peace talks. But the very fact that West Bank leaders publicly expressed views not identical with those of the PLO on such a key issue meant that local leaders were not ready to rubber-stamp PLO resolutions that had direct implications for their political future.

Under these circumstances, could the PLO assure West Bank compliance and cooperation or guarantee West Bank obedience if Jordan were to change its negative position and join the peace talks? Despite Jordan's rejection of the Camp David agreements and its refusal to join the autonomy talks, King Hussein did not exclude the possibility of negotiation along the lines of his federation plan of March 1972. During and after the Camp David summit, King Hussein maintained that his plan still provided the best solution to the Palestinian problem. Moreover, pro-Jordanian dig-

---

1. Yehuda Litani, "Leadership in the West Bank and Gaza," *Jerusalem Quarterly* 14 (1980):100.
2. Ibid.

nitaries on the West Bank still regarded a link between the two banks as an essential element in any future settlement.[3]

Indeed, Jordan's initial response to the Camp David agreements demonstrates that King Hussein's federation plan continued to influence Amman's position toward a future settlement of the Palestinian problem. As long as Hussein saw a possibility of exploiting the Camp David accords to assure Amman's domination of the West Bank, he was "willing to help implement the agreement . . . [and to] give Sadat his support."[4] On January 1, 1978, during a meeting with President Carter, Hussein spelled out Amman's view on a solution to the West Bank problem were it to join the Camp David accords. "The people of the West Bank–Gaza should have the right to self-determination but not the right to claim independence."[5] According to a Jordanian official, it was the "Israeli Prime Minister's violation of his promise to President Carter to freeze settlements on the West Bank for five years and not, as Begin claimed, for three months, which led Amman to repudiate the agreements."[6]

Jordan's decision to join the Arab opposition to the Camp David agreements should therefore be seen as a tactical position deriving from a practical consideration—not to join the peace process without assurances of tangible benefits—rather than as resulting from ideological opposition to the agreements. That Egypt and the U.S. regarded Jordan's participation at the negotiating table as vital increased PLO fears that a formula might be reached that would allow Jordan to join the peace process.

A basic question for PLO leaders at the time was whether they could rely on a united Arab front to oppose a Jordanian move to join negotiations, as the Arab states had always been willing to

3. For more details on King Hussein's position, see *Newsweek*, Sept. 25, 1978; Asher Susser, " ʿEmdat Hussein be-sheʾelat ʿatid ha-Gada ha-Maʿaravit" (Hussein's position on the future of the West Bank), *Hamizrah Hehadash* (The new East) 28/3–4 (1979):241.

4. Jimmy Carter, *Keeping Faith: Memoirs of a President* (New York: Bantam, 1982), 404.

5. Ibid., 300.

6. See Bernard Avishai, "Looking over Jordan", *New York Review of Books*, April 28, 1983: 38.

defend the Palestinian cause only as long as it coincided with their particular interests. This political uncertainty led the PLO to conclude that the best way to impede the peace process was to become more deeply involved in West Bank politics and to exercise greater control over the actions of the local leadership. Assurance of an intra-Palestinian united front was perceived as a far more promising way to prevent an unwanted solution than reliance on inter-Arab support. "Internal sumud [steadfastness]," argued Hani al-Hasan, ʿArafat's adviser, had become more essential than "external sumud."[7] A heightened political presence on the West Bank, according to this view, would increase the PLO's maneuverability and improve its independent decision-making capability. As a result, following Camp David, all the PLO factions devoted immense energy and resources to the political struggle in the West Bank.

However, radical factions within the PLO such as Hawatma's Democratic Front and Habash's Popular Front fundamentally disagreed with ʿArafat's Fatah over the nature of the relationship to be established between the PLO and the leadership in the occupied territories: Fatah sought to define it in centralizing terms, while the Democratic and the Popular fronts leaned toward decentralization; Fatah strove for control from above, while its rivals preferred a loose interaction between the two parties. Fatah therefore opposed the distinction made by Hawatma and Habash between "outside," that is, PLO leadership, and "inside," or West Bank and Gaza-Palestinian leadership. Behind this distinction lay Hawatma's and Habash's desire to allow local leaders to decide how to conduct the struggle against the autonomy plan. Fatah, in contrast, emphasized the need for unity of command and for full compliance by the local leadership.

The dispute between Fatah and the Democratic and Popular fronts was aired openly at the July 1981 seminar, "Problems of National Struggle in the West Bank and Gaza," held by the PLO Research Center in Beirut and attended by representatives of all leading PLO factions. Majid Abu Sharara, a member of Fatah's Revolutionary Council and head of Fatah's Information Depart-

---

7. See the interview in *al-Nahar al-ʿArabi wal-Dawli* (Paris), Jan. 29, 1979; also Yasir ʿArafat in *al-Watan al-ʿArabi*, Oct. 31, 1979.

ment, stated that "[it] is quite impossible to make a distinction between what goes on inside the occupied territories and what goes on outside. The majority of moves made inside, at the political and all other levels, reflects the policy of all the organizations outside. Similarly, the nature of the relations between the nationalist forces outside reflects the nature of the relations between these forces inside." Abu Sharara stressed

that the nature of relations inside the occupied territories is such that it is still necessary to take action to promote them and that greater attention should be devoted to them, and this can only be achieved through the establishment of an effective Occupied Territories Office outside the homeland. . . . [The Office] would undertake the tasks of coordination, issue political directives, and take decisions on alliance inside the occupied territories, in trade union elections and other issues. . . . It would then take the appropriate decisions to ensure more effective Palestinian national actions in the face of the Israeli occupation and in resistance to the Camp David schemes and the schemes of the Jordanian regime which still had influence inside the occupied territories.[8]

Yasir ʿAbd Rabbu, Deputy Secretary-General of the Democratic Front, argued in response that

the various communities of the Palestinian people, whether inside or outside the occupied homeland, live in differing political and social circumstances. This situation has taken shape over a long period of time, since the disaster of 1948. . . . This being the case, it is not possible to deal with the relations with the forces and organizations struggling inside the occupied territories in the same way as we discuss the relations of the leadership center in Beirut with the organization in Tyre or that in Sidon. . . . it is very natural that the task of directing the struggle and working out its tactics should fall on the shoulders of this or that organization inside the occupied territory.[9]

Behind the radical factions' position lay the suspicion that Fatah's quest for direct and full control over the local leadership was actually intended to facilitate its adjustment to the new political reality and might presage partial or complete acceptance by Fatah of the peace process. This suspicion was well founded. Although

8. *Journal of Palestine Studies* 11/2 (1982): 153–54.
9. Ibid., 155.

Fatah's leaders opposed the West Bank leaders' appeal for participation in the autonomy talks between Egypt, Israel, and the U.S., they encouraged them to hold covert "consultations" with Israeli and American officials to ascertain whether autonomy talks might further Palestinian interests.[10] Indeed, Rashad al-Shawwa of Gaza and Elias Freij of Bethlehem continued to meet American and Israeli officials despite Fatah's public position of refusing to enter into any negotiations based on the autonomy plan.[11]

Fatah's position explains why radical factions within the PLO were in favor of loose relations with the West Bank, which would permit the local leadership "to decide on its tactics and the day-to-day tasks of its struggle. . . . "[12] A loose relationship would allow local anti-Fatah elements to coalesce, strengthening opposition to Fatah in the occupied territories and weakening Fatah's ability to promote a political solution rejected by radical Palestinian factions.

On the practical level, the dispute between Fatah and the radical PLO factions on the issue of relations with the West Bank leadership was reflected by the two sides' opposing positions regarding local initiatives to form a central leadership. While the PLO's radical factions enthusiastically supported such a move, Fatah very often acted against it. The effect of these contradictory responses on the ability of local West Bank groups and individuals to play more significant political roles can be discerned in two major attempts by the West Bank political leadership—one by the Palestine National Front (PNF) and the other by the National Guidance Committee—to become a vanguard that could represent all West Bank political interests.

Fatah, the Radical Factions, and the PNF

President Sadat's visit to Jerusalem in late 1977 was followed by an initiative on the part of Communist activists and supporters of the Democratic and Popular fronts in the West Bank to reestablish

10. Interview with an anonymous Israeli, formerly a senior official in the Judea and Samaria Area Command, March 15, 1982.

11. For more on these meetings see *Middle East Contemporary Survey* 3, ed. Colin Legum, Haim Shaked, and Daniel Dishon (New York: Holmes & Meier, 1980), 316, 318.

12. *Journal of Palestine Studies* 11/2 (1982):155.

the PNF. The PNF, which had been active in the West Bank in 1973–75 now sought to become the "sole political instrument of the PLO in the occupied territories."[13] The initiative received a frosty welcome from Fatah.

The PNF's past record of adopting Soviet views and positions on the Palestinian issue played a significant role in Fatah's negative response. After the October War of 1973, for instance, the PNF followed the U.S.S.R.'s appeal to the PLO to participate in the Geneva Conference and accept a Palestinian state in the occupied territories of 1967 as a final solution to the Israeli-Palestinian conflict. From Fatah's point of view, this PNF readiness to adopt Soviet positions without consulting the PLO and before the PLO had even formulated a position on these issues showed that the PNF's loyalty rested primarily with Communism, and only secondarily with Palestinian nationalism. Fatah suspected that support for re-establishment of the PNF might lead to the emergence of a local leadership that would take an independent stand on key issues, choose its own tactics, and endanger Fatah's attempt to become the dominant actor in West Bank political life.

In contrast, the radical PLO factions welcomed the emergence of an independent West Bank leadership, since it served the basic goal of limiting Fatah's political power in the occupied territories. So determined were the Democratic and Popular fronts to prevent Fatah from gaining excessive influence in the West Bank that they were prepared to support the PNF's request to lead the PLO's political struggle in the occupied territories despite the PNF's unstable political record. Yasir 'Abd Rabbu, deputy secretary-general of the Democratic Front, argued that it was "absolutely unjustifiable and illegitimate" that Fatah should be afraid lest the PNF "inside the occupied territory could become a center independent of or parallel to the PLO." Instead, Rabbu claimed that the PNF represented all Palestinian forces within the occupied territories. More than any other force, the PNF had "raised the banner of the PLO and affirmed that the criterion of nationalism in the occupied territories is recognition of the PLO as the sole legitimate representative of all the Palestinian people. . . . " Rabbu

---

13. *al-Hadaf* (Beirut) (PFLP organ), Oct. 13, 1979.

stressed "the need to make every effort to rebuild the National Front." He noted, too, that "various forms of cooperation and solidarity already exist in the occupied areas . . . in spite of occasional manifestations of conflict or disagreement, which are usually managed in a more democratic way than that which governs relations outside the occupied territory."[14] Abu ʿAli Mustafa, Deputy Secretary-General of the Popular Front, concurred, maintaining that the PNF had to remain the controlling force that established all institutions inside the occupied territories and deployed "all the Front's committees in all localities."[15]

During the fourteenth Palestine National Council session, held in January 1979, Fatah moderated its position toward the PNF. It agreed to a compromise formula that called for "strengthening the structure of the Palestine National Front inside [the occupied territories] . . . and giving it all forms of political and material support . . . to mobilize the masses of our people in the interior to confront the Zionist occupation."[16] In reality, however, Fatah did whatever it could to minimize the PNF's influence on West Bank political life. Thus, while in 1979 the Democratic Front's organ *al-Hurriyya* and the Popular Front's *al-Hadaf* reported at length on the PNF's activities within the occupied territories, Fatah's *Filastin al-Muhtalla*, which was devoted entirely to the occupied territories, referred only to activities of the municipal councils and other local bodies, without once mentioning the PNF. *Filastin al-Muhtalla* did not even report to its readers on the 1979 Palestine National Council resolution to renew PNF activity in the occupied territories.[17]

Against this backdrop, it is hardly surprising that the PNF's attempts to initiate anti-Israeli political activities in the occupied territories met with a lack of enthusiasm by Fatah. This was the case with the PNF's initiative to declare October 8, 1979, as "Pris-

14. *Journal of Palestine Studies* 11/2 (1982): 156–57; for similar arguments see also *al-Hurriyya* (Beirut) (DFLP organ), Oct. 29, 1979.

15. *Journal of Palestine Studies* 11/2 (1982): 159; for similar arguments see also *al-Hadaf*, Oct. 27, 1979.

16. *Shuʾun Filastiniyya* (Feb. 1979): 263.

17. On the DFLP and the PFLP criticism of Fatah's policy toward the PNF, see e.g., *al-Hurriyya*, Oct. 29, 1979, and *al-Hadaf*, Sept. 22, 1979.

oner Day" for the 5000 Palestinian prisoners being held, according to the PNF, in Israeli jails. The designated day was to include a hunger strike by the prisoners and a sit-in by the public and local leaders in the West Bank and Gaza.[18] While the PNF's initiative gained the blessing of the Democratic Front, Fatah refused to endorse it. As a result the initiative ended in failure: the PNF could not mobilize either the prisoners or their relatives, except for a few who gathered in the Red Cross Office in East Jerusalem.[19] Fatah's support for the Palestine National Council's resolution approving the formation of the PNF was merely lip service. Fatah actually continued to view the PNF as an obstacle to its political hegemony on the West Bank.

Fatah's anti-PNF stand, together with Israel's warning to the PNF's Preparatory Committee members to cease their activity in an organization considered by Israel as illegal, appeared to have crippled the PNF.[20] But the PNF bypassed opposition by Fatah and Israel and found an alternative vehicle for influencing West Bank politics: the National Guidance Committee (NGC).

The PLO, the PNF, and the NGC

The NGC was established in the West Bank by local political and professional bodies in October 1978 to aid the political struggle against the autonomy plan. The NGC numbered twenty-two members and was composed of pro-PLO mayors from various regions of the West Bank and Gaza, representatives of voluntary organizations, trade and students' unions, the religious establishment, business circles, and journalists.[21]

18. For more details see *al-Hurriyya*, Oct. 15, 1979.

19. See ʿal-Hamishmar (Tel Aviv), Oct. 9, 1979. It is worth noting that the East Jerusalem dailies *al-Shaʿb* and *al-Fajr*, affiliated to Fatah, reported only a few days later on the "Prisoner Day" strike, without mentioning the PNF. See *al-Shaʿb*, Oct. 10, 1979, and *al-Fajr*, Oct. 11, 1979.

20. The Preparatory Committee was composed of eight members: former Ramallah mayor Karim Khalaf, former Nablus mayor Bassam Shakʿa, former Halhul mayor Muhammad Milhim, ʿAzmi Shuʿaybi of al-Bira, Hani Nasser of Ramallah, Muhammad Jarrar of Nablus, Dr. Ahmad Hamza al-Natsha of Hebron, and Dr. Haydar ʿAbd al-Shafi of Gaza.

21. For more details see *Middle East Contemporary Survey* 3 (1978–79), 334, and 4 (1979–80), 273–74.

The initiative for the establishment of the NGC came from the PNF's Preparatory Committee, so that, although the NGC did include members who were affiliated with Fatah, most of its key positions were controlled by the PNF. For example, three out of four seats in the NGC's Executive Committee were held by members of the PNF's Preparatory Committee: Nablus's mayor, Bassam Shak'a, Ramallah's mayor, Karim Khalaf, and the head of the Palestinian Red Cross in Gaza, Dr. Haydar 'Abd al-Shafi. Only the fourth member, Hebron's mayor, Fahd al-Qawasma, was affiliated with Fatah.

The composition of the NGC's Executive Committee explains why radical factions within the PLO welcomed the NGC's establishment and supported its activity. As in the PNF's case, they viewed the organization as another means by which to narrow Fatah's political influence in the occupied territories. Yet unlike the PNF, the NGC succeeded during its formative stage in gaining Fatah's—and, to a lesser extent, Israeli—support. This tripartite backing by radical factions, Fatah, and Israel would later enable the NGC's leaders to make independent decisions regarding the struggle against Israel and the autonomy plan, often violating Fatah's instructions.

Why did Fatah's response, and that of Israel, to the NGC differ from their reaction to the PNF? After all, PNF support meant that any NGC achievements would strengthen the PNF's position. It would appear that the initial Israeli response was rooted in the Camp David accords, and derived from Israel's need to find Palestinian partners in the occupied territories for negotiations within the autonomy framework. Israel assumed that the NGC's political activity could create an open channel for dialogue with local leaders on a political arrangement. Israeli Defense Minister Ezer Weizman permitted the NGC to hold public meetings and ordered Israeli military governors to tolerate anti-Israeli rallies organized by the NGC on the West Bank and Gaza during the first months of its existence.[22]

---

22. For more details on Israeli policy in the occupied territories after the Camp David agreements see *Middle East Contemporary Survey* 3, 333–34; Pinhas Inbari, *Meshulash 'al ha-Yarden: ha-maga'aim ha-sodiyyim ben Artzot ha-Brith, Yarden*

Although the initial responses by Israel and Fatah to the NGC were similar, Fatah's position resulted from very different considerations. Fatah believed that the NGC coalition structure provided an opportunity to advance its own interests. The inclusion within the NGC of various segments of West Bank political and economic circles nourished Fatah's hope of controlling the NGC's political activity and minimizing the influence of radical elements. Furthermore, Fatah assumed that the leading NGC figures' lack of national political experience would increase its ability to manipulate the NGC position according to its own political line.

In the first year of the NGC's existence, tension with Fatah was hardly noticeable. During the period between October 1978 and October 1979 the NGC's anti-Israel activities served the interests of all PLO factions. The NGC activities were directed against the 1978 autonomy plan, the 1979 Egyptian-Israeli peace treaty, and Israel's settlement policy. However, once the Likud of Menahem Begin came to power in 1977, settlement policy was considered by the West Bank Palestinians as the most disturbing issue. Certainly, for both the Labor party and the Likud, settlements in the occupied territories were seen as an essential element to assure Israel's national security. Yet a comparison of the settlement policy of the Labor party vis-à-vis the Likud's might explain why the Likud policy increased the West Bank Palestinians' fear more than ever that the ultimate goal of Israel was to drive them from their land to make way for Jews.

The settlement policy of the Labor party was guided from 1968 to 1977 by what has been known as "the Allon Plan." The plan is named after Yigal Allon, who served as a deputy prime minister under the Labor rule. Though the Allon Plan was never formally accepted, it gradually became the territorial and ideological blueprint for the West Bank settlement policy pursued by the Labor government up to 1977. The plan was based on three major premises. First, after the 1967 war Israel had to assure itself a defensible border with Jordan by incorporating parts of the West Bank into Israel. Second, a defensible border needed to be strengthened by

---

ve-Ashaf (Triangle on the Jordan: Secret Contacts between the U.S.A, Jordan, and the PLO) (Jerusalem: Cana, 1983), 44–53.

a thick complex of Israeli civilian settlements. Third, Israel had to exclude annexation of densely populated Arab areas in order to maintain its Jewish character and to encourage Jordan to enter peace negotiations. Following the logic of these premises, Allon suggested that a strip along the Jordan River, on its western side, between twelve and fifteen kilometers wide, should stay under Israeli control; Jerusalem should enjoy a viable geographic belt to stay under Israeli rule, and Gush-Etzion (south of Jerusalem) should also stay under Israeli jurisdiction.[23] (See map 1.)

While up to the October War of 1973 the Labor settlement policy was in line with the Allon Plan, after the war Labor deviated from one of Allon's premises, that relating to settlement in densely populated Arab areas. In 1975, Labor added to its settlement map a strip of ten kilometers in the northwest of the West Bank, an area comprising a population of more than 50,000 Palestinians, that was to stay under Israeli control in the future. The reason for this change was increasing security concern, in the wake of the 1973 war, regarding the narrowest part of Israel—the fourteen kilometers between Natanya on the Mediterranean shore in the west and Tulkarm and Qalqilya in the east. But a closer examination shows that Labor continued to devote most of its efforts to establishing settlements in unpopulated areas.

Until 1977, of 34 settlements established under labor, 30 were situated in unpopulated areas. The other four settlements were Kiryat Arba ͨ, established beside the Arab city of Hebron in September 1970;[24] Qadum (later Kedumim), near Nablus, and Offra,

---

23. For more details, see William Wilson Harris, *Taking Root* (New York: John Wiley & Sons, 1980), 32–38. See also Shmuel Sandler and Hillel Frisch, *Israel, the Palestinians and the West Bank*. (New York: Lexington, 1984), 105–15, 134–35.

24. Shlomo Gazit, the head of the Israeli military administration in the West Bank under Defense Minister Moshe Dayan, argues: "Had Dayan not been very ill during the weeks when Kiryat Arba ͨ was established, it would have never come into existance." See *Koteret Rashit* (Jerusalem), May 29, 1985. It is worth noting that Kiryat Arba ͨ was authorized by the government after a long conflict with a group of Jewish fundamentalists led by Rabbi Moshe Levinger, who demanded the resettling of the old Jewish quarters of Hebron. Though the final authorization placed the settlement outside the city, certain political observers saw in it a precedent that triggered Gush Emunim's later illegal settlement activities. See Harris, *Taking Root*, 108.

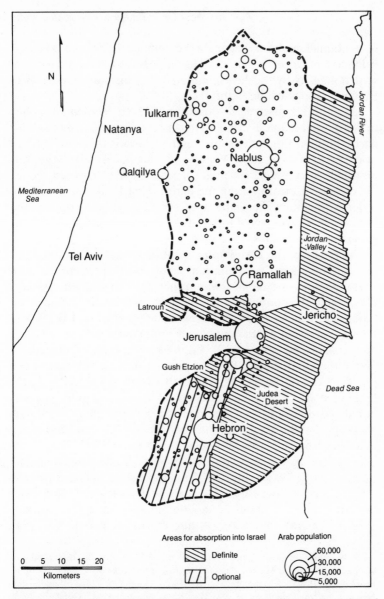

Map 1   *The Allon Plan for the West Bank and the Distribution of Arab Population, September 1967 (adapted from Harris,* Taking Root, *39)*

near Ramallah, both begun in September 1975; and Ma'aleh Edomim in December 1975. The last three were founded and settled illegally by the Jewish national religious movement, Gush Emunim (Block of the faithful).[25]

After the Likud came to power in 1977, the settlement policy took a new direction. Faithful to the historical doctrine of the Herut party, Premier Begin saw Judea and Samaria (the West Bank) as inseparable parts of Eretz-Yisra'el (the land of Israel). Begin was unwilling to consider any political settlement that would reduce the chance of incorporating the entire West Bank into Israel. In order to maintain the viability of the incorporation option, the West Bank was subjected to an intensive settlement policy without geographic limitations. (See map 2.)

The policy of the Likud administration closely approached Begin's ultimate goal. Ariel Sharon, who served as agriculture minister in Begin's first cabinet, was in charge of the settlement policy. He became the dominant figure in implementing the Likud's ambitious settlement plan. The overwhelming efforts of the Likud found expression in the number of settlements, settlers, and the budget allocated (see table 7). From 34 settlements existing at the end of the Labor rule in 1977 the number jumped to 98 at the end of 1982. And of the 64 additional settlements founded during the first five years of the Likud rule, only 7 were set up in the sparsely populated zones of the Allon Plan. At the same time, the Jewish population in the West Bank jumped from 5023 at the end of the labor government's rule to 27,500 at the end of 1983.[26]

Summing up the expenditures on West Bank settlements, we find an average expenditure of 5 million dollars per year prior to 1977; a jump to over 10 million per year during 1977 and 1978; and an average of about 36 million annually from 1979 through 1983. Moreover, allocations during the Labor party's rule were

25. For more on Gush Emunim activities under the Labor and the Likud governments, see Moshe Ma'oz, *Palestinian Leadership in the West Bank* (London: Frank Cass, 1984), 183, 188–93; Harris, *Taking Root*, 115, 133–38; Sandler and Frisch, *Israel, the Palestinians and the West Bank*, 118–26, 135–42, Gershon Kieval, *Party Politics in Israel and the Occupied Territories* (London: Greenwood, 1983), 150–55.

26. Benvenisti, *West Bank Data*, 50, 61.

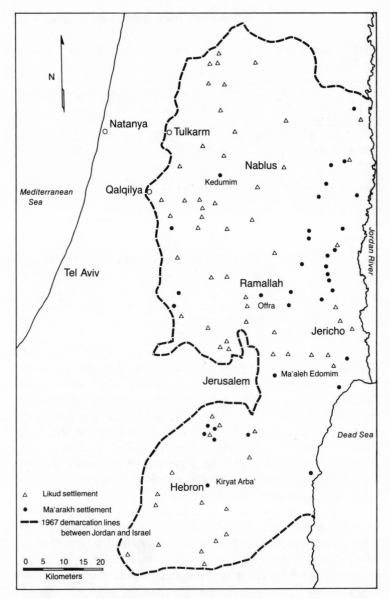

Map 2   *Israeli Settlements on the West Bank: Labor versus Likud (adapted from Benvenisti,* The West Bank Data Project, *91, and Harris,* Taking Root, *107, 129)*

Table 7   Expenditure on West Bank Settlements, 1974–83 (millions of U.S dollars)

	1974	1975	1976	1977	1978	1979	1980	1981	1982	1983
Jordan Valley	3.87	3.90	3.11	5.22	3.70	11.15	13.70	12.85	12.65	12.89
Rest of West Bank	1.22	1.20	0.72	5.06	10.14	18.59	23.40	28.20	22.14	21.24
Subtotal	5.09	5.10	3.83	10.28	13.84	29.74	37.10	41.05	34.79	34.13
Jewish National Fund (JNF) Land	0.47	0.36	0.29	0.30	1.20	3.53	3.10	3.27	1.94	1.40
Total	5.56	5.46	4.12	10.58	15.04	33.27	40.20	44.32	36.73	35.53
% spent in rest of West Bank[a]	24	24	19	49	73	63	63	69	64	62

Source: Benvenisti, *West Bank Data*, 51.
[a]not including JNF land

divided so that three-quarters of the budget was directed to the development of comparatively vacant areas of the Jordan Valley. The proportion was inverted the year the Likud came into power. From then on, three-quarters of the budget was allocated to heavily populated areas in the West Bank. This shift in the scope and direction of Israel's settlement policy under the Likud, in addition to the autonomy plan and the Egyptian-Israeli treaty, brought about a series of civil disturbances, public strikes, riots, and demonstrations initiated by the NGC.

In response to the NGC's anti-Israel activities, Israel tried to return to its pre-Camp David policy of restricting political activity beyond the municipal level. However, the radical mayors, now the NGC's leaders, often violated Israeli orders, counting on Israel's reluctance to take such far-reaching steps against them as dismissal or expulsion. The radical mayors were aware that Israeli measures of this kind would draw sharp criticism from the Egyptian and American delegations to the autonomy talks, as they still hoped to see Palestinian representatives at the negotiating table. Thus, despite Israeli warnings, influential radical figures in the NGC—Mayor Bassam Shakʿa of Nablus, Mayor Karim Khalaf of Ramallah, and Mayor Muhammad Milhim of Halhul—continued to initiate protests, lead rallies, and participate in demonstrations against Israeli policy on the West Bank.

Within a year of its inception the NGC dominated the West Bank political scene. Shakʿa and Khalaf emerged as national Palestinian figures. They were able to determine the local political agenda and challenge Israeli orders without facing serious threat of dismissal or deportation. Mayor Fahd Qawasma of Hebron, a known Fatah supporter and NGC member who leaned toward more self-restraint in relations with Israel, was shunted aside, and Fatah's efforts to place two moderate mayors, Freij of Bethlehem and al-Shawwa of Gaza, on the NGC were unsuccessful.[27] But the NGC's refusal to accept Fatah's instructions extended far beyond the appointment issue, for as it gained strength, the NGC became increasingly daring in challenging Fatah's decisions concerning the conduct of the political struggle against Israel within the occupied territories.

The best example of the increasing readiness by radical elements within the NGC to challenge Fatah's discretion is the Shakʿa affairs. This began with the November 8, 1979, decision by Israeli Defense Minister Ezer Weizman to arrest the mayor of Nablus on November 11 and expel him from the West Bank forthwith. Weizman's decision came two days after a meeting held between the Israeli coordinator of government activities in the administered area, Major-General Danny Matt, and Mayor Shakʿa. The Israeli officer claimed that during the meeting Shakʿa "justified the killing of thirty-four bus passengers on the Haifa–Tel Aviv coastal road in the PLO attack in March 1978." The Israeli major-general added that the mayor also said that "as long as the Palestinian problem remained unresolved, operations of such types were legitimate, effective and natural."[28]

After the Israeli decision became known, Shakʿa's wife appealed to the Israeli Supreme Court to suspend expulsion "until the exact

27. Based on an interview with Benyamin Ben-Eliezer, former coordinator of Israeli government activities in the administrated area, Nov. 12, 1983.

28. *Middle East Contemporary Survey* 4 (1979–80): 271.

circumstances surrounding the decision could be clarified in court."[29] Mayor Shakʿa claimed that he had neither justified nor identified with the PLO's operations, and that the Israeli officer had lifted his words out of their context. The mayor explained that what he had actually said was that "as long as there is occupation and killing, many such actions could be expected and . . . they might be effective."[30]

In the absence of minutes of the meeting the Israeli authorities could not challenge Shakʿa's claims. However, this did not change the Israeli decision to deport the mayor. Israeli leaders argued that the deportation decision was not just an outcome of the talk with Danny Matt, but also derived from Shakʿa's involvement in illegal activities, "which no democratic and tolerant society can put up with."[31]

The Israeli decision met with harsh criticism and condemnation by all West Bank mayors. Behind the scenes, however, radical leaders of the NGC such as Khalaf of Ramallah and Bashir Barghuthi of al-Bira, the more moderate mayors led by Qawasma of Hebron and Sweitte of Jericho, and non-NGC members Freij of Bethlehem and al-Shawwa of Gaza disputed the proper response to the deportation. While Khalaf and Barghuthi advocated the immediate resignation of all the mayors as a response to the Israeli decision, the moderate and non-NGC mayors counseled self-restraint. They hoped to modify the Israeli position, offering a conciliatory formula involving cancellation of the deportation order, and advocating resignation only as a last resort.

This moderate position reflected Fatah's directive to the mayors to remain in their posts. Behind Fatah's position lay the fear that resignation might play into either Israeli or Palestinian radicals' hands—in both cases threatening Fatah's ability to maintain a strong influence on West Bank political life. Nevertheless, thirteen mayors submitted their resignation to the Israeli military authority on November 13. In response to Mayor Freij's request to postpone the resignation, Khalaf explained that "we know better [than the PLO] the situation inside [the occupied territories]." The mayor

29. Ibid.
30. *Haʾaretz* (Tel Aviv), Nov. 12, 1979.
31. *Jerusalem Post*, Nov. 12, 1979.

of Halhul, Muhammad Milhim, concurred: "We have the true picture. Our friends outside do not."[32]

The NGC's public rejection of Fatah's instructions on this key issue was an unprecedented event in relations between Fatah and the local leadership. Prior to the Shak'a affair radical members of the NGC had criticized Fatah's policy on issues such as its relations with Jordan and its stand toward the United States. In April 1979, for instance, the NGC had sent a secret memorandum to Beirut opposing Fatah's willingness to initiate a dialogue and strengthen relations with Amman. NGC radicals had also criticized Fatah "for what they believed were overtures to the U.S. and what they felt was tantamount to agreeing to the exclusion of the U.S.S.R. from a key role in the Middle East."[33] However, in these cases the NGC had not translated its criticism into acts that contradicted Fatah's line.

The NGC's violation of Fatah's instructions in the Shak'a affair was a calculated risk based on the assumption that Fatah was limited in its capacity to react negatively against the NGC. First, the NGC enjoyed the support of the radical factions in the mayors' decision to resign. Second, NGC leaders assumed that because of the autonomy talks, Israel would hesitate to take harsh measures against the resigning mayors. And in the absence of a strong Israeli response, Fatah would be hard put to act directly against its rivals within the NGC to assure adherence to its political line. Moreover, the NGC expected the radical factions within the PLO to support it, while its own leaders continued to emphasize publicly their identification with the PLO.

The NGC's gamble was successful. The Democratic and Popular fronts did indeed side with the resignations, in part because they welcomed an opportunity to reduce Fatah's influence over West Bank politics.[34] Israel, on the other hand, refrained from taking immediate punitive action against the resigning mayors. As a result, Fatah reversed its initial position and ordered the rest of the

32. Monte Carlo Radio, Nov. 10, 1979; Inbari, *Triangle on the Jordan*, 82, 83.

33. See the *Christian Science Monitor*, April 15, 1979.

34. On the position of the Democratic Front see *al-Hurriyya*, Nov. 19, Dec. 3, and Dec. 10, 1979; on the Popular Front's position see *al-Hadaf*, Dec. 8 and 15, 1979.

mayors to accept the NGC's decision and to resign from their posts. A month later Israel, which sought to calm the West Bank, withdrew its decision to deport Bassam Shak'a. On December 5, 1979, Shak'a was released from jail and reinstated as mayor of Nablus.[35]

Fatah's failure to anticipate and direct the mayors' actions in the Shak'a affair led it to reassess its relations with the NGC, and it could not escape the conclusion that the price it would pay for the NGC's success in mobilizing the West Bank against the autonomy plan was too high. The more effective and popular the NGC's activity against Israeli policy, the greater its ability to maintain an independent stand in its relations with the PLO. The fact that the radical mayors were affiliated with the PNF and enjoyed the firm support of the leftist PLO factions only exacerbated Fatah's fears that the NGC might exploit its increasing political power to implement the PNF outlook on PLO–West Bank relations. Such a development would have enabled the NGC to play an intermediary role between the PLO and the West Bank inhabitants, blocking Fatah's direct access to the local population. Fatah would be more dependent on the goodwill of the radicals than on its own discretion, and its desire for maximum influence over West Bank politics would suffer a setback.

Fatah's fears and suspicions were confirmed by efforts made by the NGC after the Shak'a affair to gain control over the "steadfastness" financial aid allocated to various institutions in the occupied territories by the joint Jordanian-PLO Committee. The committee had been set up in early 1979, in accordance with the 1978 Baghdad Arab summit decision to provide $150 million to the occupied territories to support resistance to the Camp David agreements and the autonomy plan.

Shortly after the joint Jordanian-PLO Committee began its activity, radical mayors associated with the NGC criticized the PLO's representatives on the committee for inefficiency and unsuitability and attacked them for enabling Jordan to direct most of the financial aid to its supporters on the West Bank and in Gaza. They called upon Fatah to replace PLO members on the joint committee with representatives better informed about the occupied territo-

35. See *Ha'aretz* and *Jerusalem Post*, Dec. 6, 1979.

ries, who would limit Jordan's influence in the committee.[36] At this stage the NGC position was still tolerable as far as Fatah was concerned. Its attacks concentrated more on PLO members on the committee and less on the Fatah leadership. The NGC request to replace the PLO representatives on the joint committee was perceived as a dispute over tactics rather than as a challenge to the basic principle of cooperation with Jordan on West Bank issues.

After the Shakʿa affair, however, the NGC position toward the joint committee changed significantly. In early 1980 the NGC called upon the PLO to resign from the committee and transfer to the NGC sole authority to distribute the "steadfastness" financial aid to local institutions. The NGC's request reflected a desire to be recognized by the PLO as an official body with a capacity to make its own decisions on issues concerning the West Bank. As in the Shakʿa affair, on this issue, too, the NGC enjoyed the support of the Democratic and Popular fronts. The threat posed by this development to Fatah's position encouraged it to act forcefully against the NGC.

ACTIVITY BY PROXY

Although the worsening situation called for a response of some type, Fatah appeared to be in a no-win situation. A direct confrontation with the NGC might significantly narrow the NGC's growing influence and help Fatah to confirm its central position on the West Bank. However, such a move could also lead to a political vacuum that would allow Israel to enhance its military presence, increase the number of settlements, and block movement toward Palestinian self-determination in the occupied territories. Direct conflict with the NGC could expose Fatah to accusations by rivals that it had delivered the Palestinian population and territories into Israeli hands.

This dilemma led Fatah to look for a way to dismiss the NGC's leaders without either leaving a leadership vacuum or exposing itself to accusations that it was sacrificing the West Bank for narrow

36. For more details see Inbari, *Triangle on the Jordan*, 94–95; *al-Hadaf*, Oct. 13, 1979.

factional interests. Its solution was to act indirectly against the NGC through the joint Jordanian-PLO committee.

In retrospect, this decision by Fatah to rely on cooperation with Jordan to weaken the NGC's influence stood little chance of success. Cooperation and rapprochement with Amman after the September 1970 civil war in Jordan would constitute a clear deviation from the official PLO position. At the tenth Palestine National Council held in 1972, Fatah and all the other PLO factions had adopted a hard line toward the Hashemite regime. The PLO viewed Jordan as an obstacle to the liberation of Palestine and denied its right to exist. The PLO was unequivocal in its opposition to Jordan and sought a united front of the Palestinian and Jordanian people to establish "a democratic state on Palestinian and Jordanian soil to assure the national sovereignty of both peoples."[37]

The twelfth Palestine National Council in 1974 drew up resolutions that reflect this official PLO position toward Jordan, and the 1974 meeting is renowned for the resolution calling for the establishment of an "independent national fighting authority... over every part of Palestinian territory that is liberated [from Israeli occupation]."[38] However, the PLO also made it very clear that the independent fighting authority would be the first step in a prolonged struggle against both Israel and Jordan to achieve the establishment of a Palestinian democratic state in all of Palestine. The 1974 resolution stated that the PLO would "struggle along with the Jordanian-Palestinian National Front, whose aim will be to set up in Jordan a democratic national authority in close contact with the Palestinian entity that is established through the struggle."[39]

Citing these anti-Jordanian PNC resolutions, the radical factions

37. See "The Proposition for a Political Program submitted by the Political Committee to the Tenth Meeting of the Palestine National Council," as cited in *ʿArab ve Yisraʾel* (The Arab and Israel) 3–4, ed. Yehoshafat Harkabi (Jerusalem: Truman Institute, Hebrew University, 1975), 184.

38. See art. 2 of "Political Program for the Present Stage of the Palestine Liberation Organization drawn up by the Palestine National Council in Cairo," June 9, 1974, *WAFA*, June 9, 1974; *Journal of Palestine Studies* 7/4 (1974): 224.

39. Ibid., art. 5.

opposed any attempt by Fatah to initiate a dialogue with Amman. Rapprochement between the PLO and Jordan was perceived by the radicals not only as a deviation from the PLO's official stand but also as a contradiction to basic PLO interests. Since the 1974 Arab summit in Rabat, Palestinian radicals had regularly cited Jordanian policy toward the PLO and Amman's views concerning the political future of the West Bank in order to emphasize the gap between the PLO and Jordan. Although Jordan supported the Rabat resolution recognizing the PLO as the sole representative of the Palestinian people and was willing to open a PLO political office in Amman, it consistently rejected the PLO's request for a military and organizational presence in Jordan. Furthermore, PLO members are reported to have been apprehended and even executed by Jordanian authorities.[40]

Jordan has consistently interpreted Palestinian rights to self-determination in a way that coincided with the 1972 federation plan. "Self-determination," stated ʿAdnan Abu-ʿAwda, the Jordanian minister of information, "means possession by the Palestinians of the freedoms and rights specified by the Human Rights Charter. These freedoms encompass the social, cultural, and economic rights necessary for free political self-expression." In rejecting the sovereignty sought in the PLO's version of self-determination, Abu-ʿAwda cited the historical context of the

links between the Jordanian and Palestinian people that were cemented upon the unification of the West and East banks of Jordan in April 1950. Because of this merger, more than half of the Palestinian people, including the inhabitants of the West Bank, are Jordanian passport holders, and as such their legal status is internationally recognized. In 1950, the Jordanian Parliament, representing both banks, had specified in its decisions to unify them that it confirms the complete union of the East and West banks into one state, and the Hashemite Kingdom of Jordan with its Hashemite Majesty . . . as its head.[41]

Abu-ʿAwda believed that a federation of a Palestinian and a Jordanian region, as originally proposed by King Hussein in 1972,

---

40. See interview with Fatah leader Abu Iyad in *al-Mawqif al-ʿArabi* (Beirut), June 22, 1981.

41. *Jordan Times* (Amman), May 9, 1981.

was the proper solution for the Palestinian problem on the West Bank. The former Jordanian prime minister 'Abd al-Hamid Sharaf expressed a similar view: "The Palestinians and the Jordanians do not belong to separate nationalities. We have not forsaken our rights in the West Bank."[42]

Such views regarding the PLO and the West Bank were exploited by PLO radicals in an attempt to block rapprochement between Fatah and Jordan. They failed because Fatah, in seeking to build a working relationship with Jordan, presented collaboration with it as a tactical move essential in the pursuit of the Palestinian interests of sovereignty and self-determination, rather than as the ideological acceptance of the existing political order in Amman. Fatah, in other words, was confident of manipulating the Palestinian radicals' anti-Jordanian position. It assumed that the better it could justify its participation in the joint Jordanian-PLO committee in terms of PLO and West Bank interests, the easier it would be to challenge its rivals' positions.

Palestinian radicals, although opposed to Fatah's conciliatory stance toward Jordan, found it difficult to challenge this policy. All the PLO factions recognized the strategic importance of the East Bank for the PLO's military and political struggle against Israel. They were all aware that, without a political or military presence on the East Bank of the Jordan—the only common Arab border with the West Bank—access to the Palestinian population would be jeopardized, and, as Ahmad Jibril, head of the PFLP-GC, stated, the PLO would "remain in a very dangerous bottleneck."[43]

Under these circumstances, debate and disagreement between Fatah and its rivals within the PLO focused not so much on the importance of Jordan's East Bank territory for the Palestinian struggle as on how to gain a presence there. Fatah believed that for the time being the best tactic was dialogue and cooperation with Amman. But the PLO radical factions rejected such a move as wishful thinking: "We should not be misled by Hussein's declaration confirming that the PLO is the sole representative of the Palestinian people. We know that he hopes to see us eliminated

42. Interview with *Le Monde* (Paris), March 8, 1980.
43. Interview with *al-Safir* (Beirut), July 19, 1980.

in Lebanon so he can reclaim the title of the representative of the Palestinian people. . . . "[44] Nevertheless, by presenting its willingness to cooperate with Jordan in tactical terms, Fatah was able to minimize the political symbolism of its move and reduce the likelihood of being accused by its rivals of clearcut deviation from the PLO's anti-Jordanian position.

The fact that the initiative to form a joint Jordanian-PLO committee came from the Arab states also allowed Fatah to bypass its rivals' anti-Jordanian stance. First, Fatah was able to share the ideological burden of the decision with other Arab parties. Second, Fatah was better able to mobilize support for the establishment of the joint committee from organizations such as al-Sa'iqa and the Arab Liberation Front sponsored by Syria and Iraq, who stood behind the 1978 Arab summit resolution.

Such radical assent for Fatah's participation in the joint committee served as a springboard for its struggle against the NGC. Using the joint committee as a proxy, Fatah provided its supporters on the West Bank with both strong political backing and financial aid in the challenge they mounted, together with Jordan's supporters, to the NGC's power positions within key local bodies.

Fatah's efforts were directed primarily toward four West Bank universities—Bir Zayt near Ramallah, al-Najah National University in Nablus, Frère in Bethlehem, and the Islamic College in Hebron—as well as the General Association of the West Bank Workers, composed of twenty-two trade unions. During the late 1970s almost 5000 students, 300 lecturers, and 40,000 union members had been exposed to the strong influence of the NGC.[45] Most of the nine seats on the Executive Board of the West Bank Council of Higher Education, which was established in December 1977, were occupied by people associated with the NGC.[46] And in the

44. Ibid.
45. For more details on the political activity of the universities in the West Bank, see e.g., *Ha'aretz*, Dec. 5, and 12, 1980. On the trade unions' political activity see Tim Coone, "West Bankers Discover Union Power," *Middle East* (March 1980): 18–20.
46. *Middle East Contemporary Survey* 2 (1977–78), 298; for more details on the functions of the West Bank Council of Higher Education see *al-Quds*, Dec. 17, 1977.

1979 student council elections held in Bir Zayt and Frère, supporters of the DFLP, PFLP, and Palestinian Communist Organization had gained complete control over the student body.[47]

As for the General Association of the West Bank Workers, its key positions were also held by NGC supporters. The general secretary of the association, ʿAdil Ghanim of Nablus, his deputy George Hasboun of Bethlehem, and the secretary of the blue-collar Trade Union of Ramallah, Hussein aι-Tawil, were known as activists in the West Bank Palestinian Communist Organization. All three assisted the NGC in mobilizing support within the General Association.[48]

From 1980 onward, Fatah's activity via the joint Jordanian-PLO committee led to far-reaching changes in the composition and status of the three above-mentioned bodies. In October 1980 the chairman of the Council of Higher Education, Dr. Gabi Baramki of Bir Zayt University, who maintained close contact with radical mayors, was forced to resign. He was replaced by Dr. Qaʾid ʿAbd al-Haq of al-Najah University, who had served on the staff of the Jordanian Ministry of Education. Simultaneously, Mayor Freij of Bethlehem and Mayor al-Shawwa of Gaza, who were known for their close contact with Amman and Fatah, were appointed members of the executive board of the council.

Similar changes took place in the student councils. In the December 1980 elections at Bir Zayt University, for example, a coalition of Fatah and the Muslim Brothers eroded the dominant influence of the radical left over the student council, winning three seats out of nine. In the elections held at al-Najah and the Islamic College in Hebron in mid–1981, the Fatah-Muslim Brothers coalition achieved an impressive victory, winning all the seats on the student council and defeating NGC candidates.[49]

Turning to the unions, Fatah exploited conflicts and rivalries between the Communists and the PFLP's supporters over positions of power within the General Association of the West Bank Work-

---

47. Based on an interview with an anonymous Israeli official of the Judea and Samaria Area Command, Jan. 8, 1980.

48. Ibid.

49. For more details, see Inbari, *Triangle on the Jordan*, 144.

ers to weaken the NGC's hold there.[50] Fatah encouraged its supporters to join the PFLP in forming a new workers' association that enjoyed the financial aid of the joint Jordanian-PLO committee. As a result the NGC lost its influence over the trade unions.

Fatah's struggle against the NGC extended beyond the West Bank trade unions and the institutions of higher education. To undermine the political status of the radical mayors within the municipalities, Fatah agreed to Jordanian moves against these West Bank mayors, such as the reopening of passport offices and the formation of cooperative associations for marketing agricultural produce in villages of the West Bank northern district. Until January 1980, West Bank inhabitants "whose passports had expired and who could therefore not go to Amman, had to apply for renewal through their mayors or village headmen. By reopening the local passport offices, the Jordanian government was able to choose its own trusted officials and bypass the radical mayors."[51] Similarly, in early 1980 Amman exploited tensions and rivalries between Mayor Bassam Shak'a of Nablus and the rural populace, led by a former member of the Jordanian parliament, 'Abd al-Ra'uf Faris, to support the latter in organizing farmers in forty villages into cooperative associations. By late 1980 the Jordanian initiative had extended to Jenin, Tulkarm, and Qalqilya, and included 160 villages. These moves eroded Shak'a's power base and undermined the NGC's influence in the northern areas of the West Bank.

All told, the steps taken by Fatah and Jordan weakened the NGC's ability to function as an all–West Bank body, to take independent decisions, and to initiate activities that departed from Fatah policy and instructions. The Israeli decision in March 1982 to dissolve the NGC following the dismissal of seven West Bank mayors affiliated with it further narrowed the radical-left threat to Fatah's power in the West Bank.[52]

Israel's opposition to the NGC was directed ultimately at elim-

50. Ibid., 172.

51. *Middle East Contemporary Survey* 4 (1979–80), 284; for more on this issue see the *Economist* (London), Jan. 19, 1980; Inbari, *Triangle on the Jordan*, 115–16.

52. *Ma'ariv* (Tel Aviv), March 19, 1982.

inating PLO influence. Following the 1981 appointment of Ariel Sharon as Israel's minister of defense, Israel stepped up its attempt to cultivate an anti-PLO, alternative West Bank leadership. It focused primarily on the Village Leagues, first established in the Hebron region in 1979. Behind this attempt lay the knowledge that almost 70 percent of the West Bank population was rural, and that key leaders of the Village Leagues—such as Mustafa Dawdin and Muhammad Nasser of Hebron and Yusuf al-Khatib of Ramallah—rejected the PLO's claim to be the sole representative of the Palestinian people and declared their readiness to negotiate a political settlement with Israel. Israeli officials hoped that political and material support for the Village Leagues would help weaken the PLO's standing on the West Bank and reduce to a minimum its influence over the local population.[53]

However, as in the case of the NGC, collaboration between Fatah and Jordan succeeded in minimizing the threat posed by the Village Leagues' activities. The Village Leagues' leaders' willingness to maintain close contact with Israel and to accept publicly a peaceful solution to the Israeli-Palestinian conflict within the framework of the Camp David accords, was exploited by the joint Jordanian-PLO committee, which portrayed the league leaders as traitors prepared to sacrifice Palestinian national interests for personal gain. A Jordanian order issued in March 1982 prohibited membership or activity in the Village Leagues under threat of death and confiscation of property.[54]

The implementation of these harsh countermeasures shattered Israeli hopes of assisting the Village League leaders to narrow the influence of PLO leadership on the West Bank. The Leagues were structurally fragile, financially weak, and ideologically too controversial to be able to challenge the PLO's authority or damage its political reputation among West Bank inhabitants. In the words

53. On this argument see e.g., Reuven Pedatzur, "Anatomyya shel kishalon" (Anatomy of failure), *Ha'aretz* (Tel Aviv), May 5, 1983, and Amnon Dothan, "Inconvenient Peace" *Jerusalem Post*, Oct. 7, 1983. On the political perception that lay behind Israeli support of the Village Leagues see Menahem Milson, "How to Make Peace with the Palestinians," *Commentary* 71/5 (May 1981), 25–35.

54. For more details, see Uri Moor, "Le'an mu'adot panav shel Dawdin?" (Where is Dawdin going?) *Ha'aretz*, Sept. 27, 1983.

of Shlomo Ilya, the former Israeli head of the Judea and Samaria Civil Administration, the attempt by the leagues to form an all–West Bank anti-PLO movement turned into "a joke."[55]

The increasing attention devoted by the PLO to the West Bank as a result of President Sadat's peace initiative intensified the dispute between Fatah and the radical factions over the status and role of Palestinian leadership in the occupied territories. This dispute was exploited by the PNF, the NGC, and later the Village Leagues to undertake political activity beyond the municipal level and to seek leadership at an all–West Bank level.

All three bodies sought to assure the influence and participation of West Bank leaders in decisions concerning both daily issues and the political future. However, beyond this similarity, they differed fundamentally as to what political perception should guide West Bank leadership activity. The PNF and the NGC emphasized cooperative relations with the PLO based on collaboration and mutuality, while seeking a status of internal leadership. The Village Leagues sought to become an alternative leadership to the PLO, composing and conducting their own "music" without outside interference.

What was the effect of these two opposing perceptions? To build up their status as an internal leadership, the PNF and the NGC relied on the support of the radical factions within the PLO to challenge Fatah's policy of assuring full subordination of the West Bank to the PLO's political command. They adopted a policy of noncompliance with Fatah's views and instructions on issues concerning West Bank politics and economics. By continuing, however, to declare publicly their ultimate adherence to the PLO as the sole legitimate power to decide on the occupied territories' political future, they were able to downplay their deviation from the Fatah line. The noncompliance policy represented not so much the outcome of a straightforward conflict or of competing interests with Fatah as a disagreement over practical, day-to-day matters.

The Village Leagues' activity, on the other hand, rested on close cooperation with Israel and adoption of the Israeli line of emphasizing differences between the PLO and the Palestinians on the

55. *Jerusalem Post*, Oct. 27, 1983.

West Bank and treating the PLO as an external element. As a result, Village League leaders viewed their relationship with the PLO as a straightforward conflict, a zero-sum game. Gains for the PLO meant losses for the West Bank.

One might assume that the Village League's leadership, in comparison to the PNF and NGC, represented the greatest threat to the PLO's influence, and especially to Fatah's strength, on the West Bank. Of the three, the Village Leagues were the only group to challenge the PLO's claim to represent Palestinians everywhere, and thereby to question the PLO's raison d'être and right to interfere in West Bank political life. The Village Leagues were also ready to recognize Israel publicly and to reach a political solution to the West Bank problem independent of the PLO.

However, it was much easier for Fatah to act successfully against the Village Leagues than against the PNF and the NGC. Fatah's rapid success in rendering the leagues impotent demonstrated that the major threat to Fatah on the West Bank rested not so much on the activity of those who challenged its raison d'être as on the PLO's middle-of-the-road supporters, who bowed publicly to PLO values and symbols, but in practice gave them a different, local significance. Fatah's problem was not so much to defend itself against the "nonbelievers" as against those who did not comply.

Fatah's success in the early 1980s in reducing modes of noncompliance was made possible by its ability to act against its rivals through proxies. Such activity sometimes required close cooperation with Amman, a clear deviation from the official PLO line. However, Fatah's success in finding effective ways to justify such cooperation in terms of the PLO's national interest reduced the risk of its being accused of sacrificing the future of the West Bank for factional rewards. Yet despite its power to maneuver, Fatah was not completely successful in imposing its position on the West Bank political leadership. Thus the organization found it difficult entirely to prevent local political actors from initiating political activity that did not concur with its interests. But it was effective enough to neutralize local attempts based on alternative or competitive perceptions whenever they threatened to upset the PLO quest for hegemony.

CHAPTER 7

Why Not a Daring Strategy?

At the beginning of the 1980s, Chairman ʿArafat could look back with satisfaction. No Palestinian organization had ever done so much for the Palestinian cause as had the PLO under his leadership. The organization was now recognized as the sole legitimate representative of the Palestinian people by all the Arab nations and by much of the international community. The Palestinian people had gained the sympathy of world public opinion: in the 1970s more states maintained diplomatic relations with the PLO than with Israel. The PLO had become the only nongovernmental body to gain observer status in the United Nations, and it had managed to get a series of anti-Israeli resolutions passed by the General Assembly.[1] And it had emerged as a significant force in Middle East politics: the notion that a peaceful settlement to the Arab-Israeli conflict would require a solution to the Palestinian problem had taken firm root.

The PLO's diplomatic achievements were accompanied by successes within its own camp. During the 1970s, the PLO formed overarching institutions, establishing effective interorganizational collaboration by means of which it was able to mitigate conflicts, manage tensions, and deal effectively with noncompliance. Although ideological cleavages, political mistrust, and suspicion had not disappeared, no serious Palestinian political or military group

1. For more details see Aaron David Miller, *The PLO and the Politics of Survival* (Washington: Georgetown University Center for Strategic and International Studies, 1983), 97–98.

existed outside the PLO's sphere of influence. All the major groups were either affiliated or identified with the PLO. It had become the dominant force in Palestinian political life. Its symbolic status, charismatic leadership, and political influence among the Palestinian people were beyond question.

Still, the Israeli occupation of the West Bank and the Gaza Strip remained a military and political fact of life, and the PLO's quest for an independent state no more than an aspiration. What had generated this gap between political success and territorial failure? Why was the PLO unable to make effective use of growing world sympathy for the Palestinian cause and support for the PLO as a legitimate representative of the Palestinian people?

Much of the answer lies in PLO policy since the Arab-Israeli war of 1973, which has consisted of a certain degree of flexibility within conformity: saying yes to the notion of territorial concessions, but no to ideological reconciliation. The policy was based on willingness to reach a settlement through a peaceful process, but only so long as recognition of Israel's right to exist and of U.N. Resolution 242 were not the basis for political negotiations. Thus, the PLO was ready to call for the establishment of a Palestinian state in the West Bank and Gaza—as long as it did not have to give up publicly the ultimate vision of a Palestinian state in all of Palestine. The organization was willing to agree on the prose of reality while at the same time maintaining the poetry of its ideology.

In this chapter I present the following arguments. First, the yes-no policy was sufficient to endow the PLO with international support for the idea of a Palestinian state in the West Bank and Gaza. But PLO reluctance to recognize both Israel's right to exist and U.N. Resolution 242, as well as to accept the West Bank–Gaza state as a permanent solution, hampered its ability to cope effectively with Israel's opposition to such a settlement. Second, until the 1982 war in Lebanon, Israel's attempts to undermine the PLO's international status and to diminish its military capability had been unsuccessful. This led the PLO to believe that its yes-no policy could be effective. Third, while the war in Lebanon dashed this hope, 'Arafat nevertheless remained reluctant to embark on a new path—to stray from the yes-no line—because he feared the uncertainties of any radical policy change.

THE MAKING OF PLO POLICY

In previous chapters I have described those post–1973 war political circumstances that played a major role in shaping the PLO's yes-no policy. Readiness on the part of Egypt, Jordan, and Syria to consider diplomatic initiatives for regaining the occupied territories increased PLO fears that a political settlement might be reached on the West Bank and Gaza without its participation. This fear led the PLO to conclude that a demonstration of political flexibility and willingness to consider territorial compromise would increase its chances of playing a role in any negotiated settlement. However, considering the fragmented structure of the PLO, endorsement of territorial compromise entailed the risk of disrupting its various factions' coexistence under one umbrella. Political flexibility, although needed to improve the PLO's chance for participation in any peace negotiations, could cause irreparable damage to PLO unity. Moreover, considering the PLO's uncertainty regarding the outcome of peace negotiations, flexibility could leave it without an organization and without a territory. Under these circumstances, the PLO could seriously endanger its status as the sole representative of the Palestinian people.

It is here that one should seek to understand why the PLO mainstream factions, especially Fatah, searched for a political formula that could be presented to the outside world as a far-reaching change in its all-or-nothing position, and, at the same time, to the Palestinian camp as a tactical move that did not alter the PLO's basic outlook. In earlier chapters I dealt with the major components of Fatah's formula and the way in which it was implemented. I have shown that Fatah initiated and welcomed peace proposals that called for territorial compromise along the lines of a two-state solution: Israel and, alongside it, a Palestinian state in the West Bank and Gaza Strip. However, Fatah made its willingness to consider such a solution dependent upon a number of preconditions. First, a complete Israeli withdrawal from the occupied territories would precede the establishment of a Palestinian state in the West Bank, the Gaza Strip, and East Jerusalem under the PLO's leadership. Second, the Israeli withdrawal and the establishment of the Palestinian state would precede any negotiations between the PLO and Israel. Third, major issues such as recognition, a peace treaty, and security guarantees to Israel would be discussed within the framework of multilateral negotiations with the participation of international and inter-Arab parties (the U.N., the superpowers, European states, and the Arab League). Fourth, the international or inter-Arab parties would guarantee both Israel's security and the settlement itself.

The logic behind such tactics is clear. By making the establishment of the Palestinian state a prerequisite to any move on the issues of recognition and a peace treaty with Israel, and by sharing or transferring responsibility for such concessions to a third party's shoulders, Fatah was able to play down its deviation from the PLO's official policy of no concessions to Israel. These tactics bore positive results. Within the PLO, Palestinian radicals were hard put to present Fatah's political moves as an ideological sellout or a betrayal of fundamental beliefs. In the international arena, Fatah's very readiness to move away from the official PLO stand helped to blur the PLO's image as an intransigent organization. In many diplomatic circles, the PLO's notion of a Palestinian state in the West Bank and Gaza encouraged the hope that it would be only a matter of time and expense until the PLO recognized Israel and accepted the West Bank–Gaza Strip state as a permanent solution.

'Arafat, however, drew a different inspiration from these achievements: the hope that he could mobilize enough diplomatic support to play a role in any negotiations and to gain territorial rewards, but without prior acceptance of either U.N. Resolution 242 or Israel's right to exist. This partially explains 'Arafat's response to Palestinian critics in the occupied territories who argued that the yes-no policy did not provide an adequate answer to Israel's creeping annexation.[2] 'Arafat proclaimed that time was on

2. See, for example, the statement by Mayor Elias Freij of Bethlehem that "in ten years there will be nothing left for the Palestinians to talk about," *al-Fajr* (East Jerusalem), Jan. 29–Feb. 4, 1982. See also *Ha'aretz* (Tel Aviv), Jan. 22, 1982.

the Palestinians' side. Israel, he claimed, suffered from an inherent weakness: its small population and sensitivity to human life played into the hands of the more numerous Arabs. Moreover, Israel's economic dependence on the United States had turned it into a nation with "imported strength"; any change in U.S. policy could overturn the situation drastically. Therefore, claims that Israel's creeping annexation of the occupied territories reduced the options for a Palestinian state were "ideological terrorism" and "fake realism."[3]

THE LIMITATIONS OF PLO POLICY

The period between 1978, when the Camp David accords were signed, and 1982, the year of the war in Lebanon, was not a favorable one for the PLO. The organization's attempts to mobilize diplomatic support in order to ensure a favorable political environment during future peace negotiations did not bear fruit. But this failure did not result in any change in the yes-no policy. The PLO continued to believe in its ability to further a settlement without either prior recognition of Israel's right to exist or acceptance of the West Bank–Gaza state as a permanent solution. Two developments during this period encouraged the organization to sustain this belief. First, the Soviet Union rejected the Camp David accords because they did not include the PLO—a reaction shared by many Western European nations. Second, Israel's policy toward the PLO in the 1980s led to increasing Israeli military pressure on the organization, but did not enable Israel to reduce the PLO's strength drastically.

The PLO and Camp David

At first glance, the PLO had every reason to be pleased with the Soviet and the Western European responses to the Camp David accords. Both the Soviet Union and the Western European nations considered a solution to the Palestinian problem unachievable

3. Voice of Palestine, May 29, 1982, as cited in *Middle East Contemporary Survey* 6 (1981–82), ed. Colin Legum, Haim Shaked, and Daniel Dishon (New York: Holmes and Meier, 1984), 335. See also *al-Musawwar* (Cairo), Dec. 31, 1982.

without the PLO's participation in any negotiated settlement. Consequently, the Soviets and the Western European community dismissed the Camp David accords as a proper basis for negotiations. Indeed, as noted in chapter 4, both of these parties proposed alternative peace plans comprising three principal elements. First, they insisted on the need to bring an end to the Israeli occupation of the Arab territories seized in 1967 and the need to recognize the right of the Palestinian people to a state (according to the Soviets) or to self-determination (in the Western European version). Second, they held that a solution to the Palestinian problem must be part of a comprehensive settlement of the Arab-Israeli conflict, reached through negotiations between all parties involved, including the PLO. Third, both plans called for the active involvement of international parties in the achieving and guaranteeing of the settlement.

Significantly, neither the 1981 Brezhnev plan nor the 1980 European Economic Community declaration met with the PLO's prerequisites for a political settlement. The Soviet peace initiative called for a permanent settlement that required the PLO to accept the "sovereignty of all states in the [Middle East] region including Israel," while the European plan referred to a settlement based on "the right to existence and to security of all states in the region including Israel. . . . "[4] Thus, although the PLO was able to assure broad international support for its participation in any negotiated settlement, it was far less effective in recruiting international backing for a settlement that would not require clear public recognition of Israel's right to exist.

By the same token, the rejection of the Camp David accords by the vast majority of the Arab nations could not compensate the PLO for lack of international support for a settlement under its favored conditions. It is true that the Arab summit convened in Baghdad in November 1978 called the accords "harmful to the rights of the Palestinian people" and agreed upon the duty of all Arab nations to "furnish aid and facilities to the struggle of the Palestinian resistance in all its forms through the PLO . . . for the

---

4. For more details on the Soviet peace proposal see *Current Digest of the Soviet Press* 23/3 (March 25, 1981): 8. On the European proposal see "European Community, Venice Declaration, June 13, 1980," (AP release).

sake of the liberation and the recovery of the national rights of the Arab people of Palestine, including their right to return, to self-determination, and the establishment of an independent state on their national soil."[5] But Arab verbal opposition to Camp David could not hide the discrepancy that has always existed between Arab public commitment to the Palestinian cause and actual practice.

The Arab states back the PLO either (as in the case of Saudi Arabia) because they use it as an instrument in their inter-Arab policy to push their adversaries into a defensive stance. Or because they find it convenient to pretend, through qualified support of the PLO, that they accept the resolutions of all the Arab conferences while they are actually following a different policy (Jordan). Or they do so as a derivative of a broader policy in the global context (South Yemen).[6]

In this sense, Arab opposition to Camp David should be read more as the outcome of narrow calculations by each Arab nation than as genuine concern for the PLO and the Palestinian cause. It is this discrepancy between Arab words and deeds regarding the Palestinian cause that led Shafiq al-Hut, chief of the PLO's Beirut bureau, to argue that "none of the Arab leaders has ever been committed to an independent Palestinian state. I have checked President Carter's assertion that no Arab leader has ever spoken to him about a Palestinian state. . . . They do not see a need for a Palestinian state. . . ."[7]

Despite the PLO's failure to assure sufficient diplomatic support for a settlement along yes-no lines, the organization still believed that time was on its side. The difficulties encountered by the three parties to the Camp David accords—the U.S., Egypt, and Israel—in persuading Jordan and West Bank Palestinian leaders to join the autonomy talks led the PLO to the conclusion that the likelihood of furthering a settlement without its participation was negligible. The deadlock reached in the autonomy talks strengthened this assessment, and American and Egyptian attempts to overcome

5. See *Journal of Palestine Studies* 8/2 (1979): 203.

6. Dan Schueftan, "The PLO after Lebanon," *Jerusalem Quarterly* 28 (1983): 13.

7. Shafiq al-Hut to the Saudi weekly *al-Sharq al-Awsat* (Riyadh), Oct. 21, 1983.

the deadlock by persuading the PLO to let Palestinian leaders in the Israeli-occupied territories participate in the talks on its behalf also made it clear that the PLO's role in any further settlement had not been significantly undermined by the Camp David agreements.[8]

The PLO and Israel in the Early 1980s

The autonomy talks, then, encouraged the PLO to pursue its yes-no policy. But this policy became increasingly problematic due both to developments in the Arab world and to increasing Israeli military pressure. In September 1980 a war broke out between Iran and Iraq that soon caused a sharp division within the Arab world—between supporters of Iran and of Iraq—and pushed the Palestinian problem away from the center of the Arab world's attention.[9] This deterioration in the PLO's position in the inter-Arab arena was followed by an increasing number of Israeli military operations against the organization. South Lebanon, the PLO's only autonomous base and its main area of concentration, became a frequent target for Israeli air, sea, and land raids. In the period between September 1980 and August 1981 alone, forty-six such attacks were carried out.[10]

The massive operations reflected a new Israeli policy of preemptive strikes against the PLO, which derived from the inability of the six-thousand-man United Nations Interim Force in Lebanon (UNIFIL)—formed by the Security Council in 1978—to prevent the PLO from shelling and infiltrating Israel's northern settlements. Israel's new policy sought "to keep up constant pressure against PLO bases; to cause maximum losses to those stationed there and maximum damage to base installations; to ob-

8. For more details on these American and Egyptian attempts see chapter 4.

9. For more details see Miller, *The PLO and the Politics of Survival*, 101–02. On the military and political implications of the Iran-Iraq war for the Arab world, see Mark A. Heller, *The Iran-Iraq War: Implications for Third Parties*, 23 (Tel Aviv: Jaffee Center for Strategic Studies, Tel Aviv University, 1984).

10. For more on Israeli military activities against the PLO in South Lebanon, see Helena Cobban, *The Palestinian Liberation Organization: People, Power and Politics* (London: Cambridge University Press, 1984), 108, 111–12: *Middle East Contemporary Survey* 5 (1980–81), ed. Colin Legum, Haim Shaked, and Daniel Dishon (New York: Holmes and Meier, 1981), 214.

struct their operations and generally to direct their main efforts and energies to defense."[11]

The new Israeli policy was also supposed to serve a broader political goal. Prime Minister Menahem Begin, who came to power in 1977, and his minister of agriculture, Ariel Sharon, assumed that the more intense its military operations against the PLO, the better the chances of weakening the organization's standing in the international and local arenas. If it succeeded, Israel would be able to further a political settlement of the West Bank issue through negotiations with local Palestinian leaders in the occupied territories—without PLO participation.[12]

However, based on the immediate results of Israel's military activity in South Lebanon, the PLO decided that it would be able to withstand Israeli pressure, upsetting Israeli political intentions regarding the West Bank. The PLO was encouraged by the fact that, despite the Israeli attacks, it was still able to reciprocate by shelling Israeli settlements or carrying out attacks within the West Bank or Israel proper.[13]

Israel's preemptive-strike policy also made the PLO revise its military structure and its operational modes. In 1980 the PLO reached the conclusion that, under the changed circumstances, its strategy of revolutionary guerrilla warfare was no longer suitable. In order to withstand Israeli air attacks and artillery bombardments, the organization decided to regroup its forces into regular military units under a single command (*jaysh nizami*).[14] This move in effect transformed PLO units in Lebanon into a semiregular army and led both to the formation of battalion and company units and to a massive influx of heavy armaments, including artillery pieces, tanks, and anti-aircraft missiles.[15] The PLO's new artillery

11. *Middle East Contemporary Survey* 5 (1980–81), 214.

12. On the effects of this Israeli policy on the West Bank see Moshe Ma'oz, *Palestinian Leadership on the West Bank* (London: Frank Cass, 1984), chap. 4.

13. In the period between September 1980 and August 1981, the PLO carried out 136 artillery and Katyusha attacks against Israeli cities and towns in Galilee, and 174 operations within Israel, the West Bank, and Gaza. For more details, see *Middle East Contemporary Survey* 5 (1980–81), 220.

14. *Shu'un Filastiniyya* (Aug. 1980): 35, 46–47.

15. For more details see *al-Nashra al-Istratijiyya* (London), July 30, 1981; also *al-'Amal* (Beirut), Nov. 11, 1981.

deployment came into full play during the July 1981 military confrontation with Israel.

In mid-July 1981, following five consecutive days of Israeli air raids against PLO strongholds in South Lebanon and against Fatah and DFLP headquarters in West Beirut, the PLO commenced a massive shelling of Israel's north. Over ten days the PLO fired 1230 advanced Katyusha rockets and artillery shells on settlements stretching from Nahariya along the Mediterranean coast to Kiryat Shemona in the east.[16] Despite its military sophistication, the Israeli High Command was unable to counter the PLO artillery successfully, and the shelling continued. The Israeli air force was hard-pressed to pinpoint the location of the artillery and Katyusha launchers, which were fired and then immediately camouflaged. Also, the air force chose not to attack PLO artillery positions in the Syrian-controlled Biqaʿ Valley. "Although day by day, more PLO guns were put out of action . . . some 40 percent of the population of Kiryat Shemona fled the town. . . . Never had Israel witnessed such a mass exodus from a settlement under attack."[17]

The Israeli cabinet's decision to respond positively to a U.S.-initiated cease-fire agreement in July and its rejection of the military's proposal for a large-scale ground operation against the PLO reinforced the PLO's assessment of Israel's difficulties in driving it out of, or even drastically reducing its military presence in, South Lebanon. Thus, in the summer of 1981, the PLO did not think Israel could possibly push it to the sidelines by initiating peace negotiations without its participation.

Waiting for Sharon

The 1981 appointment of Ariel Sharon as minister of defense in Menahem Begin's second cabinet marked a turning point in Israel's attitude toward the PLO. While many Israeli political figures doubted Israel's ability to diminish the PLO either militarily or politically, Sharon held a very different view. He believed that Israel could achieve both goals by bringing an end to the PLO's presence in Lebanon and creating a new political order there based

16. Zeʾev Schiff and Ehud Yaʿari, *Israel's Lebanon War* (New York: Simon and Schuster, 1984), 36.
17. Ibid.

on a strong central government that would sign a peace treaty with Israel. "Unless Lebanon has a government that will sign a peace treaty with Israel, everything can revert to its former state. And a government of that kind cannot come into being as long as the [Palestinian] terrorists control southern Lebanon and two-thirds of Beirut, and as long as the Syrians control whole sections of Lebanon. . . ."[18]

Sharon assumed that expulsion of the PLO from Lebanon and the establishment of a strong Lebanese government would increase the PLO's dependence on Syria and other radical Arab nations. As a result, the PLO's political maneuverability in the international, inter-Arab, and Palestinian arenas would decrease, and alternative local leadership, willing to enter into negotiations with Israel about the establishment of a self-governing authority in accordance with the autonomy plan, would emerge in the West Bank. This would allow Israel to maintain its military presence and political influence in the occupied territories for the foreseeable future.[19]

The PLO's leaders closely followed political developments within Israel, and were aware of Sharon's growing influence within the second Begin cabinet. In Begin's first cabinet there were, in addition to Sharon, three other senior ministers with wide military experience: Minister of Defense Ezer Weizman, Foreign Minister Moshe Dayan, and Deputy Prime Minister Yigael Yadin. All three shared a common pragmatic view toward the Arab world and the PLO. Absolute truths and millennial visions were alien to their political thought. And, in contrast to Sharon, they were aware of the factors that would limit any Israeli attempt to solve the Palestinian problem through military means. The absence of these three from Begin's second cabinet enabled Sharon to emerge as Begin's chief adviser on security matters. In his new position as minister of defense he was able to convince the prime minister of the necessity of taking strong measures against the PLO.

In addition to Begin, the new foreign minister, Yitzhak Shamir, the IDF chief of staff, Rafael Eitan, and Israel's ambassador to the United States, Moshe Arens, were known within Israeli po-

---

18. Ibid., 42.
19. See Sharon's interview in *Time*, June 21, 1982; also *Ha'aretz*, May 23, 1982.

litical circles as supporters of a hard-line policy toward the PLO. In February 1982, Ambassador Arens declared that an Israeli invasion of Lebanon was "only a matter of time."[20] And in May of that year, Chief of Staff Eitan stated that "having built up a military machine costing billions, I must put it to use. . . . Tomorrow, perhaps, I will be in Beirut."[21]

The PLO was also aware of diplomatic efforts undertaken by Begin and Sharon aimed at securing U.S. support for, or at least acquiescence in, a large-scale military operation against the organization. The Begin government was "attempting to persuade President Reagan's administration that there could be no real sequel to the Egyptian-Israeli peace treaty unless the Palestinians' base in Lebanon was eliminated."[22] Given the fact that President Reagan and Secretary of State Haig held far more hawkish views toward the PLO than their predecessors in the Carter Administration, the PLO could not dismiss the possibility that Begin and Sharon would convince the Americans that, if they wished Israel to be more forthcoming in eventual peace negotiations, the PLO must first be made powerless.

The PLO was also aware of contacts between Israel and the Christian Phalangist militias in Lebanon, which had grown closer after the Lebanese civil war of 1975–76. The Phalangist militias were formed by Pierre Gemayal in 1936. In the 1970s they were led by him and his sons, Bashir and Amin. Their major goal was the preservation of the Maronite Christians' political and economic might in the face of a growing challenge from the Muslim community. Over the years, the influx of 'foreigners,' Palestinian refugees, increased this challenge. The PLO's success in becoming a major political and military power among the Palestinian population in Lebanon, and its cooperation with the Lebanese left, composed of Sunni Muslims and Druze, presented a grave threat to Maronite political hegemony in Lebanon.[23] Thus Sharon's mil-

20. *Washington Post*, Feb. 26, 1982.
21. As cited in *MERIP Reports: Middle East Research and Information Project* 12/6–7 (Sept.–Oct. 1982): 4.
22. *Economist* (London), June 12, 1982.
23. For more on the Maronite Christians and their role in Lebanon's politics see

itary plan to rid Lebanon of the PLO had the Phalangists' blessing. High-ranking Israeli officers, including Sharon himself in January 1982, who visited Phalangist leaders perceived a growing readiness among the Phalangists to cooperate with Israel in order to expel the PLO from Lebanon.

Finally, the PLO had managed to obtain accurate military information on Israel, including many of the operational details of the Israeli invasion plans. It knew the Israelis intended to launch a large-scale military operation against the PLO that would include the destruction of PLO headquarters in Beirut.[24] However, encouraged by the results of its July 1981 confrontation with Israel, the PLO assumed that once again Israel would be unable to remove it from the Middle East political game by military means. On the contrary, the PLO was convinced that an Israeli invasion of Lebanon would strengthen its stand in the international political arena and increase its chances of furthering a settlement under favorable conditions.

The PLO's assessment was based on four assumptions. First, in the event of a genuine Israeli invasion, the PLO would be capable of delaying a swift Israeli advance. PLO military units located within the Palestinian refugee camps would prevent unimpeded Israeli maneuverability in South Lebanon. Then too, factors of geography and improved weaponry enhanced the PLO position. "Our missiles," claimed a high-ranking PLO officer,

are spread out through all the wadis of South Lebanon. . . . If the Jews so desire, they will be able to destroy all of them. But that will take a long time and cost them many casualties. Further, we have more sophisticated weapons than ever before. Their air force will not be able to solve the problem. The Israelis may destroy a position here or there, but there will always remain enough positions in order to turn the north [of Israel] into hell on earth. It will take them many days to destroy our forces in the south [of Lebanon].[25]

Itamar Rabinovich, *The War for Lebanon, 1970–1983* (Ithaca: Cornell University Press, 1984), 61–65.

24. See, for example, the interview with ʿArafat's deputy Abu Jihad in *al-Majalla* (London), March 13, 1982; also *Yediot Ahronoth* (Tel Aviv), May 31, 1985.

25. *Bamerhav*, (June 1982): 14.

Second, the longer the PLO held out against the Israelis—Yasir ʿArafat estimated ten days—the greater the chances that Syria would join the fighting. "The Syrians must enter if the fighting lasts, otherwise the way to Damascus will be open to Sharon's forces."[26] Syrian participation in the fighting would lead to the involvement of other Arab states: "It is enough that only one Arab state makes war on Israel . . . in order that all the Arab states join in" stated Fatah leader Abu Iyad. "The Fedayeen in South Lebanon . . . can carry out a war against Israel that will lead to such a development."[27]

Third, a new Arab-Israeli war would jeopardize the security and stability of a region crucial to the West, and particularly to the United States. An Arab-Israeli war endangers "the fragile stability of Saudi Arabia and other pro-Western regimes in the region, threatening to tilt the inter-power balance in the region in the U.S.S.R.'s favor and to generate an even broader and more perilous conflict."[28] Even if Israel managed to gain U.S. support for initiating a military operation, it would be hard-pressed to drum up support for completing it. The U.S. and its allies, fearing the results of all-out war, would pressure Israel to cease military operations before achieving its major goal of eliminating the PLO's political and military presence in Lebanon.[29]

Fourth, there was a good chance that the invasion of Lebanon would make the U.S. increase pressure on Israel to agree to a compromise formula that would enable the PLO to participate in the peace process. This was because the West, fearing continued political instability from the persistence of the Palestinian problem, would recognize the key role that the PLO should play in any negotiated settlement.

In sum, the PLO leadership was convinced that an Israeli in-

26. Ibid.

27. Interview in *Le Matin* (Paris), March 2, 1982; cited in ʿal-Hamishmar (Tel Aviv), March 10, 1982.

28. Schueftan, "The PLO after Lebanon," 10.

29. For more details on this argument see Zvi Lanir, "Tfisat derekh ha-maʾavak ha-mezuyyan shel Ashaf be-mivhan milhemet shlom ha-Galil" (The PLO's perception of the armed struggle in the light of Operation Peace for Galilee), *Maʿarakhot* 284 (Oct. 1982): 17.

vasion of Lebanon would end in a Palestinian political victory. The possibility that the invasion would lead to the opposite result seemed unlikely. "We await Sharon and welcome him. Let him come and see who we are," exclaimed a high-ranking PLO officer to a *Bamerhav* correspondent. "Did not [President] Nasser [of Egypt] say the same thing to [Israeli Chief of Staff] Rabin in 1967?" asked the correspondent. "We are Palestinians, not Egyptians," was the reply.[30]

THE WAR IN LEBANON AND THE FEAR OF FRESH STARTS

The Israeli invasion of Lebanon proved the illusory nature of the PLO's assessments regarding its ability to delay the Israeli military move. On June 6, 1982, 40,000 Israeli troops in hundreds of tanks and armored personnel carriers rolled across the 33-mile-long border into South Lebanon. Two days later, Israeli seaborne troops landed on the Lebanese coast at Sidon near the mouth of the Zaharani River. The Israel air force meanwhile continued an intense bombing attack upon Palestinian refugee camps in the south and around Beirut that had begun two days earlier.

The Israeli invasion took the form of a three-pronged attack (see map 3). On the west, the forces advanced toward Tyre, situated thirteen miles north along the coastal road. Beaufort Castle, long a PLO stronghold, was the initial goal of the force that moved through the central area under UNIFIL control. And in the east, Israeli troops advanced in the direction of the Biqaʿ valley, then occupied by Syrian forces, and the site of Syrian anti-aircraft missile positions. On the ground, the Syrians suffered heavy losses trying to prevent the Israeli advance. In the air, more than ninety Syrian jets were brought down by the Israel air force. In addition, Israeli planes destroyed the Syrian anti-aircraft missile installations in the Biqaʿ.

PLO units in someʿ of the Palestinian camps along the coast initially held their positions in the face of an intense land, sea, and air bombardment. Yet this did not halt the Israeli advance. The Israelis bypassed these trouble spots and moved swiftly northward.

30. *Bamerhav* (June 1982): 14.

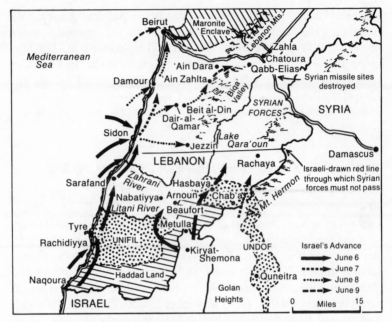

Map 3   The Israeli Invasion of Lebanon (from the Economist, *June 12, 1982)*

Within two days, Israeli forces had conquered Sidon and Damour, to its north. By June 9, the Israel Defense Forces were entering the outskirts of Beirut.[31]

With Israeli forces nearing Beirut, and Syria reluctant to take any initiative against the invading troops, the PLO was in a difficult situation. All of South Lebanon, the Lebanese skies, and the coastline were under Israeli control. Beirut was cut off by land and by sea.

The reluctance of the Arab nations and the Soviet Union to intervene on behalf of the PLO weakened its chances either to break the Israeli siege of Beirut or to negotiate an agreement that would allow PLO forces to remain in the city. With the Israelis determined to see the PLO out of Lebanon, the most the PLO

31. For a more detailed description of the Israeli invasion of Lebanon, see Rabinovich, *The War for Lebanon*, 135–43, and Schiff and Ya'ari, *Israel's Lebanon War*, chaps. 8 and 9.

Table 8   Distribution of PLO Forces, August 1982

	Lebanese Estimate	Israeli Estimate	Affiliation of Evacuees
Syria	8125	7448	Varied
Tunisia	982	973	Varied
Southern Yemen	700	518	Varied
Algeria	588	560	Mostly Fatah
Sudan	488	472	Mostly Fatah
Yemen	446	415	Fatah
Jordan	265	265	Palestine Liberation Army (PLA)
Iraq	132	132	Arab Liberation Front
Total	11726	10783	

Source: *New York Times*, Sept. 2, 1982.

could do was to seek an American guarantee for the safe evacuation of its fighters to other Arab states. The Israeli invasion of Lebanon and the siege of Beirut caused the withdrawal of 11,000 PLO members from Lebanon and their removal to seven Arab states in late August 1982 (see table 8). Only about 6000 Palestinian guerrillas remained in the Syrian-controlled part of Lebanon.

The destruction of the PLO infrastructure in Lebanon and the scattering of its units to the four corners of the Arab world severely undermined its military capability as well as its political freedom of action. Thus the PLO's ability to continue thwarting political initiatives that ran counter to its interests suffered a setback. This weakness was most apparent during the talks held between King Hussein and Yasir ʿArafat in the fall of 1982 and winter of 1983— talks aimed at reaching a formula that would enable the PLO to participate in President Reagan's Middle East peace initiative of September 1982.

The key point in the Reagan plan was that a peaceful settlement of the West Bank and Gaza problem could not be achieved through "the formation of an independent Palestinian state in those territories. Nor [could it be] achieved on the basis of Israeli sovereignty or permanent control over the West Bank and Gaza." Instead, President Reagan regarded the establishment of a self-governing Palestinian entity, located in the West Bank and Gaza Strip and linked in some kind of association with Jordan, as "the best chance for a durable, just and lasting peace."[32]

In order to encourage Jordanian and other Arab participation in the negotiations, Reagan demanded an Israeli settlement freeze in the occupied territories. "Further settlement activity is in no way necessary for the security of Israel and only diminishes the confidence of the Arabs that a final outcome can be freely and fairly negotiated." In addition, President Reagan reaffirmed U.S. support for U.N. Security Council Resolution 242 and stated that, in return for peace, the "withdrawal provision of Resolution 242 applies to all fronts, including the West Bank." Finally, the President stated that "the permanent status of Jerusalem should be decided by negotiation."[33]

In comparison to previous peace plans, the Reagan proposal came closest to the 1972 Jordanian plan for a federation between the West and East banks and the Gaza Strip. This similarity between the two plans could explain why King Hussein and other Jordanian officials publicly supported Reagan's peace plan, calling on the PLO and the Arab nations to back it. The American plan, claimed Amman, provided a unique opportunity for a political breakthrough toward Israeli withdrawal from the occupied territories.[34]

The PLO response was far less enthusiastic. A statement issued by the PLO's Central Council, a sixty-member consultative group, denounced the Reagan plan for ignoring "the right of our people to self-determination and to establish its own independent state under the leadership of the PLO, without which there can be no lasting peace in the Middle East."[35] The council's statement also criticized President Reagan for not recognizing the PLO as the

32. *New York Times*, Sept. 2, 1982.

33. Ibid.

34. See, for example, the interview with the Jordanian foreign minister Marwan al-Qasim in *al-Hawadith* (Beirut), Nov. 14, 1982; also Asher Susser, *Bein Yarden le-Falastin* (Between Jordan and Palestine) (Tel Aviv: Hakibutz Hameuhad, 1983): 187–88.

35. *New York Times*, Nov. 27, 1982.

sole legitimate representative of the Palestinian people. However, the council did not reject the Reagan plan outright.

ʿArafat's response was similar in tone. He cautiously noted that the American plan "contains positive aspects."[36] Going into detail, ʿArafat stated in an interview to the Egyptian weekly *Akhir Saʿa*, that "it is the first time that the American administration has regarded the West Bank and Gaza as occupied territory and has spoken of an end to the establishment of new [Israeli] settlements. However, the plan does not relate to the basic needs of the Palestinians: recognition of our legitimate rights and particularly the right to establish an independent state."[37]

ʿArafat's decision not to reject the U.S. plan outright derived from his growing belief that the war in Lebanon had significantly enhanced the U.S. position in the Middle East. Having lost its only autonomous base for political and military maneuvering, PLO willingness to consider some form of participation in the American peace initiative seemed the most viable option open to it to reduce the dual risk of political isolation and negotiations without its participation.

As Jordan became the focus of American diplomatic efforts in the Middle East, the likelihood of the PLO joining the peace process without working through Jordan was narrowed. And given the similarity between the American and Jordanian plans regarding the political future of the West Bank and Gaza, incorporation of the PLO into the American peace initiative entailed the risk of being steered toward a settlement that would not meet the PLO's quest for sovereignty. However, ʿArafat assumed that as long as the Arab world remained faithful to its official stand of recognizing the Palestinian right to an independent state, King Hussein's ability to join the peace process along the lines of Reagan's plan was limited.

Following the war in Lebanon, political trends that emerged within the Arab world appeared to support ʿArafat's assessment. The Fez summit of September 6–8, 1982, rejected President Rea-

36. *Newsweek*, Sept. 20, 1982.
37. *Akhir Saʿa* (Cairo), Jan. 19, 1983.

gan's notion of a self-governing Palestinian entity in the West Bank and Gaza linked to Jordan. Instead, the Fez resolutions emphasized the Palestinians' right to a state of their own under the leadership of the PLO.[38] King Hussein's response to the Fez summit decisions supported ʿArafat's assessment concerning the limitations of Jordanian readiness to enter into peace negotiations solely on the basis of the Reagan plan. In interviews with the Western media, the king described the Fez resolutions as "a major milestone in the annals of the Arab world."[39] Going further, Hussein invited ʿArafat to hold discussions to define future relations between Jordan and the PLO within the framework of a peace agreement.[40] ʿArafat took these developments as an indication of Jordan's awareness that participation in any peace negotiation would depend on its willingness to cooperate with the PLO. To achieve such cooperation meant taking into account the PLO's demand for a Palestinian state in the West Bank and Gaza. With this assessment, ʿArafat responded positively to Hussein's invitation.

As the talks progressed, however, it became clear that there was little chance of King Hussein making any concessions on the issue of Palestinian sovereignty. During his meetings with ʿArafat, Hussein was willing to discuss the idea of a Palestinian state in the West Bank and Gaza in confederation with Jordan. In practice, however, he proposed the confederation solution in a way that drastically narrowed the possibility of an independent Palestinian state. To ensure that in any future settlement the West Bank would remain under Amman's authority, King Hussein insisted on setting up the confederation *prior* to the establishment of the Palestinian state in the West Bank and Gaza, rejecting categorically ʿArafat's demand for doing things in the opposite order.[41]

Amman's hostility to the Palestinian state idea also affected its

38. For more on the Fez summit resolutions, see *Daily Report: The Middle East and Africa*, Sept. 10, 1982.

39. King Hussein's interview on BBC-TV, Sept. 13, 1982, cited in the *New York Times*, Sept. 15, 1982.

40. See ibid., Sep. 22, 1982.

41. For more on King Hussein's position in negotiations with ʿArafat on the confederation issue, see Thomas L. Friedman, "Arafat-Hussein Talks: Reagan Peace Plan at Stake," *New York Times*, Oct. 11, 1982; Eric Rouleau, "The Future of the PLO," *Foreign Affairs* 62/1 (1983): 151.

position on the issue of Palestinian representation in peace talks. While 'Arafat called for a joint Arab delegation to the peace negotiations including PLO and Jordanian representatives as well as additional Arabs, King Hussein wanted a delegation of only Jordanians and Palestinians. At a meeting with Jordanian leaders in early 1983, the king noted that future ties between Jordan and the Palestinians were "a matter for the two sides only. No one else must be allowed to interfere in the forging of these ties or the weakening of them, be he Arab or foreigner, from the east or the west.... An agreement between the [two] sides will constitute the correct Arab position...."[42]

Later on, when 'Arafat retreated from his original position and agreed to a joint Jordanian-Palestinian delegation, the king refused to accept the PLO as the sole negotiating party on behalf of the Palestinians. Instead, Amman insisted on the inclusion of West Bank Palestinian representatives in the Jordanian-Palestinian mission.[43] Behind Amman's position lay the assessment that in any eventual peace negotiation, the existence of divergent, sometimes conflicting interests between the PLO and the West Bank would make it difficult for the PLO to enforce a united position among the Palestinian members of the delegation. Under such conditions Jordan would have a better chance to cope effectively with those PLO demands that ran counter to Jordanian national interests.

King Hussein's tactics of agreeing in principle to the Palestinians' quest for self-determination and a state of their own while in practice taking safety measures to prevent such a development are not a new phenomenon. Since Jordan took over the West Bank in 1948, the political goals of the Jordanian regime and the Palestinians have seldom coincided. Recovery of Palestine from the Jews and the establishment of Palestinian or Arab rule over the entire territory of Palestine (which was divided among Israel, Jordan, and Egypt) has been the central political aspiration of many Palestinians. Amman, by contrast, has sought to gain the loyalty of

---

42. *Akhir Sa'a* (Cairo), Jan. 19, 1983.

43. See "Mismakhee Hussein-Ashaf: ha-Heskem shelo nehtam" (The Hussein-PLO documents: The agreement that was not signed), *Koteret Rashit* (Jerusalem), July 13, 1983.

and control over the Palestinians in order to integrate part of Palestine—the West Bank—into the Kingdom of Jordan.

In so doing, Amman kept the Palestinians' ultimate goal outside the realm of discussion. It continually declared that its political objectives were identical with those of the Palestinians. Thus, it was careful not to challenge publicly the resolutions of the highest inter-Arab forum, the Arab summit, which recognized the Palestinians' right to have their own political organization (the PLO), to cultivate their own entity, and to establish their own sovereign state. Indeed, any differences between the two parties were, as presented by the Jordanian government, artificial and temporary, derived not so much from a dispute over the Palestinian right to self-determination as over the best choice of tactics. This distinction between the fundamental and the tactical levels—the hereafter and the here and now—enabled Jordan to carry out a policy that was, in fact, incompatible with the PLO's political goal.

Nowhere was this ability to manipulate PLO national aspirations more apparent than in the post–1973 war era. In 1974, for example, Jordan endorsed the Rabat summit resolution that recognized the PLO as the sole legitimate representative of the Palestinian people. Jordan also supported the Rabat resolution that stated that any territory in the West Bank evacuated by Israel would be handed over to the PLO. In 1978 Jordan joined in a Baghdad summit resolution supporting the Palestinian right to a state. Jordan also conformed with the Baghdad summit resolution to form a joint committee with the PLO for distribution of $150 million in funds to West Bank local bodies. However, these Jordanian gestures toward the PLO were really tactical moves enabling Jordan to maintain its political influence in the West Bank, not signs of its willingness to lose the West Bank to the PLO. While Jordan publicly endorsed the Arab summit resolutions concerning the Palestinian issue, it continued in close contact with local West Bank institutions and established high-level committees to deal with day-to-day issues. Jordan also continued to pay the salaries of West Bank officials who served under the Jordanian administration in the pre–1967 period. Moreover, in 1979 Jordan decided to issue new identity cards to residents of both the East and West banks,

emphasizing the strong ties between the two areas.[44] Amman justified its activity by claiming that the West Bank was still a part
of Jordan; therefore it was in duty bound to continue caring for
the interests of its inhabitants.

Yet, despite Amman's success in legitimizing its activity and
maintaining its influence on the West Bank, it is worthwhile noting
the stumbling-blocks Jordan encountered in furthering a settlement
that ran counter to PLO interests. These found vivid expression
in the Hussein-'Arafat talks on the issue of a Jordanian-Palestine
confederation. On the one hand, King Hussein rejected 'Arafat's
demand that Jordan agree to the establishment of a Palestinian
state prior to the confederation, thus bringing the talks to a close
in April 1983. On the other, due to changes in Israeli policy toward
the West Bank in the early 1980s, Amman's unwillingness to make
concessions to the PLO on the issue of sovereignty seemed to place
the kingdom in an intolerable position.

Until the late 1970s, one might argue, Jordan, in contemplating
a political settlement that might require far-reaching concessions
to the PLO, regarded the continuity of an Israeli occupation as
the lesser of two evils.[45] Amman's position could be seen as a
product of the Israeli policy of the time, which excluded annexation
and favored negotiation with Jordan regarding the future of the
occupied territories. After 1981, however, Jordanian fears of Israeli annexation of the West Bank were exacerbated because of
various steps taken by the second Likud government. These included a marked increase in the rate of settlement accompanied
by a heavy-handed policy toward West Bank leaders and institutions. In addition, Israel encouraged the cultivation of an alternative Palestinian leadership on the West Bank, one that would
be willing to cooperate with Israel.

Most of all, Jordanian officials suspected that the annexation
process would lead to the emigration of thousands of Palestinians
from the West Bank into Jordan. This appraisal was based on
public statements by central figures in the Likud cabinet—partic-

---

44. Susser, *Bein Yarden le-Falastin*, 173–4.
45. For more on this argument see ibid., 145.

ularly Minister of Defense Ariel Sharon and Foreign Minister Yit-zhak Shamir—who claimed that "Jordan is . . . the Palestinian state." A series of political and military moves by Israel, including the bombing of the Iraqi nuclear reactor in May 1981, the annex-ation of the Golan Heights in December of that year, and the invasion of Lebanon in June 1982, augmented Amman's fears "that Israel will also use force against Jordan in order to create an al-ternative Palestinian homeland."[46] Under these circumstances, Jordan did not appear to have much choice but to accelerate move-ment toward a political settlement, even if it necessitated political concessions to the PLO.

However, a broader look at the complex relations between Jor-dan and the PLO on the one hand, and Jordan and Israel on the other, lead one to doubt Jordan's readiness to adopt such a line. Considering Jordan's and the PLO's longstanding political disputes and conflicting motives and aspirations, Jordanian concessions to the PLO on the issue of sovereignty could radically undermine Amman's ability to maintain its control over the Palestinian pop-ulation of the East Bank. Such a development would increase the threat to the Hashemite dynasty's existence. On the other hand, the prolonged history of Israeli-Jordanian collaboration, based on a de facto coalition against Palestinian aspirations for statehood, as well as a broad-based opposition within Israel to the Likud government's stand toward the West Bank and Jordan, minimized the actuality of the Israeli threat to annex the West Bank and expel its population.

The probability of Jordan's making concessions to the PLO on the sovereignty question decreased even more following the May 1983 mutiny within Fatah and the July 1984 formation of a new government in Israel headed by Labor Party leader Shimon Peres. Ostensibly, the mutiny in Fatah broke out as a result of ʿArafat's appointment of two officers to high military posts as a reward for their loyalty, even though, according to the rebels, they had failed to carry out their duties during the 1982 war in Lebanon. But it soon became clear that the quarrel over appointments reflected a fundamental disagreement over ʿArafat's decision not to exclude

46. Ibid., 185, 186.

the possibility of a political settlement and especially focused on his willingness to hold negotiations with King Hussein on the confederation issue. The rebels, led by two members of the Fatah Central Committee, Abu Salih and Ahmad Qadri, and by two colonels, Abu Musa and Khalid al-ʿAmla, feared that ʿArafat might reach an agreement with King Hussein based on the Jordanian conditions. Nor were they placated when ʿArafat refused to sign a memorandum of agreement with Hussein because the king failed to meet ʿArafat's demands on the issues of sovereignty and Palestinian representation in eventual peace talks. "He [ʿArafat] did not sign," the rebels announced, "but nearly did so. If it were not for our efforts, ʿArafat would be in Washington today."[47]

In the course of talks between Fatah and the rebels, the latter agreed to end the mutiny only if ʿArafat opposed any compromise with Israel, rejected the Reagan and Fez plans, and refused to renew talks with Jordan. They also demanded that the PLO rely exclusively on armed struggle "to liberate all of Palestine."[48] Syrian military aid to the rebel forces, together with active support from Jibril's PFLP-GC, the pro-Syrian al-Saʿiqa, and the Fatah military units stationed in the Syrian-controlled parts of Lebanon, strained relations between the rebels and Fatah to breaking point. The ensuring battles fought between the rebels and ʿArafat's supporters in North Lebanon—which led to the exodus of ʿArafat and his men from Tripoli in December 1983—threatened to turn the rift within the PLO into a permanent split.

Under this threat of inner division, ʿArafat's bargaining power dwindled, and his chances of gaining concessions from Jordan on the issue of Palestinian sovereignty in the West Bank were reduced. But ʿArafat refused to accept the rebels' demands and turn away from the political process. Moreover, after Tripoli, he renewed the dialogue with Jordan. His decision to convene the seventeenth Palestine National Council in Amman in November 1984 and his agreement with King Hussein on the confederation issue three

47. *al-Kifah al-ʿArabi* (Beirut), May 30, 1983.

48. On the rebels' demands from ʿArafat see *al-Hawadith*, June 17, 1983; *al-Safir*, June 28, 1983; also Adam M. Garfinkle, "Source of al-Fatah Mutiny," *Orbis* 27/3 (1983): 631–38.

months later, at the price of an unprecedented split within the
PLO (see appendix 2), indicate just how far ʿArafat was prepared
to go to maintain contact with Jordan.

ʿArafat and his followers' refusal to embrace the rebels' hard-
line insistence on armed struggle as the only way to liberate Palestine is understandable. Were they to adopt such an intransigent
line, they would only increase the Palestinian movement's isolation
on the inter-Arab and international scenes. "The missing side is
always the one that loses," claimed ʿArafat's political adviser Hani
al-Hasan. It was in the PLO's interest to be involved in political
activity and not to exclude the possibility of a settlement through
political means.[49]

Yet the PLO's need to rely on diplomacy to assure participation
in any negotiated settlement does not explain ʿArafat's decision
to exert so much effort to maintaining his dialogue with Jordan.
Certainly Fatah could produce ample arguments to justify the importance of political cooperation with Amman irrespective of the
fundamental disagreements between the two sides. Given the desire of the Palestinians in the West Bank to see an end to the Israeli
occupation in the near future, an uncompromising PLO position
toward Jordan would increase the risk of losing support from the
local population and pushing it into the Jordanian camp. Thus,
noted Hani al-Hasan, "No Palestinian strategist can afford to take
his eyes off Jordan for even a moment. The only Arab state able
to replace us [as a partner to a political settlement] is Jordan."
Moreover, "No Palestinian strategist can ignore the geographical
fact that the Palestinian state-to-be will have two entrances: one
from the East Bank and the second from Gaza. To ensure free
access to the West Bank there can be no chance but to have
cooperative ties with Jordan."[50]

However, given the sharp decline in ʿArafat's bargaining power
in the aftermath of the war in Lebanon and his meager chances
of generating a radical change in the Jordanian position regarding
the Palestinian state, one wonders what motivated ʿArafat to maintain his reliance upon a third party. Would it not be more promising
for ʿArafat to replace the lazy ox—reliance on a third party—for

49. Interview in *Filastin al-Thawra* (Beirut), April 21, 1984.
50. Ibid.

the strong and quick-footed horse of prior recognition of Israel, dramatically increasing his chances of getting the PLO's wagon out of the mud and leading it to its territorial goal?

Such a decision would carry political risks within the PLO rank and file, and the PLO could not be sure that prior recognition would soften Israel's opposition to a Palestinian state. Nevertheless, prior recognition would dramatically raise the PLO's international prestige and legitimacy in the United States and Western Europe. Prior recognition of Israel would also release the U.S. administration from the bonds of its 1975 memorandum of understanding with Israel, which committed the United States not to recognize or negotiate with the PLO unless it accepted Resolution 242 and Israel's right to exist.[51] And recognition of Israel would undoubtedly lead the way to the formulation of new American and European peace plans more favorable to the PLO's demand for a state in the West Bank and Gaza strip.

The PLO was also aware of the sharp disagreement within Israeli society over the Palestinian issue, which was exacerbated during and after the invasion of Lebanon. 'Arafat said, "There are intelligent Israelis who realize that Israel cannot base its existence upon force alone. . . . [Force alone] will not solve the dead end into which it has forced itself [on the Palestinian issue]."[52] His deputy Abu Iyad added, "There are [Israeli] youth who want to recognize the existence of the oppressed Palestinian people. There are [Israeli] pilots who describe their actions [during the war in Lebanon] as brutal. For the first time, there is no consensus in Israel on a war."[53] Under these circumstances, prior PLO recognition of Israel and readiness to accept a state in the West Bank and Gaza as a permanent solution might cause an upheaval in Israeli public opinion like the one that followed President Sadat's trip to Jerusalem (November 1977). The Greater-Land-of-Israel camp would be on the defensive. Wrenching reassessments would have to take place among Israeli decision makers. A new beginning in relations between Israel and the Palestinians would become more likely. Prior

---

51. See "The Memorandum of Agreement between the United States and Israel," *Washington Post*, Sept. 16, 1975.

52. Interview in *al-Musawwar*, Dec. 31, 1982.

53. Interview in *al-Watan* (Kuwait), March 24, 1983.

recognition "might have moved the PLO from its position on the sidelines into the game; from its position on the sidelines, the PLO was not closer to actually regaining an inch of Palestine than when it was founded in 1964."[54]

'Arafat declined, in spite of all this, to embark on a new path. He hesitated to maximize the PLO's chance to participate in a negotiated settlement involving prior recognition of Israel. It appears that the more he recognized the advantages of such a move, the more he became aware of its enormous risks. 'Arafat was afraid of an irreparable loss of control both inside and outside the PLO because of his uncertainties regarding any territorial rewards in return for prior recognition of Israel. He was reluctant to lose the obedience and compliance of broad segments of the Palestinian people and of his old comrades. Angry opponents might seize power and even eliminate him, or, if they failed, might form a new aggressive PLO, dissipating his influence. And if he somehow managed to go his way, there still remained the possibility of Israel's exploiting the turmoil both to question his right to power and to place obstacles that would prevent him from pursuing a negotiated settlement. Whatever the circumstances, there always existed the possibility that prior recognition would yield no positive results, leaving 'Arafat stranded. If this occurred, the PLO and the idea of Palestinian sovereignty would have become but a mere passing political episode.

'Arafat had no guarantee that continued reliance on the services of a third party would ensure that these developments would not occur. If negotiations with Israel took place through King Hussein, 'Arafat's angry opponents might still do their best to block them, and Israel would have an equal interest in bringing about 'Arafat's downfall. Moreover, 'Arafat had to take into account the heavy price he might have to pay for the Jordanian cooperation. In return for their services as a third party, the Jordanians might try to restrict his freedom of action, or, were he to attempt to act against their will, to refuse to collaborate. 'Arafat also could not exclude the possibility that Jordan would hold talks with Israel behind his

54. Aaron David Miller, "The PLO: What Next?" *Washington Quarterly* 6/1 (Winter 1983): 17.

back to reach a common stand regarding disposal of the PLO if it neared its territorial goal: the West Bank and Gaza.

Nevertheless, negotiation through a third party has remained 'Arafat's best alternative. It minimizes the intensity of the shock his supporters would experience if he recognized Israel prior to any territorial reward. A slower pace promises better control over events and allows for modification according to developments. It provides 'Arafat with the opportunity to take safety measures and to plan his responses ahead of time. Reliance on third-party mediation cannot prevent the possibility of a catastrophe. But, in contrast to prior recognition without territorial rewards at hand, reliance on a third party diminishes the chance of such a catastrophe occurring without 'Arafat's being able to foresee and plan for it.

In describing the advantages of negotiation through a third party, I do not mean to imply that under radically different political circumstances a shift in 'Arafat's position is impossible. Far-reaching changes in the PLO's immediate external or internal environment might encourage 'Arafat to make the daring move of recognizing Israel. On the external level, such a development might be a sharp and prolonged decline in the PLO's standing in the Arab world, which might sour relations between the PLO and Jordan to a point where continuous reliance on cooperation with Jordan would radically endanger 'Arafat's role as a leading spokesman of the Palestinian people. Similarly, a change in Israeli or American attitudes or behavior that would enhance the PLO's chance to gain territory might also push 'Arafat toward prior recognition of Israel.

On the internal level, radical developments to 'Arafat's advantage within the power structure of the PLO might lead him to decide that, no matter how strong the resistance, prior recognition of Israel and acceptance of the West Bank–Gaza state as a permanent solution would not damage his status as the high priest of Palestinian nationalism. This means confidence in his ability to assure the support and compliance of a large portion of the PLO's rank and file and the Palestinian community on the West Bank after recognition *even if it does not result* in immediate territorial gains.

As long as there is no clear indication of such developments, whether internal or external, ʿArafat's PLO will maintain its yes-no policy and reliance on a third party to advance a territorial settlement, not adopting a new and daring strategy that would risk the political survival of the Palestinian national movement. The yes-no policy and reliance on a third party may preclude the chance of a rapid solution to the Palestinian problem. Yet it offers ʿArafat's followers hope that something may be saved rather than all being lost.

A P P E N D I X 1

PLO Structure

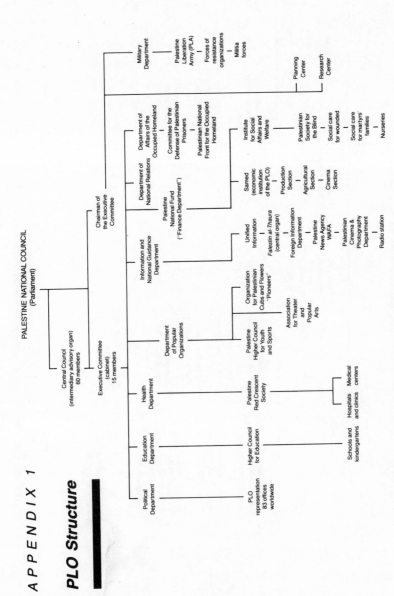

PLO Structure 1a. Palestine National Council: Executive Branches

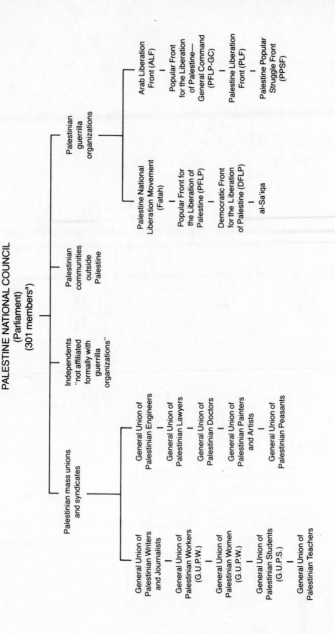

PALESTINE NATIONAL COUNCIL
(Parliament)
(301 members[a])

Palestinian mass unions and syndicates

General Union of Palestinian Writers and Journalists
–
General Union of Palestinian Workers (G.U.P.W.)
–
General Union of Palestinian Women (G.U.P.W.)
–
General Union of Palestinian Students (G.U.P.S.)
–
General Union of Palestinian Teachers

General Union of Palestinian Engineers
–
General Union of Palestinian Lawyers
–
General Union of Palestinian Doctors
–
General Union of Palestinian Painters and Artists
–
General Union of Palestinian Peasants

Independents "not affiliated formally with guerrilla organizations"

Palestinian communities outside Palestine

Palestinian guerrilla organizations

Palestine National Liberation Movement (Fatah)
–
Popular Front for the Liberation of Palestine (PFLP)
–
Democratic Front for the Liberation of Palestine (DFLP)
–
al-Sa'iqa

Arab Liberation Front (ALF)
–
Popular Front for the Liberation of Palestine—General Command (PFLP-GC)
–
Palestine Liberation Front (PLF)
–
Palestine Popular Struggle Front (PPSF)

[a]The number is not constant.

Adapted from Americans for Middle East Understanding, *The Link* 15/3 (1982)

PLO Structure 1b. Palestine National Council: Constituent Bodies

PLO Split, 1985

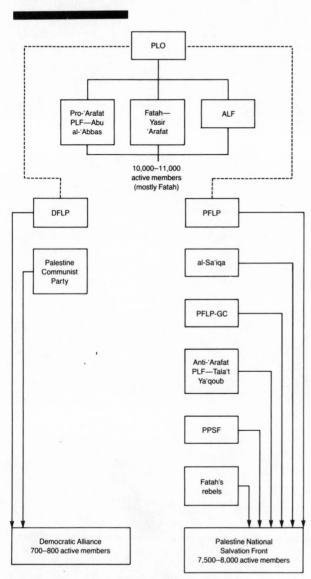

Source: Newsweek, January 13, 1986, and interviews with Israeli officials.

Index

▬

ʿAbd al-Haq, Dr. Qaʿid, 144
ʿAbdallah, King (Jordan), 27–27n
ʿAbd al-Nasser, Jamal. *See* Nasser, Jamal ʿAbd al-
ʿAbd al-Shafi, Dr. Haydar, 128
ʿAbd Rabbu, Yasir, 125–26; quoted, 123
Abu al-ʿAbbas, 44, 46
Abu ʿAli Mustafa, 126
Abu ʿAmmar (ʿArafat's nom de guerre), 60
Abu-ʿAwda, ʿAdnan, 141–42
Abu Iyad, quoted, 21, 45, 52, 162, 175
Abu Majid, Sharara, quoted, 122–23
Abu Musa, Colonel, 173
Abu Salih, 173
Abu Shilbaya, Muhammad, 31, 97
Akhir Saʿa (Egyptian weekly), 167
Algeria, 4–5, 42, 63, 81
Algiers, Arab summit in, 18, 20, 84, 115
Allon Plan, 129–32
All-Palestine Government, 27. *See* Gaza Strip
al-ʿAmla, Colonel Khalid, 173
Amman (Jordan), PLO bases in, 13, 15. *See also* Jordan
ʿAmmar ibn-Yasir, 60
al-Ansar (Palestinian guerrilla organization), 105, 106
Arab Higher Committee, 4

Arab-Israeli wars: *1948*, 4, 24, 26, 46, 57, 103, 111, 123; *1967*, 6, 8, 31, 33, 39, 61, 65, 66, 68, 76, 78, 82, 99, 102, 104, 105, 112, 129, 154, 163; *1973*, 16–17, 20, 41, 44, 46, 47, 57, 72, 76, 94, 99, 106, 115, 125, 130, 150
Arab League, 3, 34, 66, 152
Arab Liberation Front (ALF), 12, 44–47 passim, 143
Arab nationalism. *See* Pan-Arabism; Palestinian national goals
Arab Nationalists. *See* Qawmiyyun al-ʿArab
"Arab Revolution" approach (PFLP), 42–43
Arab summit meetings, 16–20 passim, 35, 143, 154, 155, 167–68, 170, 173; and international peace plans, 81, 84; and West Bank, 115, 138, 141
ʿArafat, Yasir: at U.N., quoted, 1; and West Bank, 8; becomes PLO chairman, 7; and radical left, quoted, 37, 38, 39; and Palestinian national goals, quoted, 52, 53, 57; nom de guerre, 60; advisers to, 65; and international peace plans, 75, 77, 80–81, 85; and West Bank, 122; successes of, 149–50; and yes-no policy, 150–51; and Israeli invasion of Lebanon, 162, 167; talks with Hussein, 165–75 passim;